KU-301-244

Pregnancy
& Birth

Pregnancy & Birth

Revised Edition

Gill Thorn

hamlyn

For my husband, Dennis

First published in Great Britain in 1995 by
Hamlyn, an imprint of Octopus Publishing Group Ltd
2–4 Heron Quays, London E14 4JP

This revised edition published in 2001

ISBN 0 600 60329 6

Copyright © Octopus Publishing Group Ltd 1995, 2001

The moral right of the author has been asserted.

All rights reserved. No part of this work may be reproduced or utilized in any form or by any means, electronic or mechanical, including photocopying, recording or by any information storage and retrieval system, without the prior written permission of the publisher.

A CIP catalogue record for this book is available from the British Library

Printed and bound in China

NOTE

While the advice and information are believed to be accurate and true at the time of going to press neither the author nor the publisher can accept any legal responsibility or liability for any errors or omissions that may be made. The reader should always consult a physician in all matters relating to health and particularly in respect of any symptoms which may require diagnosis or medical attention.

Contents

Introduction

It's exciting to be expecting a baby and there are many things to think about and learn. This book will tell you all you want to know about pregnancy, birth and the early weeks with your new baby. It includes up-to-date information, reassurance and practical tips from other parents to help you to enjoy this special time.

The days when parents passively accepted whatever was offered are long gone. Most parents want to consider their choices and share the decisions that affect them, from the type of antenatal care or pain relief they receive to how much technology is used during labour. *Pregnancy & Birth* offers a comprehensive guide to the options available and help to make intelligent choices among them. Information is empowering, but everyone's experience is different so it doesn't tell you what you ought to do. The decisions are up to you.

I have learned how varied the individual experience of having a baby can be from the thousands of parents who have shared their joys, hopes and fears with me in over 25 years of teaching. I'd like to acknowledge my debt to them, and to the many childbirth educators, writers and midwives who have influenced my thinking over the years.

I'd like to thank Sue Copello and Val Gardner, psychologist and doctor respectively, for reading the manuscript and making helpful comments; also Helen Gill, sometime editor of *Practical Parenting* magazine; and my daughters Joanna and Annabel, who have always prevented me from taking anything for granted.

Gill Thorn

1

Planning Pregnancy

‘ *Parenthood is a privilege, not a right. Thinking about why I wanted a child – the responsibilities as well as the joys – made me feel confident and ready to commit myself. I plan to enjoy pregnancy and give my baby a good start in life.* ’

WHY PLAN YOUR PREGNANCY?

It may seem calculating to plan something that is so natural such as having a baby, but thinking ahead can help you to start pregnancy in good health and a positive frame of mind. It can enhance your chances of conceiving, reduce the likelihood of problems during pregnancy, and spare you a certain amount of worry. Pregnancy today has actually never been safer but it can be an anxious time, not least because of all the information available and the tests to make sure you and the baby are alright. Thinking carefully about it in advance helps you to get everything in perspective.

Sharing the preparations for a new and exciting phase of your lives can bring you and your partner closer together. There are ups and downs and anxieties with any aspect of life and advance planning for pregnancy cannot get rid of them all, but it can make your journey smoother and help you to get the most out of a very special experience.

How you may feel about parenthood

For most women, deciding to have a baby is exciting and brings a new sense of purpose to life. You can re-enter the world of childhood in a new role, think about the little garments and nursery items to buy, and remember forgotten childhood pleasures. There is the challenge of raising a child your way, using some of your parents' tried-and-tested methods and re-inventing others. You may suddenly feel closer to friends and relatives with children, and look forward to carrying on family traditions and forming new ones.

You will probably also experience some less positive feelings. You may worry about giving up your freedom, losing out in your career, becoming dependent on your partner or just facing the responsibilities of parenthood. If you have had a miscarriage you may fear that it will happen again. You may worry about the physical demands of pregnancy, any illness that might affect your baby, or having a child with a disability. You may be concerned about being a good mother, coping with day-to-day childcare, and about how much your partner will really help you.

Any major change in life involves losses as well as gains, and a few mixed feelings will stop you viewing motherhood through rose-tinted spectacles. You will have to work through some of your doubts, but others will disappear once you are pregnant.

Your partner's feelings

Many men take great delight in young children, are proud to think of becoming a father, and are enthusiastic and eager to share the preparations. Others are pleased, but reserved about it. Like you, your partner will have moments of doubt. He may worry about being a good father, about taking on the financial responsibility for you and the baby and about your safety during pregnancy and birth. He may also be concerned about changes in your social life, your sex life and your relation-ship with each other.

Worries about the future can outweigh optimism when it comes to fatherhood. If your partner's reactions are lukewarm try to find out why. He may have unhappy memories of his own childhood, be afraid of the changes a baby will

' The hardest thing about having a baby was taking the plunge. We kept putting it off, first until I'd got my promotion, then until the house was straight or we'd had our holiday. There was always a good reason, but really I think we were scared of making the commitment. It seemed such a grown-up step to take. ' LIZZIE

bring, or not feel ready for the responsibilities of parenthood. Some men may feel concerned because they have no interest in babies although they like older children. Others may simply not be drawn to children at all.

All relationships are different and you may be happy to accept most of the parenting responsibility yourself. Only you can decide if you would resent this as time goes on. On the other hand, some men who are adamant that they do not want children change their minds as soon as a baby arrives!

PREPARING FOR PREGNANCY

It's never too late to improve your state of health, but if you and your partner have the chance to do so before you become pregnant, take it! Healthy parents tend to have healthy babies and fit mothers tend to experience fewer problems during pregnancy and birth.

A child will be dependent on you for many years even if you return to work, so your life will and should change; pregnancy starts the process of adapta-tion. It can be frustrating to find that your body slows down and you can't concentrate on much beyond your own and the baby's needs as pregnancy advances, but the less rushed, new rhythm is more suited to the needs of a baby. Many women are glad of a reason to find a slower but more satisfying pace of life. Most preparation for pregnancy is simply common sense and ideally should involve both partners. For example:

- Look at ways of reducing the stress in your life. Try to shed unnecessary work commitments or reorganize your social life.
- Go to your GP for a check-up so that you start pregnancy with a clean bill of health. Your doctor can prescribe folic acid supplements and may recommend you to take them for at least a month before becoming pregnant.
- Look at the balance between work and play, activity and relaxation, your own needs and those of others in your life. If one aspect dominates another, try to modify it.
- Concentrate on taking more exercise and improving your diet.
- Change habits you know are bad for you such as smoking and excessive drinking of alcohol.

Getting fit

The special needs of pregnancy often become obvious to women too late, when they realize how much harder everything is if they are unfit! If you increase your suppleness, strength and stamina before becoming pregnant you'll be able to carry a baby more easily, reduce the risk of backache and other discomforts, and find you get less tired. It's not wise to start a rigorous exercise programme during pregnancy and any activity that you are not used to doing should be treated cautiously. Swimming and brisk walking are safe for most women, but ask your doctor for individual advice.

Women have been discouraged from taking part in activities such as skiing and horse riding during pregnancy, but there is little evidence for a blanket ban. It depends on individual circumstances. If your pregnancy is normal and you are fit and skilled at an activity you'll probably find you can carry it on in a modified form. Marathon runner Ingrid Kristiansen competed at international level when she was seven months pregnant, but most women are content with more modest goals!

Eating healthily

Good nutrition is the basic foundation for good health. It protects the body against infection by building a strong immune system and helps rid the system of toxins. It improves the feeling of well-being and increases the chances of conceiving and having a successful pregnancy.

Research suggests that drinking more than three cups of coffee (or the equivalent) per day can delay the chance of conception. Caffeine is addictive and you may want to cut down for other reasons, such as its interference with sleep patterns and the fact that it is a diuretic.

It may seem incredible that your body can provide everything needed to grow a healthy baby using the simplest of essentials: water, oxygen and good food. Try to eat some foods like these every day to help ensure that you and your baby get the best nourishment possible.

WHOLESOME FOODS

◆ *Take salad items such as carrot and celery sticks to work in a plastic container, to eat with a wholemeal roll.*

◆ *Choose fruit or low fat yoghurt for dessert.*

◆ *Eat snacks of nuts, sunflower seeds, dried apricots or raisins instead of crisps and biscuits.*

◆ *To make the transition from white rice or flour to brown easier, mix them in equal quantities at first.*

◆ *Vegetables from large supermarket chains are usually very fresh. Stir-fry or steam them to retain vitamins and minerals.*

◆ *Buy a wholefood cookery book and try out a new recipe every week.*

◆ *See page 40 for foods to avoid when you're pregnant.*

A wholesome diet should include fresh vegetables and fruit, unrefined carbohydrates like wholemeal bread and brown rice, and protein such as meat, fish, milk, eggs, nuts and pulses. You should get all the vitamins, minerals and other nutrients you need from foods like these. If your diet consists mainly of processed or fat-laden foods try to improve it for your own and your future baby's sake .

Stopping contraception

If you are taking the Pill or using an intra-uterine device (IUD) you might want to use another form of contraception for about three months before attempting to get pregnant. This will allow your body to return to normal as both forms of contraception can alter the balance of nutrients such as zinc, copper and certain vitamins. Good nutrition, plus a short break from the Pill or an IUD, will help to put you in a healthy condition for pregnancy. Allowing your periods time to settle down to a regular pattern also makes dating your pregnancy much more accurate.

RISKS IN PREGNANCY

Being pregnant today may appear a risky process because bad news always gets more attention than good news. However, the risks are actually less than they used to be because women in general are better nourished, better housed, have fewer children and are able to plan when to have them more easily. These factors are very important in making pregnancy safer than it was for previous generations.

If you make yourself aware of the avoidable risks and take action to reduce them, you can get the others in proportion and relax knowing that you have done your best.

Older motherhood

Physically, the best time to have a baby is in your early 20s. However, many of the risk factors associated with giving birth when you are older could affect any woman, whatever her age; being overweight, and having had several babies or suffered infertility problems just happen to be more common in older women.

The risk of chromosomal abnormalities does increase with age (see page 55) but most problems, including heart defects, spina bifida, cleft palate and club foot, are no more common in older mothers. Some problems, for example, congenital dislocation of the hip (clicky hips), are actually less common. Keep an eye on your weight and take regular exercise to improve your fitness before becoming pregnant. There is sound evidence that older women who are fit and of average weight for their height suffer fewer problems in pregnancy and birth. They also cope just as well physically as younger women when having a baby.

If you are over 35 and smoke you are five times as likely to have a baby who suffers poor growth (see page 103) and who could have problems in early life. The risk of minor malformations in the baby is significantly increased. So it is even more important for older women to stop smoking (see page 41).

In general, the older you are the better you know yourself and the more motivated you may be to help yourself by planning ahead. You may also be more financially secure and able to get the most out of the emotional and spiritual side of pregnancy.

Weight before pregnancy

If you eat a balanced diet, are physically active and have plenty of energy most of the time, your weight is probably about right for you. The Body Mass Index chart (right) shows the best weight range for good health, regardless of your age or body build.

Band **A** (under **17**): Women who are very underweight may find it harder to conceive. If you're poorly nourished when you become pregnant your baby may lack nutrients before the placenta is fully developed and can supply them from your blood.

Band **B** (**17-19**): Being a little underweight can be perfectly healthy and your baby should be fine if you gain at a reasonable rate during pregnancy. If your baby isn't growing you may be weighed over several weeks (to assess the trend)while you rest more and improve your diet. Postnatally you may need extra food to make sufficient milk for breastfeeding.

Band **C** (**20-25**): This is the weight range to aim for if you're planning a pregnancy and it's associated with the fewest problems during pregnancy. If you're generally healthy and fall within this range you will not benefit from gaining or losing weight, so concentrate on the quality of the food you eat.

Band **D** (**26-30**): This is a little on the heavy side. Women towards the top end of the range are more likely to suffer discomforts during pregnancy, including breathlessness, tiredness, heartburn, varicose veins or skin irritation caused by friction and perspiration.

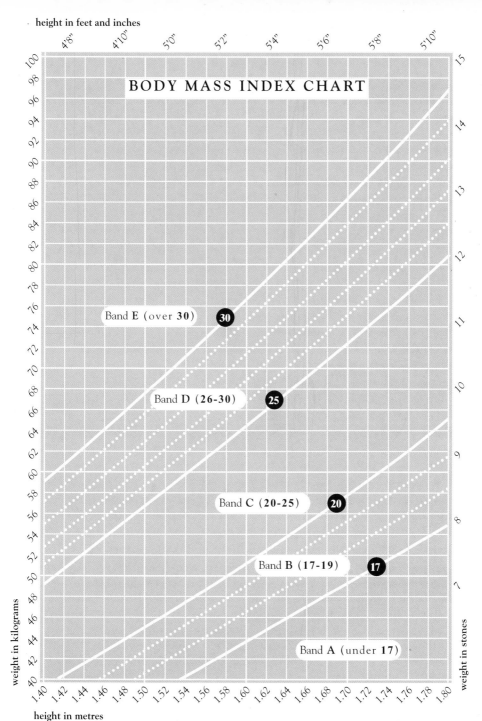

BODY MASS INDEX CHART

Band E (over **30**) 〔**30**〕

Band D (**26-30**) 〔**25**〕

Band C (**20-25**) 〔**20**〕

Band B (**17-19**) 〔**17**〕

Band A (under **17**)

weight in kilograms

weight in stones

height in metres

Band **E** (over **30**): Women in this band tend to suffer from health problems that can complicate pregnancy, such as high blood pressure and diabetes. Medical procedures such as epidurals and fetal heart monitoring can be more difficult to carry out and the baby may be slightly heavier than average.

‘ *It's a good idea to plan your pregnancy if you can. I gave up smoking before I was expecting my son, and cut out chips and burgers in favour of salads and greens.*

There are risks in everything, even in crossing the road, and you have to get them in proportion. Of course I worried when I was pregnant. It's part of caring for the baby. Basically I just follow sensible advice and use common sense. If you become paranoid you spoil that lovely special feeling you get when you're expecting a baby. ’ JANICE

Smoking

Smoking is one of the main culprits in a range of pregnancy problems from miscarriage through to pre-term delivery. The major cause of infant illness and death is being born too small (see page 103). About one-third of low birthweight babies are like this because their mothers smoked during pregnancy. The risks continue as the child grows up; babies of mothers who smoked during pregnancy are less healthy, more likely to be hyperactive and more at risk from cot death.

If you continue to smoke during pregnancy you'll either choose to believe that your baby will escape harm, or you'll suffer agonizing guilt and self reproach. It's best to tackle the problem before you conceive. There are some ideas to help you stop smoking in Chapter 3.

Passive smoking also affects the developing baby, so ask your partner to give up smoking, or to smoke outside or in another room. Try to negotiate a special area for smokers in your workplace if there isn't one already.

Drugs

All illegal and addictive drugs potentially cause harm to the developing baby. We know as little about the use of marijuana and cocaine in pregnancy as was known about cigarette smoking 20 years ago, so more problems will probably be discovered. Cocaine crosses the placenta and may damage it, leading to poor fetal growth (see page 103) and some serious complications of pregnancy, including stillbirth. Long term effects for the baby include irritability, excessive crying and abnormal brain wave patterns. Marijuana can interfere with conception and has been linked with severe pregnancy sickness and complications such as abnormally long or rapid labours. It affects placental efficiency and can lead to low birthweight babies.

Medicines

Most women know not to take any pills or medicines, such as multi-vitamins, common cold remedies and pain killers including aspirin and paracetamol, without advice from a doctor or pharmacist during pregnancy. Some prescription drugs have withstood the test of time and are perfectly safe. Others, including common drugs such as tranquillizers, may carry risks to the baby. In certain cases the risk may be outweighed by the benefits of taking the drug.

If you need to take regular medication check with your doctor, who will have access to the latest information, before attempting to become pregnant.

There may be other forms of treatment or lower-risk medication that you could try. You could discuss taking smaller doses for a shorter time or using an alternative therapy, if appropriate. Women's Health (see Appendix) may provide helpful information.

MEDICAL AND PHYSICAL CONDITIONS

If you suffer from a condition such as chronic backache or have a pre-existing infection it makes sense to get it treated before you conceive. Once you are pregnant it may be harder to clear up, either because of the effects of hormones or because the appropriate medication is unsafe in pregnancy.

It's useful to find out about how pregnancy could affect any chronic medical condition you may have. Knowing what to expect can be reassuring and it's easier to look after yourself well. For example, asthmatics whose condition is well controlled usually have normal pregnancies. About two-thirds find their condition stays the same or improves, although the most severe sufferers may find that it worsens, especially after the fourth month. Diabetics who keep the disease under control have as good a chance as anyone else of having an uncomplicated pregnancy these days, provided they always follow medical advice.

Women with a physical disability often feel isolated when they are pregnant. Access to buildings, facilities and information can be restricted. Some disabled women have said that control was subtly denied and decisions taken for them, or they got the impression that they were an interesting medical condition rather than a person! You will probably have to find information for yourself (see Appendix) but planning can minimize problems and enable you to enjoy pregnancy as much as anyone else.

Genetic problems

Most people probably have a few less-than-perfect genes without knowing it. For the majority of serious genetic conditions, a baby has to inherit a faulty gene from each parent before being affected.

It's worth seeking advice if you know you're at higher risk of suffering from a particular defect. This includes regional or ethnic groups in which a condition is more prevalent, such as people of Eastern European Jewish origin for Tay-Sach's disease, and couples where one partner suffers from a congenital problem. Couples who know about an inherited disorder in either family, or who are closely related, should also seek advice.

There are about 5,000 rare single-gene defects known at present, so testing everyone randomly for them would be like looking for a needle in a haystack. Where a defect is known or suspected a genetic counsellor can give you the odds on your child being affected, help you decide whether to take the risk, and tell you if there is a test that could find out if a baby is affected.

QUESTIONS AND ANSWERS

Q: We have a smallholding and keep a few sheep, goats and chickens as well as having a sheepdog and two cats as pets. Are there any risks from looking after the animals during my pregnancy?

A: The main risk from household pets is toxoplasmosis, an infection that can damage the fetus in the early weeks of pregnancy or be passed directly to the baby in the later months, although only about one in 10,000 babies is born with it. If your pets have an active infection they could pass it to you; or you could acquire it by drinking unpasteurized milk. On the other hand you may already be immune to the disease.

Ask your doctor to test for antibodies before you become pregnant. If you are immune this will give you peace of mind; if not you could be re-tested if you develop a slight fever and swollen glands followed by a rash. Any toxoplasmosis antibodies discovered would be the result of a recent infection.

You should be careful about hygiene when caring for the farm animals. In particular, an infection that causes sheep to miscarry (*Chlamydia psittaci*) poses a similar threat to women. When you are pregnant ask someone else to milk your ewes and help with lambing. Call your GP if you experience flu-like symptoms after you have been in contact with sheep.

Q: My lifestyle is busy and my work involves a great deal of travelling. I don't always eat very well. Should I take vitamin and mineral supplements before becoming pregnant?

A: Have a word with your doctor before taking pills of any sort. As you are aware, a poor diet may not supply all the nutrients that you need, so you could start pregnancy with a deficit.

Experts have differing views about the wisdom of taking supplements, other than folic acid which is currently recommended. Some feel that food habits are hard to change but deficiencies can be avoided with a pill; others point out that excesses of certain vitamins are damaging and may rob the body of other vitamins because of the complex interactions between nutrients. There is little research into this problem as yet.

Nutrients ought to come from a healthy diet because that is how the body uses them most effectively. A poor diet plus a vitamin and mineral supplement does not equal a good diet! Even the best pill cannot supply nutrients that have not yet been isolated in food – and there may be many of these. It would be better to try to improve your eating habits before conceiving.

Q: I work in a nursery where we have a child who was damaged by rubella. Is there any way I can find out if I'm immune to this illness and if not can I be immunized before pregnancy?

A: About 85 per cent of women are immune to rubella (German measles), having already had it or been vaccinated against it. It's no longer a common disease in the community, so even if you have no immunity you are unlikely to contract it.

For peace of mind, your blood could be tested for antibodies before conception. Alternatively your GP may suggest vaccinating you just in case and advise you to delay pregnancy for three months afterwards as a precaution. Even if you were vaccinated and later discovered that you were pregnant your baby will probably be fine. Damage caused by the live virus has not been reported after vaccination.

Q: **I am 38, single, and would dearly love to have a baby. A close friend has offered to be the father provided he has no further contact with the child. As time is running out I can see the advantages to this, but what are the pitfalls?**

A: Your friend might find it hard to relinquish responsibility for his child. Although a man who donates sperm to a licensed clinic escapes the attention of the Child Support Agency, private arrangements do not. At the very least you could be under considerable pressure to name your friend.

How would you react if the baby inherited a defect, or if your friend had second thoughts and came back to make a claim on the child, for instance? Apart from this your child would one day want to know about, and possibly search for his father.

The issues are very complex and personal and you need to think them through carefully. The Family Planning Association (see Appendix) can give you information and helpful advice.

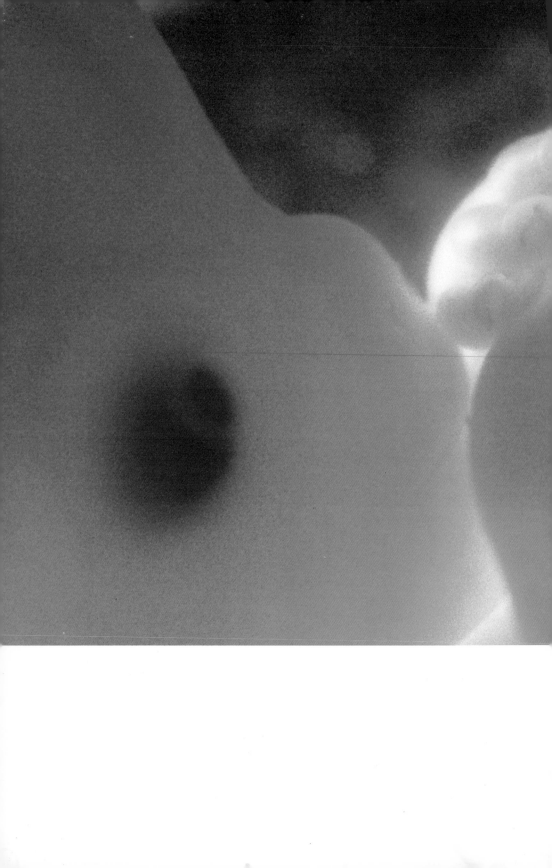

2

Conception

‘ *I dithered on the brink of having a baby for ages, but when it happened I was bowled over! Becoming pregnant is the best thing I've ever done and I can't get the grin off my face.* ’

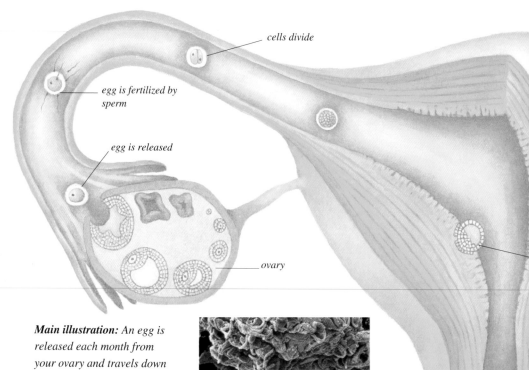

cells divide

egg is fertilized by sperm

egg is released

ovary

Main illustration: An egg is released each month from your ovary and travels down your Fallopian tube. If it is fertilized the cells divide rapidly before implanting in the lining of the uterus about six days after conception.
Right: *Sperm attempting to penetrate the egg.*

HOW CONCEPTION OCCURS

About halfway through each menstrual cycle an egg is released from your ovary and drawn into the opening of your Fallopian tube. There are about 400 million sperm in each male ejaculation and they can survive for up to three days in your body. Unless the egg is fertilized within about 24–48 hours your body reabsorbs it. You are fertile for about seven days each month.

During this period the mucus in your cervix changes to a fern-like structure through which the sperm can swim towards the egg. Many sperm take a wrong turn or get lost in the folds of the Fallopian tube, but even so thousands reach and surround the egg. When one of them penetrates its outer coating the membrane instantly changes to prevent others from following.

The victorious sperm burrows inwards until its nucleus fuses with the nucleus of the egg. Fertilization results in a single cell, smaller than this full stop. From this tiny, dynamic beginning a new life is formed.

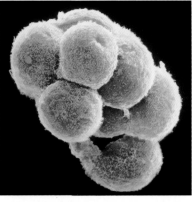

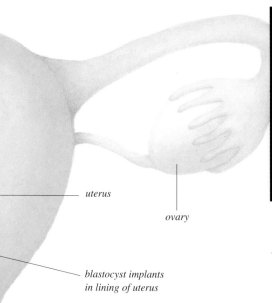

uterus

ovary

blastocyst implants
in lining of uterus

Above: *The fertilized egg divides to
form a blackberry-like cluster of cells
called a morula. The inner cells of
the morula will form the embryo and
the outer cells will become the
placenta and amniotic sac.*

Twins

If two eggs are released and fertilized by separate sperm, the result is non-identical twins. If a fertilized egg splits to form two embryos, you get identical twins who will always be the same sex.

Non-identical twins (or triplets) have separate placentas and can be different sexes, like brothers and sisters who happen to share the same uterus. They are more common in families with a history of non-identical twins, women over 35 and people of African origin. The rise in multiple births, which has increased from about one per cent to almost two per cent over a generation, is largely due to the use of fertility drugs.

Identical twins share a placenta and have the same genes as they come from the same egg and sperm. About a third of twins are identical and they are equally spread throughout the population.

Genes and chromosomes

Most living cells contain deoxyribonucleic acid, better known as DNA, a substance that includes the chemical formula to make the cell individual. It resembles two strands that spiral around each other and this famous double helix is packed into each of the thousands of genes which in turn are threaded like beads into the 23 pairs of chromosomes that form the nucleus of a human cell.

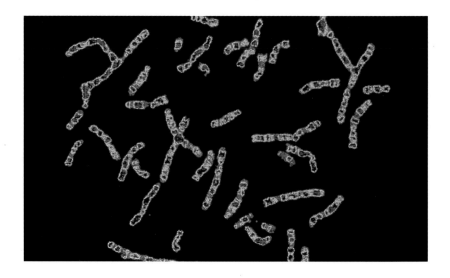

Your egg and your partner's sperm each contribute 23 chromosomes to your baby. Most chromosomes look

Chromosomes are composed mainly of the genetic material DNA.

like a little 'x' under the microscope but the chromosome that determines sex in the sperm can be an 'x' or a 'y'. Fertilization by an 'x' sperm results in a girl while a 'y' sperm gives a boy.

DNA, genes and chromosomes are the master plan for your baby's individual characteristics, determining everything from his temperament to the colour of his eyes. Half of the thousands of bits of information come from your partner's side of the family and half from yours. Environment and life experiences will alter certain aspects of your child's physiology or personality, but his essential being is determined at the moment of conception.

CHANGES IN YOUR BODY

During pregnancy your blood supply increases, your heart works harder, your lungs expand to provide more oxygen and up to 7 litres (12 pints) of extra fluid circulates around your body.

Hormones are released to stop your periods, although your cycle can also be temporarily upset by other things such as medication, sudden weight changes, fear of pregnancy, stress, travel or exhaustion.

❛ It was a bit of a shock, getting pregnant so soon. I came off the Pill and never had a period. The first I knew about it was that my boobs felt firmer and blue veins showed up on them. Then I started to fall asleep as soon as I got home from work. ❜ MARILYN

Pregnancy hormones enable you to carry on with daily life while your baby grows and your body changes, but they also produce mood swings and some of the less welcome symptoms of early pregnancy. For example, oestrogen and progesterone relax the smooth muscles of your internal organs so that your body can adapt as your uterus grows; but they contribute to heartburn, constipation and varicose veins. Relaxin helps to make your ligaments flexible ready for the birth, but this increases the likelihood of overstraining yourself by lifting or poor posture. However, many of the discomforts caused by pregnancy hormones can be avoided (see page 72).

' *Every time we saw my husband's family someone asked me when we were going to have a son. When I found out I was pregnant all I could think of at first was that I would let them down if the baby was a girl. I was so worried about it that I made myself ill.*

My husband said I should take no notice of them, because it was our baby and we would welcome either a girl or a boy. He told his family that we wanted a daughter and he made me realize that you can't live to please other people all the time. I'm enjoying my pregnancy now, but I've discovered a strange craving for pickle with everything! ' SHEENA

HOW YOU MAY FEEL

When you first suspect you are pregnant you may be over the moon with excitement. If you have been actively trying to conceive your success will be a cause for great celebration and will help you to make light of any minor discomforts.

However, many women feel neutral or negative about pregnancy at first. Even if it was half expected or planned, discovering that it has actually happened may be a shock. Some women take a while to realize how much they really want the baby.

If pregnancy is unwelcome you may feel guilty, anxious about telling your partner or your family, or uncertain about what to do. You may not want to think about pregnancy, and this is not a bad instinct for a week or two. Once the turmoil settles down you will be able to think more clearly. Many children in loving families were conceived at the wrong time or in the wrong circumstances. Far from being the disaster they seemed at first, unwelcome pregnancies often turn into much loved babies.

RELATIONSHIP WITH YOUR PARTNER

Some men are fascinated by the development of a baby and the progress of pregnancy. Others regard the whole process in the way that women often feel about cars: so long as it keeps going they do not wish to know what goes on under the bonnet. Although it can be disappointing if your partner feels like this, it's no more a reflection on his ability to be a good father than wielding a spanner in a car engine shows you are a good driver!

Changes usually have more impact on those who are experiencing them than the spectators. However interested your partner may be, he can only experience pregnancy through you. Even if he is less than enthusiastic about the personal details of having a baby, he will probably want to share decisions about antenatal care, tests, and the place where your baby will be born.

Along with the joy of expecting a baby there are moments when every mum-to-be wonders what she has let herself in for. Ideally your flashes of worry will coincide with your partner's moments of confidence and you'll help each other through them. But life isn't always like this! You may hit doubts together, and feel as though you are rowing a boat in opposite directions. It's scary to feel that your relationship is under strain when you need it to be strongest, but many people take time to adjust to a new future, however welcome the change.

PREGNANCY TESTS

Your doctor or family planning clinic can provide a pregnancy test, although some will make a charge for this. Many chemists also offer them for a fee, or you can buy a home test. Laboratory tests are slightly more accurate, but home tests have the advantage of speed and privacy.

Pregnancy tests differ slightly, but they work by detecting the presence of HCG (human chorionic gonadotrophin), a hormone that is secreted into your blood and passed in urine a few days after conception. If you do the test as soon as your period is overdue a positive result is more likely to be accurate. A false negative could occur because insufficient HCG is being secreted, so some kits include a second test to confirm a negative result a few days later. If your test is positive, or you still 'feel' pregnant after two negative results, visit your GP.

Announcing the news

Finding out that you are pregnant can be one of the most exciting moments of your life, comparable only to holding your baby in your arms for the first time. Like any highly charged emotional event, it makes you see the world in a different light. Although it can be tempting to shout the news of your pregnancy from the rooftops, many women wait until after the first 12 weeks or so, when there is less likelihood of miscarriage before telling the world. Others delay announcing the news until tests for fetal abnormalities (see page 55) have been completed, and some women decide not to tell their employer or workmates, at least for a while.

‘ *I was hysterically excited when my test was positive. We went out for a meal to celebrate, and I drank orange juice virtuously all evening while my partner drank enough wine for both of us and told complete strangers he was going to be a Dad!*

We'd been trying to conceive for so long that we decided not to tell anyone else except our parents, but somehow the secret got out. In no time at all everyone at work was coming up to congratulate me. ’ SHARON

ADJUSTING TO PREGNANCY

◆ *Remember your body is built for pregnancy and knows what to do.*
◆ *Extra rest will help you cope with the changes of early pregnancy, making it easier to handle personal relationships.*
◆ *Share your feelings about pregnancy and parenthood with your partner. Some worries disappear when brought into the open; others can be handled better by two people.*
◆ *Borrow a book or video to discover together how a baby grows from a seed as small as a grain of sand into a little person.*
◆ *Uncertainty is part of life, so get it in proportion and take pleasure together in celebrating this special time.*
◆ *Give yourself a few weeks to adjust. Women who are pregnant for the first time often feel disorientated and unsure of themselves.*

MATERNITY CARE

As soon as you know you're pregnant, see your GP or contact a midwife directly. The receptionist at your GP's surgery or the supervisor of midwives at your local hospital can give you a number to call. A midwife specializes in normal pregnancy; if there's any complication she refers you to an obstetrician. Some women like to involve their GP, but your routine antenatal care will be done by midwives, so it's up to you.

Antenatal care has been reorganized over the past few years to improve continuity and give more individual attention to those who need it. If your pregnancy is normal you may have no more than five or six routine checks. Some people worry that important symptoms might be overlooked, but good care means identifying women who might have a problem and offering more visits as necessary. In between checks you can contact your midwife if you're concerned about anything.

Most women prefer continuity of care during pregnancy and birth. Some areas have teams of 6-8 midwives, or groups of 12-15 who work in hospital, rotating between the antenatal clinic, labour and postnatal wards so that you see some familiar faces as you progress.

In other areas midwives look after women on a one-to-one basis, working in a partnership or small team and taking responsibility for all your antenatal, delivery and postnatal care, in hospital or at home. Some areas have a drop-in clinic where you can see a midwife (or the consultant in late pregnancy) in addition to your routine antenatal checks.

It's the duty of your GP (or the supervisor of midwives) to arrange antenatal care that is acceptable to you. You are not obliged to accept a form of care you dislike, or treatment from someone who upsets you.

CALCULATING YOUR EXPECTED DATE OF DELIVERY

The average length of a pregnancy is 266 days, or 280 days from the start of your last menstrual period (LMP) because you conceive about 14 days later. Your expected date of delivery (EDD) is calculated as nine calendar months plus one week from this date. For example, LMP started 17 September, plus nine months = 17 June, plus seven days = baby due 24 June. To use the EDD chart, find the month and day your last menstrual period started on the top line (bold type). The month and day your baby is due is on the line below.

Your EDD is really a guide for measuring your baby's progress. It is imprecise for several reasons. Some months are longer than others; you may have a longer or shorter cycle than the 'average' of 28 days; you may bleed a little while pregnant or miss a period before conception without realizing and so on. If you don't know the date of your LMP, or if other signs such as the size of your uterus do not accord with this date, your doctor may suggest a scan (see page 56). This is the most accurate way of dating a pregnancy.

January	1	2	3	4	5	6	7	8	9	10	11	12	13	14	15	16	17	18	19	20	21	22	23	24	25	26	27	28	29	30	31
October	8	9	10	11	12	13	14	15	16	17	18	19	20	21	22	23	24	25	26	27	28	29	30	31	1	2	3	4	5	6	7
February	1	2	3	4	5	6	7	8	9	10	11	12	13	14	15	16	17	18	19	20	21	22	23	24	25	26	27	28			
November	8	9	10	11	12	13	14	15	16	17	18	19	20	21	22	23	24	25	26	27	28	29	30	1	2	3	4	5			
March	1	2	3	4	5	6	7	8	9	10	11	12	13	14	15	16	17	18	19	20	21	22	23	24	25	26	27	28	29	30	31
December	6	7	8	9	10	11	12	13	14	15	16	17	18	19	20	21	22	23	24	25	26	27	28	29	30	31	1	2	3	4	5
April	1	2	3	4	5	6	7	8	9	10	11	12	13	14	15	16	17	18	19	20	21	22	23	24	25	26	27	28	29	30	
January	6	7	8	9	10	11	12	13	14	15	16	17	18	19	20	21	22	23	24	25	26	27	28	29	30	31	1	2	3	4	
May	1	2	3	4	5	6	7	8	9	10	11	12	13	14	15	16	17	18	19	20	21	22	23	24	25	26	27	28	29	30	31
February	5	6	7	8	9	10	11	12	13	14	15	16	17	18	19	20	21	22	23	24	25	26	27	28	1	2	3	4	5	6	7
June	1	2	3	4	5	6	7	8	9	10	11	12	13	14	15	16	17	18	19	20	21	22	23	24	25	26	27	28	29	30	
March	8	9	10	11	12	13	14	15	16	17	18	19	20	21	22	23	24	25	26	27	28	29	30	31	1	2	3	4	5	6	
July	1	2	3	4	5	6	7	8	9	10	11	12	13	14	15	16	17	18	19	20	21	22	23	24	25	26	27	28	29	30	31
April	7	8	9	10	11	12	13	14	15	16	17	18	19	20	21	22	23	24	25	26	27	28	29	30	1	2	3	4	5	6	7
August	1	2	3	4	5	6	7	8	9	10	11	12	13	14	15	16	17	18	19	20	21	22	23	24	25	26	27	28	29	30	31
May	8	9	10	11	12	13	14	15	16	17	18	19	20	21	22	23	24	25	26	27	28	29	30	31	1	2	3	4	5	6	7
September	1	2	3	4	5	6	7	8	9	10	11	12	13	14	15	16	17	18	19	20	21	22	23	24	25	26	27	28	29	30	
June	8	9	10	11	12	13	14	15	16	17	18	19	20	21	22	23	24	25	26	27	28	29	30	1	2	3	4	5	6	7	
October	1	2	3	4	5	6	7	8	9	10	11	12	13	14	15	16	17	18	19	20	21	22	23	24	25	26	27	28	29	30	31
July	8	9	10	11	12	13	14	15	16	17	18	19	20	21	22	23	24	25	26	27	28	29	30	31	1	2	3	4	5	6	7
November	1	2	3	4	5	6	7	8	9	10	11	12	13	14	15	16	17	18	19	20	21	22	23	24	25	26	27	28	29	30	
August	8	9	10	11	12	13	14	15	16	17	18	19	20	21	22	23	24	25	26	27	28	29	30	31	1	2	3	4	5	6	
December	1	2	3	4	5	6	7	8	9	10	11	12	13	14	15	16	17	18	19	20	21	22	23	24	25	26	27	28	29	30	31
September	7	8	9	10	11	12	13	14	15	16	17	18	19	20	21	22	23	24	25	26	27	28	29	30	1	2	3	4	5	6	7

INFERTILITY

One couple in eight take over a year to conceive a baby. About half achieve a pregnancy without help and a fifth of the rest succeed after treatment. About 35 per cent of problems can be traced to the man, 35 per cent to the woman and the rest are shared by both partners.

Infertility can be caused by problems such as blocked tubes, hormone imbalances, infections and general ill health, or by factors such as fear of pregnancy or sexual difficulties. Overheating, stress or coming off the Pill can cause temporary problems. Finding that you can't conceive a baby when you want to, and when other couples seem to manage it so easily, is nothing short of anguish. However, although the problem seems to be growing so does research into potential solutions, including assistance such as in vitro fertilization (IVF). The Family Planning Association (see Appendix) has information about achieving a successful pregnancy.

ECTOPIC PREGNANCY

About one in 350 embryos implants outside the uterus, usually in a Fallopian tube. If the pregnancy were allowed to continue the tube would rupture, which could possibly lead to infertility.

The first symptom of an ectopic pregnancy is usually pain low down at one side of the abdomen, often between the sixth and twelfth week. It may be worse when you cough or move and there may be spotting or dark brown bleeding. If you have pain, tenderness or bleeding contact your GP.

If a pregnancy test is positive but an ultrasound scan (see page 56) shows no signs of pregnancy in the uterus, a laparoscopy may be performed. A fine instrument is inserted through the abdomen to look directly at the tubes. Early diagnosis and treatment can save the tube in 80 per cent of cases so that you have a good chance of conceiving again.

TO INCREASE YOUR CHANCES OF CONCEIVING:

◆ *You and your partner should make changes to your lifestyle to reduce stress caused by overwork and exhaustion.*

◆ *You and your partner should stop smoking and check your diet (see pages 12-13 and 39-41).*

◆ *Check if any chemicals you or your partner work with are linked to infertility.*

◆ *Your partner could try to avoid overheating from hot baths or tight underwear and jeans.*

◆ *If you are not pregnant after a year (six months if you are over 35) ask your GP to refer you to a specialist.*

MISCARRIAGE

Up to 40 per cent of pregnancies are thought to miscarry early on, before they are confirmed. Your reaction to a miscarriage depends on how you felt about your pregnancy, but it causes grief and considerable loss of confidence to many women. However, the chances are strongly in your favour when a pregnancy has been confirmed as at least 85 per cent of these continue successfully.

An abnormal embryo is the most likely cause of miscarriage in the first 10 weeks. Investigations to find a cause are usually only considered after three successive early miscarriages. This seems hard, but it's an expression of confidence that there is unlikely to be a problem and you have just been unlucky.

Miscarriages between 12 and 20 weeks occur in one to two per cent of pregnancies, but are rare where everything is otherwise normal. A fifth to a quarter of late miscarriages may be caused by the cervix opening too soon, possibly due to damage from surgical treatment or a previous birth. If you have suffered such a tragedy in the past your cervix may be closed with a stitch at 12-16 weeks to help support it.

Most women experience aches, cramps or light spotting at some stage during pregnancy without there being a problem. Emotional upsets, minor falls, sex and things like lifting toddlers or shopping do not usually cause miscarriages, but if you have a history of them your GP may suggest avoiding such activities.

Vaginal bleeding could indicate a threatened miscarriage. Some doctors advise extra rest but there is no evidence that it makes any difference. If nothing else happens the chances of your pregnancy continuing are high, with no extra risk of abnormality in the baby.

If you have a history of miscarriage, if bleeding or pain are severe, or if you pass clots or other material, seek immediate treatment from a doctor or the nearest hospital. Otherwise, contact your GP if you are worried or have any of these symptoms:

- Cramps accompanied by bleeding.
- Pain that is severe or lasts over 24 hours without bleeding.
- Bleeding that is as heavy as a normal period.
- Light spotting or staining continuing for more than three days.

After a miscarriage

Miscarriage happens to lots of women and most go on to have a baby successfully. After an early miscarriage you may be offered a D & C: the neck of the uterus is gently dilated and the lining scraped or aspirated to make sure nothing remains to cause infection. Some doctors suggest waiting three to six months before trying to conceive again (although lovemaking can resume before this) to give yourself time to recover physically and emotionally. The Miscarriage Association (see Appendix) can offer advice and support.

QUESTIONS AND ANSWERS

Q: I was shocked to discover that I was pregnant as I didn't feel ready for a baby. My partner blamed me for missing my pill and we had some spectacular rows before coming to our senses. Now we are looking forward to becoming parents, but I'm overwhelmed with guilt and fear. Could our baby have been affected by the stress we were under at first?

A: Unexpected pregnancies are not always welcome and it can be hard to relate to a baby and imagine yourselves as parents at first. Couples often think and say things that they later regret. Emotional stresses do affect the fetus but unless they are severe and prolonged they are unlikely to make more than a temporary impression. A baby only learns when he reaches the right stage of maturity for a particular experience. In the early months he is both emotionally and physically immature.

Although many studies have been carried out, there is no sound, direct evidence to suggest that emotional stress affects a baby adversely before birth. Indirect evidence suggests that the fetus is exposed to the sort of stress levels that he will have to learn to handle in everyday life, but is protected from excess stress. Most women will have some negative thoughts or a few rows during pregnancy. The positive feelings you now have about your pregnancy are probably more significant.

Q: We would like to have a daughter. Is there any way to boost our chances, and could we find out our baby's sex before birth?

A: Investigations such as ultrasound scans and amniocentesis (see page 58) can usually determine whether you are carrying a boy or a girl, but they are not always correct and would not be used for choosing the sex of your baby.

There is a new technique where 'y' (male) and 'x' (female) sperm are separated in the laboratory and artificial insemination is carried out to increase the chances of conceiving the desired sex. The Family Planning Association (see Appendix) can give you more information.

Other suggestions for increasing your chances of having a girl or a boy are less expensive but require more dedication. In 1979 doctors in a Paris maternity hospital claimed an 80 per cent success rate with a special diet. To conceive a girl the mother ate food that included starch and milk products, raw or frozen vegetables, unsalted butter, and fruit with the exception of pineapple, peaches and prunes. For a boy the diet had to be rich in salty foods, meat and fruit, and include dried vegetables and salted butter.

Another theory holds that timing intercourse is important because female sperm swim slowly but live longer than male sperm. Couples who want a girl should have intercourse two days before ovulation, so that most of the 'x' sperm will have died before the egg arrives. For a boy you should have intercourse on the day an egg is released, so that faster-swimming male sperm are more likely to fertilize it. Of course it is not always easy to know when an egg will be released. You can buy a special thermometer at the chemist to pinpoint ovulation, but would need to keep a record of your temperature for several months beforehand for it to have any degree of accuracy.

It can be fun to try to influence the sex of your baby, but don't pin your hopes on methods that can never be foolproof! Most parents are happy to welcome a boy or a girl into their family.

Q: My doctor says that I have a retroverted uterus. Will this make it harder to conceive, and does it affect pregnancy?

A: The uterus is usually tipped forward towards your pubic bone with its upper segment above your bladder. The position of a retroverted uterus is more upright, lined up with your spine. About 17-20 per cent lie naturally in this position. Very occasionally the uterus becomes retroverted as a result of disease or pelvic infection; these could cause infertility rather than the position of the uterus.

For most women with a retroverted uterus, conception is no less likely and miscarriage no more likely than for anyone else. The uterus usually moves forward spontaneously somewhere between the ninth and twelfth week and the pregnancy is just like any other.

Q: Our baby was conceived shortly before our holiday in Greece. Not knowing, I happily ate the local seafood and drank rather a lot of wine. I've had no problems but I feel guilty now as my baby's organs were forming. Is it likely that they have been harmed?

A: It's possible, but unlikely. Many actions increase a risk without turning it into a certainty. Drinking too much and eating seafood are *potential*, not inevitable causes of harm. An embryo that is damaged during the early stages of development is often miscarried, so your healthy pregnancy suggests that your baby is probably unaffected by anything you did on holiday.

It's hard to avoid all theoretical hazards, even after you have become pregnant. Your protective feelings about your baby are designed to be a positive influence on what you do from now on, not to make you feel guilty about risks you took before you knew you were pregnant.

Q: A friend says it is dangerous to have a high temperature in early pregnancy as the baby can be affected. How can I avoid it and what should I do if I get a fever?

A: An increase in body temperature to over 40°C (104°F) for a day, or over 38.5°C (102°F) for two days or more, *may* cause birth defects particularly between the third and seventh weeks of pregnancy.

You cannot isolate yourself from everyday life in case you catch something! Thousands of women who had flu or some other illness before realizing they were pregnant have gone on to have healthy babies. A strong immune system built on a good diet and a sensible lifestyle will help to protect you from infections.

If you have a high temperature, say over 38°C (101°F), don't take any home remedies. Contact your GP, who may suggest bringing it down by sponging yourself with tepid water or having a cool bath, although you should stop if you shiver. Other treatment would depend on how high your temperature was and your doctor's advice.

Q: I've read that VDUs can cause miscarriages and birth defects, and I work in an open plan office full of them. Is it true, and if so can anything be done about it?

A: No pregnancy related problems have been reported among women who use VDUs for 20 hours a week or less. Even if you work full time some experts say that modern equipment emits such low levels of radiation that they could not possibly harm a fetus, and that stress in the working situation may be more significant. But talk to your company's medical officer if there is one. Some employers have agreements that allow women who have worked with the firm for a certain length of time to move to other work during pregnancy.

More radiation is emitted from the back of a VDU than the screen, so if your desk is near someone else's VDU you could ask to be moved. Don't strain to see the screen and have a break away from your desk for a few minutes every hour. Perhaps you could alternate VDU work with other work during the day.

3

Early Pregnancy

(MONTHS 1–3)

' *When I was first pregnant I felt such pride, as though I'd grown up and proved myself at last. But then came the fears. Did I want to give up my freedom, would I be a good mother, could I bear the sleepless nights, or the pain of the birth? The first three months crept by, with sickness and self-doubt, and indescribable joy at the new life I was secretly nurturing.* '

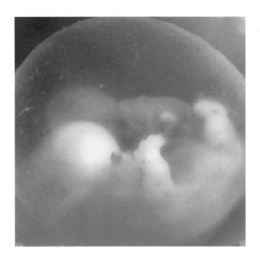

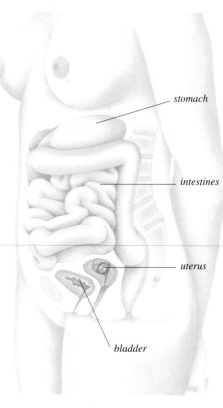

stomach

intestines

uterus

bladder

ONE MONTH

Above: An embryo at seven weeks, protected in the fluid-filled amniotic sac. All the organs of a future adult are beginning to function.
Right: First month: Your internal organs are in the same position as before conception.
Second month: Hormones soften your ligaments so that your organs can adapt as your uterus grows.
Third month: Your pregnancy may barely show but already your uterus has doubled in size.

HOW YOUR BABY DEVELOPS

After conception, the cells of your fertilized egg divide rapidly and roll down the Fallopian tube, increasing in size like a snowball. Seven days later (week three of pregnancy), dozens of cells of different shapes and sizes form a cluster. The outer layer of cells becomes the placenta and amniotic sac and the inner layer becomes the baby.

The cluster of cells (blastocyst) attaches to the lining of the uterus (endometrium) with tiny projections (villi), like ivy clinging to a wall. As the cells multiply an embryo forms, about the size of this full stop. By the fifth week the embryo is a three-layered disc as big as a lentil. The inner layer will become the baby's lungs, intestines, bladder and digestive system. The middle layer will form her heart, genitals, kidneys, bones and muscles; and the outer layer will form her brain, nervous system, external features and skin.

The embryo's head and brain develop first, followed by her body and then her limbs. By six weeks she's roughly the size of a grain of rice and her heart

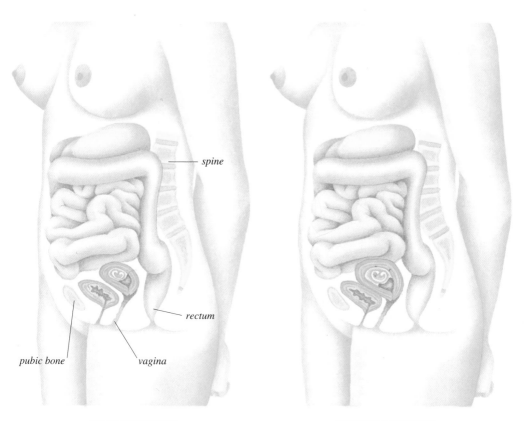

spine

rectum

pubic bone   *vagina*

TWO MONTHS   THREE MONTHS

has started to beat. By eight weeks she's the size of a peanut. Tiny limbs and muscles develop. A week later eyes and ears have formed and her fingers and toes are almost separated. When you are 10 weeks pregnant your embryo is about as long as the top joint of your little finger, and all her main body parts including the bones are formed. Finishing touches such as eyelids and finger nails are added. Twelve weeks after conception (week 14 of pregnancy) everything is beginning to function. Even egg (or sperm) cells are present.

HOW YOU MAY FEEL

If you are thrilled to be pregnant and your hormones cause little discomfort you may feel fitter and happier than ever before, and have glowing skin and shining hair. But many women experience mixed feelings in the early weeks. Although there is little to show and the outside world may be unaware of your pregnancy, enormous physical and emotional changes are taking place.

Periods of change can be stressful and unsettling. It takes time to adjust to having a baby, especially if it is unexpected or unwelcome. The demands that pregnancy makes on your body can sap your energy and make you feel exhausted. Hormone activity may cause symptoms that are distressing for you but are not considered important by anyone else because they don't harm the baby. Your feelings may swing from joy and excitement to self-doubt or despair. Common symptoms of early pregnancy include:

- A bloated, irrational feeling like pre-menstrual tension.
- Tender breasts, or painful nipples in cold weather.
- Flushes of heat or dizziness in stuffy rooms.
- A taste for strong flavours such as orange juice or pickles.
- Nausea, vomiting, or distaste for certain smells or foods.
- A need to urinate more frequently, caused by your growing uterus pressing on your bladder.
- Digestive upsets such as constipation or flatulence.
- Excessive saliva or a metallic taste in the mouth.
- Breakthrough bleeding when your period would have been due.
- Lifeless hair and greasy skin, or spots.
- Pulling pains at the sides of the abdomen, caused by the round ligaments stretching as the uterus moves into the abdomen.

RELATIONSHIP WITH YOUR PARTNER

Once a baby is on the way the relationship between you and your partner is bound to alter as you adjust to new roles. Many couples worry about this, but change is not necessarily negative.

Pregnancy may bring you and your partner closer together as you share new and exciting hopes for the future. Many fathers-to-be are both practically and emotionally supportive. However, if your partner seems bewildered or unhelpful try to talk to him about it. He may not understand your needs or why you feel the way you do. He may find it hard to adjust to your pregnancy. You become the focus of everyone's attention and he is expected to support you, but he may have his own worries. Some men feel proud of the pregnancy but ambivalent about becoming a father. Life will change and your partner may be anxious about the commitment required, new responsibilities and the loss of freedom. About 10 per cent of men suffer from symptoms of mild anxiety such as toothache, that are severe enough to make them seek help.

Accepting and talking about each other's feelings really does help. Try setting aside half an hour a week, with five minutes each to express your feelings without interruption and 20 minutes to discuss anything else that comes up. You'll learn more about each other, and you'll build a framework that makes it easier to deal with sensitive issues before they become damaging resentments that may threaten your relationship.

Relationship with your family

Babies bring great joy to the wider family. They provide a chance for other women to recall the special time when their own children were tiny, and men to take an interest they may have missed out on a generation ago. If you and your partner have children from previous liaisons your new baby will be a brother or sister to all of them, which can build positive bridges and help bring families together.

It will give other family members great pleasure if you share your pregnancy as far as possible. Phone them with news if they live far away; send them photocopies if you have a scan picture; find patterns you like if an auntie wants to knit bootees! If you are overwhelmed with offers to buy equipment explain that you prefer to wait until you have decided what you need. Meanwhile, it costs nothing to smile and say 'thank you'.

You may find yourself sensitive to unwanted advice and comments, but try to take them all in your stride. It's good to listen to other people's views, but deciding what is right for your baby is your responsibility, however well-meaning and experienced other family members may be. Family ties change, especially when you are expecting your first child, but with give and take new and rewarding relationships can be built.

YOUR LIFESTYLE

A healthy lifestyle means you're more likely to have a trouble-free pregnancy and a healthy baby. It's worth taking a look at your daily routine. Small changes can have a really positive effect for both you and the baby.

What to eat

If your diet is good you are more likely to have healthy blood, supple skin and muscles that function efficiently. The old saying, 'you are what you eat' applies equally to you and your baby. The early months of pregnancy when the baby's organs are developing are especially important. Mothers who eat a good or excellent diet are much less likely to have sickly, premature or low birthweight babies.

It's not really possible to give detailed instructions about what you should eat because nutritional needs differ with age, build, metabolic rate and so on. As a rough guide, you might aim to eat three to five portions of protein foods, plus five portions of bread and cereals and five of fruit and vegetables daily. Leafy green vegetable are especially valuable as they contain folic acid which is important for cell reproduction.

You gain more nutrients from fresh, whole foods than from processed foods. Try to eat some raw food, something containing iron, such as meat, nuts or dried fruit, and about four servings of calcium rich foods such as milk or milk products every day. Your body needs some fat, but fat is hidden in many foods

FOOD PRECAUTIONS

◆ *Avoid soft and blue-veined cheeses, unpasteurized milk or cheese,
shellfish, cook-chill foods, uncooked egg (such as in mayonnaise), paté
and undercooked meat, to reduce the risk of infection caused by listeria or
salmonella bacteria. Liver contains high levels of vitamin A which could
harm the baby and large quantities of nuts are thought to make some
babies liable to nut allergy, so eat liver and nuts in moderation.*
◆ *Buy ready-prepared food from a reputable source.*
◆ *Cook home-prepared foods thoroughly (especially re-heated foods).*
◆ *Check that the temperature of your fridge is below 4°C (39°F).*
◆ *Store raw meat separately from other foods.*
◆ *Wash all fruit and vegetables before eating.*

and is high in calories, so two servings of butter, margarine or oil per day is
adequate. If you eat poorly one day, try to make up for it the next day.

The chances are that you already think your diet is reasonably good, but
look at the labels when you're shopping. Some foods are more efficient
sources of nutrients than others. For example, a pint of semi-skimmed or
skimmed milk gives you the same amount of protein but fewer calories and
more calcium than whole milk.

Alcohol

Considerable research shows that drinking too much alcohol is harmful to
your child. The baby is unlikely to be affected if you have an occasional glass
of sherry, or a glass or two of wine each week, but cut down if you drink heavily and never binge. Your baby is at greater risk from one heavy drinking
session than if you have a small gin and tonic every evening. No one can say
what is 'safe' for an individual, so many women prefer not to drink at all when
pregnant. Others drink spritzers (half mineral water) or allow themselves the
occasional drink as a treat. Contact Alcohol Concern (see Appendix) for
advice if you're at all worried about your current drinking habits.

' *Nobody can see that you're pregnant in the
early weeks. I was so proud I wanted to shout
it from the rooftops, and when I found out it
was twins I grinned from ear to ear all the way
home! I felt so special and people were excited
in a way they usually aren't when it's not your
first baby. Of course there were moments of
panic and my husband was a bit worried as to
how we'd cope. But I was so determined to
enjoy this pregnancy.* ' PAULINE

Smoking

Smoking is a habit as well as an
addiction. Don't despair if you find
it hard to give up, but keep on
trying. Ask your GP to refer you to
a 'Stop Smoking' group, or you can
contact the Pregnancy Quitline
(see Appendix) for help.

AVOIDING RISKS

One of the down sides to any pregnancy is worry. The world can seem a dangerous place when you become aware of the growing list of what pregnant women should avoid! However, most babies are born healthy even when their mothers have been exposed to risks. Worrying about things you have no control over, or that happened in the past is pointless.

Just be sensible and avoid unnecessary risks:

- Avoid chemicals such as rain-proofing sprays for anoraks and tents, paint fumes, pesticides, other garden sprays and substances with any toxic warnings on the can. If you live in a farming area ask to be notified before crops are sprayed.
- Cats or dogs may carry active toxoplasmosis (see page 18). Pet lovers often develop immunity to this disease, but use rubber gloves to empty litter trays, or ask someone else to do it. Wear gloves for gardening and wash all home-grown fruit and vegetables as carefully as you would shop-bought produce.
- Avoid excess heat from very hot baths, saunas, electric blankets, heating pads or over-enthusiastic workouts.
- Have appliances such as your fridge (for safety of food storage), and microwave checked over to make sure they are all working properly. With your microwave always follow the manufacturer's instructions accurately and avoid standing in front when it's working.
- Tell the dentist or X-ray technician if you are or could be pregnant, although experts say modern low-dose diagnostic X-ray equipment rarely causes harm to the fetus.

REDUCE THE SMOKING RISK

◆ *Link your decision to stop smoking with an emotional incident. Many women use the joyful discovery that they're pregnant.*

◆ *Change your normal routine. Go for a brisk walk in the fresh air, or set yourself a task to complete when you would normally smoke a cigarette. Have a mint instead of a cigarette after a meal.*

◆ *Cut down by smoking only half a cigarette instead of a whole one and deliberately stubbing it out.*

◆ *Avoid smoke-filled rooms and smoking areas in public transport and restaurants. Ask your partner to go outside if he wants to smoke.*

◆ *Pay attention to what you eat, because an excellent diet gives some protection against the ill effects of passive smoking.*

◆ *Contact your Trades Union or Health and Safety representative at work if other people's smoking is a problem.*

HOW TO RELAX

◆ *Watch your posture (see page 44) to prevent causing unnecessary tension in your muscles.*

◆ *To relax your shoulders, pull them down and let go. They'll settle into a relaxed position. Check them every time you wait for the kettle to boil.*

◆ *Loosen your fingers. Tension from clenched hands travels up your arms and into your shoulders.*

◆ *Your face will reflect tension in your body. Relax the muscles around your eyes. Part your lips slightly and gently close them to relax your jaw and mouth.*

◆ *Buy a relaxation tape and spend some time each day learning the art of relaxing at will.*

Learn to relax

At this point, being pregnant may seem so full of pitfalls that it seems impossible to relax even for a minute! But life is full of risks and most people manage to come through unscathed. Certain environmental risks are unproven while others account for only a tiny proportion of birth defects or pregnancy complications. It's far more important to eat a good diet, have regular antenatal checks and avoid smoking or taking non-prescribed drugs. Try to get risks in proportion instead of feeling anxious and guilty over every little transgression. Do your best and then you can relax mentally.

Many women feel exhausted around the second and third months of pregnancy. Even after a good night's sleep they doze at their desk at work or fall asleep over the evening meal. It may not be easy to relax physically when you're working or looking after a lively toddler, but try to pace yourself during the day. Make allowances for the unseen changes of pregnancy and don't push yourself, especially if you're feeling under the weather. It's better to decline an invitation or make a meal from the freezer than end up feeling utterly frazzled. Many women feel guilty if they sit down without having a good excuse, but growing a baby is the best possible reason to rest.

' *When I became pregnant my life changed overnight. I didn't resent the changes, but I felt ill, emotional and mixed up and had no idea how to help myself or where to go for advice. I assumed if you had morning sickness you'd wake up, be sick and it would be over, whereas mine lasted all day. I lost weight and felt totally different inside. My partner was very supportive but he didn't understand why I cried all the time.*

I couldn't relate to a baby as it all seemed too remote. Everyone was delighted, but I had little enthusiasm because I felt so awful. I thought there must be something wrong with me. I didn't realize that other women also felt emotionally drained or found life very difficult in the early weeks. ' FRANCESCA

COPING WITH PREGNANCY SICKNESS

It's little comfort, but the first known record of this complaint is in a papyrus dated 2,000 BC, and some form of it is suffered by up to 70 per cent of women! It may be caused by the hormone HCG (human chorionic gonadotrophin) which is produced a few days after conception, reaches a peak at about 10 weeks and usually drops dramatically after 12-16 weeks.

Pregnancy sickness ranges from mild nausea in the mornings for a few weeks to severe nausea and vomiting lasting all day, in some cases throughout the entire pregnancy. It is often trivialized because it does not affect the baby adversely, but if you suffer badly from it you deserve everyone's sympathy and understanding.

Stress makes symptoms worse, but psychological factors such as 'unconscious rejection of the baby' are no longer thought to play a major role in the problem; neither is diet although there may be links with certain minerals and vitamins, especially B6.

Sickness is often worst at the time when your baby's organs are forming, so never take over-the-counter remedies without professional advice. This includes herbal or homeopathic preparations and vitamin supplements. If you cannot keep anything down you should certainly tell your doctor.

Otherwise, some of these suggestions may help:

- Accept the nausea and change your lifestyle temporarily. Ask your partner to do the cooking. Slow down, take extra rest, get fresh air every day and go to bed early.
- Don't worry about your diet for the time being. Eat little and often, whatever you can keep down. Take snacks like ginger biscuits or tiny sandwiches to eat at work.
- Sucking boiled sweets or crystallized ginger may banish the metallic taste in your mouth. Try root ginger in cooking.
- Ice lollies, plain water, fizzy drinks or herb teas may help.
- Find somebody to listen to your worries and to give practical help when you feel awful. There may be no remedy for your misery except time, but you need support to live through it.

ACHES AND PAINS

In early pregnancy the action of hormones softens all your ligaments so that as your baby grows your uterus can move out of your pelvic basin into your abdominal cavity. Ligaments that would normally stabilize your joints are softened too, and can be strained by poor posture when standing, sitting or lifting. Tense shoulder muscles, weak abdominal or buttock muscles, and wearing high heels that tilt your pelvis can cause backache. To avoid strains, watch your posture carefully, sleep on a supportive mattress, and roll onto your side before getting up.

Looking after your back

Pregnancy is an excellent time to review how you use your body. If you have picked up bad postural habits over the years it will take thought at first. However, good posture quickly becomes automatic, avoiding aches and pains.

Lifting: Bend your knees and keep your back straight. Try not to lift and twist at the same time – move your feet instead. Keep the weight close to your body unless it's as light as this empty bucket.

Standing: Keep your back upright with your shoulders relaxed, pelvis balanced and feet apart. Don't rest with your weight on one hip or stick your bump out.

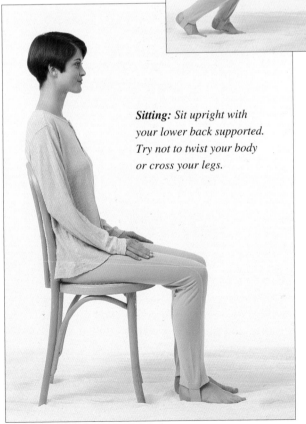

Sitting: Sit upright with your lower back supported. Try not to twist your body or cross your legs.

YOUR PELVIC FLOOR

If there is one part of the body that all women should know about it's the pelvic floor, the muscles between your legs that form the base of the pelvic basin. To locate them, look at the illustration below. Cough into your hand and you'll feel the muscles bulge a little.

They are important because they support your bladder, vagina and bowel, and control their sphincters or exits. They carry the growing weight of your uterus and baby and withstand the extra pressure when your baby's head engages (see page 52) before labour. When your baby is born the muscles guide her head to align it with your pubic arch and stretch to let her emerge. They need to be strong but flexible.

During pregnancy your pelvic floor sags a little with the extra weight, but muscles with good tone (the normal firmness of healthy tissue) return to their normal horizontal state after the birth. Over a long period, lax muscles allow your pelvic organs to change position, making it harder for the supporting muscles to function properly. This could lead to problems such as stress incontinence.

How to tone your pelvic floor

Breathing normally, slowly draw up the muscles, hold them momentarily, and release them gently. Repeat this six times, several times every day without using your abdominal and buttock muscles. Concentrate on becoming more aware of the sensations you feel. Some women find it easiest to lean forward with their knees apart and their buttocks resting on the edge of a chair seat.

Imagine that your pelvic floor is a lift in a department store. Tighten it up, pausing at each floor before moving to the next one. You may reach the second floor or the seventh depending on how much control you have. Try to stop at each floor on the way down again!

Your pelvic floor muscles are more complex, but this shows its hammock-like structure which supports your internal organs. From front to back it has three openings – the urethra leading from the bladder, the vagina from the uterus and the anus from the bowel.

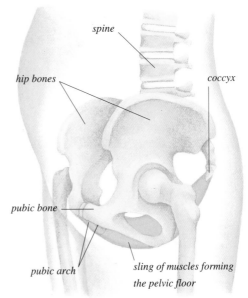

spine

hip bones

coccyx

pubic bone

pubic arch

sling of muscles forming the pelvic floor

RIGHTS AND BENEFITS

If you work during pregnancy you have legal rights that protect your health and job, and entitlements to cash benefits when you stop work to have your baby. Some apply to all pregnant women in paid employment; for example the right to paid time off for antenatal care. This includes antenatal classes although you may need a letter from your GP or midwife stating that classes are part of your care.

Others, such as rights to move from a job involving heavy lifting to a suitable alternative if one is available, and to return to your job after your baby is born, depend on qualifying employment periods. Maternity Allowance and sickness benefits depend on contributions in a qualifying period, so you may still be eligible if you are self-employed or have recently stopped work.

All pregnant women are entitled to free prescriptions and dental care. If you are on a low income you may be able to claim free milk and vitamins, help with fares to hospital and a lump sum to buy things for the baby.

There are set times to claim in order to preserve some rights but the rules are complicated. Ask your GP, midwife or local Benefits Agency (address in phone book) for leaflets on 'Maternity Benefits' and 'Babies and Children'. Note all the important dates in your diary.

Some employers offer better maternity benefits than required by law, so find out the terms that apply to you. The Maternity Alliance (see Appendix) has free leaflets on your rights at work, including one on redundancy.

YOUR PREGNANCY PLANNER – MONTHS 1-3

◆ *Your first antenatal check ('booking visit') takes place between 8 and 12 weeks, often at your home. Your midwife finds out about your health, lifestyle and medical history, takes blood samples and checks your blood pressure and urine. Ask about tests for fetal abnormalities (see page 55).*

◆ *Stop smoking, cut down on alcohol and make improvements to your diet now – it's important for you and your baby. If you need help there are useful addresses in the Appendix.*

◆ *If you are uncertain about your rights at work contact the Maternity Alliance (see Appendix) for information.*

◆ *Take advantage of free dental care to visit your dentist for a check up.*

◆ *Tell your employer when you need time off for antenatal care.*

◆ *Start thinking about various birth options and getting information about different hospitals (see page 85) and antenatal classes (see page 79).* Practical Parenting *magazine has up-to-date articles to help you to make choices.*

◆ *Look in the small advertisements for addresses to order maternity wear catalogues.*

QUESTIONS AND ANSWERS

Q: My back has always been one of my weak spots and I don't want to suffer during pregnancy. Apart from watching my posture is there anything I can do to help myself avoid backache problems?

A: You could strengthen your back muscles with gentle pelvic rocking. Stand with your feet apart and your knees bent. Tighten your buttocks and tilt your pelvis forwards, then release them and tilt it backwards, rocking it slowly and rhythmically. This movement also helps existing backache.

If you get backache under your shoulder blades, circle your shoulders to release stiffness. Try wearing a larger size of bra or let the hooks out, and make sure that you sit with your back straight and supported. For pain that is low down and to one side of your spine (probably a strained sacroiliac ligament) ask your partner to massage the area firmly and apply some gentle heat.

Q: I have been a vegetarian for 10 years but am now a vegan. Is this diet adequate for pregnancy, or should I take supplements?

A: Vegetarians who are healthy and eat a good, varied diet do not usually need supplements, as their blood mineral levels fall within normal ranges. Some nutritionists recommend that vegans take supplements of vitamin B12, vitamin D, calcium and iron during pregnancy, but check with your doctor first. You may also need to make sure that you get enough protein.

Vegetarians and vegans have the same needs as other pregnant women and any diet is only as good as you make it. Contact the addresses in the Appendix if you need more information.

Q: I'm delighted to be pregnant but I'm having nightmares about the birth. We were shown a film at school and although it was years ago the memory is still vivid. How can I overcome my fear?

A: The feelings and emotions that are part of giving birth, and can make it a special experience, rarely come over in films. In real life giving birth is not in vivid Technicolor and it's *your* baby, which makes a world of difference.

When negative thoughts float into your mind try not to dwell on them, but replace them with positive ones. For example, remind yourself that women are designed to give birth; that you won't be entering a competition or giving a performance, just doing your best. Concentrate on enjoying your pregnancy and looking forward to seeing your baby. The birth is simply the bridge between the two.

It's not too soon to look for antenatal classes (see page 79) to attend later on, as good ones often get booked up early. Part of the job of a parentcraft teacher is to explain about birth more fully and teach you ways of coping. After you have been to classes and as the birth gets closer you'll probably wonder why you ever felt so afraid.

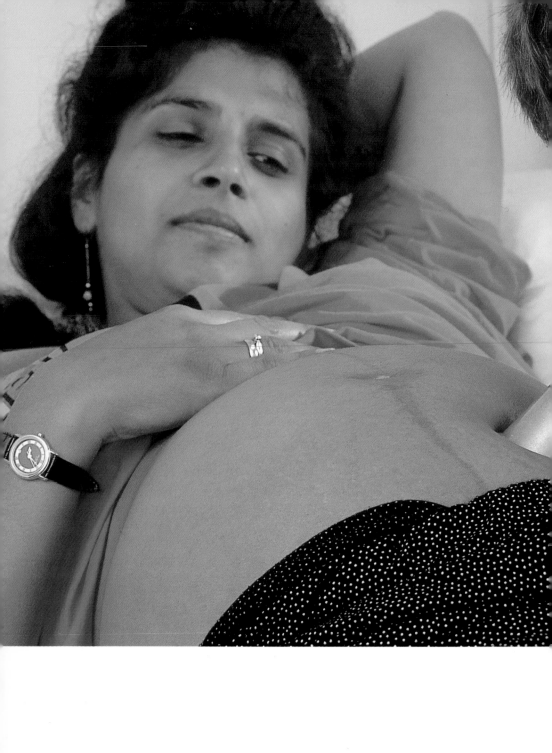

4

Antenatal Care

' Getting to know my way around the system was like learning the ropes in my first term at secondary school. I scarcely knew what I was doing but I was bowled along in a friendly way while I asked questions and learned new names for familiar things. '

WHAT IS A 'NORMAL' PREGNANCY?

Your pregnancy is normal if it progresses like the majority of pregnancies, and if any unusual symptoms you get are not generally thought to be harmful to mothers or babies. What is considered normal depends to some extent on the experience of the people concerned and on current scientific interests.

Routine antenatal checks distinguish harmless symptoms from potentially dangerous ones, so that you and your baby stay healthy and any problems are picked up early. They also give you a chance to ask questions and find out enough information to help you make informed decisions.

Pregnancy is a state of health with just an occasional problem, although doctors sometimes forget this! If you are never singled out for special attention you can rest assured that everything is going well. Even if closer attention is paid to a particular symptom it does not always mean there is a problem. Women are so individual that something could be abnormal for some women, but be normal for you.

ANTENATAL VISITS

Antenatal checks are carried out by a midwife and may take place at your home, or at your GP's surgery or the local hospital - you can take your partner or a friend along if you wish. The first (or booking visit) usually lasts about an hour, much longer than later visits. The midwife takes your history, recording details such as your job, your lifestyle, your past and present health plus that of your partner and both families if possible. The aim is to find out your individual circumstances and anything that could affect your pregnancy. Previous pregnancies, terminations or adoptions will be noted, but say if you don't want something written down.

' I had antenatal care at my GP's antenatal clinic and got to know Jane, my midwife, so well that she became a friend. Thinking about tests is the worst part of pregnancy, but she discussed it until I felt ready to make a decision. She listens to the baby's heart with an ear trumpet and the first time she heard it she stuck a stethoscope on the end so that I could hear it too. I don't know which of us was more excited.

Going for check-ups made me feel special because of Jane's attitude. I could ask anything without feeling silly. I don't have anyone to share the excitement of pregnancy with; luckily Jane seemed as interested in every little detail as I was. ' ALISON

Your height and weight may be checked, although some doctors question whether this is useful or not. The weigh-in gives a baseline for later visits. Failure to put on weight could mean your baby isn't growing properly and a sudden weight gain could indicate fluid retention. But not all gains or losses are important. For instance, you might be wearing lighter or heavier clothes because the weather has changed, or be laying down fat stores on your bottom or thighs, which are normally used up while breastfeeding.

ANTENATAL CHECKUPS

◆ *Take your partner, a friend or a book to your first antenatal visit –*
you may have to wait between examinations.
◆ *Be open about any symptoms you have and ask questions about tests*
or treatments suggested.
◆ *If your blood pressure is high because of anxiety or stress ask if it can*
be taken again in half an hour and use the time to consciously relax. This
will often bring it down to normal.

If the visit takes place in hospital or at your GP's clinic you may have a physical examination to check your current state of health, but you are unlikely to have an internal examination. Blood samples (see below) will be taken and you may be asked to provide a mid-stream urine sample (pass urine for a short time, then catch the sample in a container) to check for infection. An ultrasound scan or other special tests (see page 56) will be offered.

At each antenatal visit your urine will be tested for sugar and protein, possible signs of gestational diabetes (see page 53) and pre-eclampsia (see page 102). Your blood pressure when your heart is pumping and at rest will be taken using an inflated cuff around your upper arm. The midwife will also feel your stomach to check the height of your uterus, and later your baby's position. From about 18 weeks, or earlier with sophisticated equipment, she will listen to your baby's heartbeat, and feel your ankles to test for any swelling (see page 102). You may have more frequent antenatal checks if your pregnancy is unusual in any way, but you can contact your doctor or midwife between visits if you have any worries.

Antenatal care should be considered a partnership between you and your midwife. It's part of her job to give you unbiased information and help you make informed decisions about what tests to have, where to have your baby and so on. No examination or test is compulsory and the decisions are up to you. At each visit you can ask for advice and discuss anything that worries or interests you.

Routine blood tests

Blood samples are taken at your booking visit and later in pregnancy. The analysis varies but includes checking for blood group and the rhesus factor (see page 53) in case you need an emergency transfusion, plus tests for glucose, syphilis, rubella and possibly hepatitis B. If you have no rubella antibodies you will be offered immunization after the birth. The other diseases could harm your baby if left untreated. Some hospitals offer a full glucose tolerance test on a separate occasion (see gestational diabetes, page 53). You may be offered an HIV test as treatment can now be offered to reduce the risk

What your notes mean

If there is anything you don't understand it's better to ask than to go home and worry! Here are some common phrases and abbreviations:

Your details:

Para 0/1/2+1	You have had 0, 1 or 2 previous births. +1 means a miscarriage or termination before 28 weeks.
LB or SB	Live birth or stillbirth.
TCA 3/7 (4/52)	To come again in 3 days (or 4 weeks).
Brim	The inlet or upper rim of your pelvis.
Fundus	The top of your uterus, which rises in your abdomen as your baby grows and descends a little when the baby's head engages (see below).
BP	Blood pressure.
PET	Pre-eclampsia (pre-eclamptic toxaemia) (see page 102).
US or USS	Ultrasound scan.

Urine:

NAD	Nothing abnormal discovered.
Alb/Tr Prot+ (or ++)	Albumin/trace of protein. The plus signs indicate the amount of protein found. This could signify the start of pre-eclampsia.
0 Gluc	No glucose found in the urine. Two per cent or more glucose would be considered high.

Blood:

Bloods	Blood tests done.
Hb	Haemoglobin or blood count.
Fe	Iron tablets. The prescription (e.g. Pregaday) may be recorded.
WR	Syphilis test VDRL/TPHA or FTA-Abs are alternatives.

The baby's health:

FMF or FMNF	Fetal movements felt, or not felt.
FH	Fetal heart. H or NH means heard or not heard. The heart rate (usually between 120 and 160 beats per minute) may be recorded.

The baby's position:

LOA/ROA	Left (or right) occiput anterior or LOP/ROP posterior (see page 105).
PP	Presenting part, or the part of your baby nearest to the cervix and likely to emerge first.
Vx or Ceph	Vertex or cephalic, meaning 'head down'.
Br/Tr	Breech (bottom down), or transverse (lying across the uterus).
Eng or E	Engaged. This refers to how far down your baby's head is in your pelvis. When recorded in fifths it means the proportion of your baby's head above the brim of your pelvis. So 1/5 means the head is almost fully engaged, ready for the birth, while 4/5 means it has started to engage.
NEng or NE	Not engaged.

of transmitting HIV to the baby. Discuss it with your midwife – it's not compulsory and you can refuse.

Your haemoglobin level will be checked. Haemoglobin is the substance in red blood cells that carries oxygen around your body. The average blood count in pregnancy is about 12g. When you are anaemic (ie your haemoglobin level is too low) your heart has to work harder to supply your baby with oxygen, so you may be given iron tablets and folic acid supplements if your blood count is under about 10g.

Individual tests may be performed if you are at risk from a disease that needs special care in pregnancy, such as sickle cell anaemia, thalassaemia, toxoplasmosis (see page 18) or diabetes.

The rhesus factor: If a mother is rhesus negative and her partner, like 80 per cent of the population, is rhesus positive a problem may arise in future pregnancies if the baby inherits the father's blood group. The baby's blood will contain a D antigen and the mother's does not. If the baby's blood passes into the mother, as can happen during birth, miscarriage or termination, the mother's blood will form antibodies against the D antigen. These may attack the red blood cells of any future rhesus positive baby the mother carries.

If you are rhesus negative you will have extra blood tests to monitor your antibody status. Within three days of the birth you will be given an anti-D injection to destroy any cells from the baby's blood before antibodies are formed. About two per cent of women need treatment during pregnancy because the baby's blood cells have leaked across the placenta.

Blood pressure: Normal blood pressure is about 110/70. In pregnancy it varies, usually somewhere between 95/60 and 135/85. The systolic (upper) figure (measuring your heart when pumping) can be affected by stress, including anxiety or rushing to your appointment. The diastolic (lower) figure records your heart at rest. If it rises by 20 points above your normal baseline it could indicate pre-eclampsia (see page 102). The usual cut-off point for concern is 140/90, although in the absence of other symptoms there may be nothing to worry about.

High blood pressure can make you feel energetic just when you ought to be resting to help bring it down, while low blood pressure may make you feel faint or excessively tired. Although blood pressure outside the normal range is a potential problem during pregnancy, it is not your fault!

Gestational diabetes

Insulin regulates the glucose in your blood and eliminates any excess. To meet the needs of the baby, anti-insulin hormones in pregnancy allow extra glucose to circulate. If there is too much for the mother's and the baby's needs, the excess is excreted. About 50 per cent of pregnant women show traces of sugar in the urine at some stage, and more insulin is usually produced to compensate.

Women with gestational diabetes have high levels of sugar in their blood and urine because the anti-insulin hormones work so well that they cannot produce enough insulin, or cannot use the insulin they produce efficiently. This is rarely linked to 'ordinary' diabetes (inability to produce enough insulin when you are not pregnant), although treatments for the two conditions are similar, including a good diet and extra monitoring to keep your blood sugar at normal levels. If you have 'ordinary' diabetes your care should preferably begin before conception, but monitoring during pregnancy can greatly reduce the risks of either ordinary or gestational diabetes.

Have you any questions?

At the end of your antenatal check you'll be asked if you have any questions. When you're pregnant for the first time it can be hard to think of any questions as you feel a complete novice. Later you'll probably think of plenty of things to ask, but at your first visit there are things you might want to know, so that you don't miss out on something or find out about it too late. So it is worth preparing a list of questions to take along to your first appointment.

Ask where you could have your baby, to discover all the possibilities in your area. Some women get the impression that they have to go to a certain hospital, but this is not true. Before your visit you might like to look at the pros and cons of hospital, midwifery unit and home birth on page 84. You do not have to make your mind up immediately about where to have your baby but you can decide later when you have thought about it.

Ask what sort of antenatal care you can have. This is usually linked to where you have your baby. Look at the possibilities on page 27 and find out what happens in your area.

Finally, ask what tests are available to check that your baby is healthy. These are discussed on the next page. Some are carried out very early in pregnancy, or you might have to travel to a specialist centre to have them.

WHEN TO CONTACT YOUR DOCTOR

Even normal changes in pregnancy can be worrying when you first experience them. Here are the symptoms you should always report to your GP:

◆ *Vaginal bleeding – it may be no problem, but it's best to check.*

◆ *Abdominal pain or cramps that get increasingly severe.*

◆ *High temperature, fever symptoms or excessive vomiting.*

◆ *Severe headache that doesn't respond to the usual remedies, blurred vision, or swelling of your feet so that you can't get your shoes on. These could indicate pre-eclampsia (see page 102).*

◆ *Any other symptom that worries you.*

WILL MY BABY BE ALRIGHT?

Anxiety about whether your baby will be perfect is natural. About 4 per cent of liveborn babies have an abnormality. No one knows what causes most of these, but more than half of them are either mild, such as an extra toe or a birthmark, or moderate such as a cleft palate or congenital dislocation of the hip. They may need no treatment or an operation (sometimes very minor), and the baby will lead a normal life.

Older mothers often worry that they are at greater risk of having a child with a disability than younger mothers, but only chromosomal abnormalities increase with age. For example, there is a one in 800 chance of having a baby with a major chromosomal abnormality at age 30. At age 35 it's one in 335, at 40 it's one in 100 and at 45 it's one in 25.

Testing for fetal abnormalities is part of antenatal care. If you feel that a termination is preferable to bringing a disabled baby into the world they offer this choice. They may also offer reassurance so that you can enjoy the rest of your pregnancy.

But tests have disadvantages: they are not totally accurate, they only detect certain problems (for example, most rare single gene defects are not detectable at present), and they cannot show the degree of disability which may vary considerably.

If you are not particularly worried, think carefully before having a test just because it's available. Some hospitals offer tests with the expectation that if an abnormality is diagnosed you will want a termination, but not all women agree with this. It's better to clarify your feelings in advance rather than jump on a roundabout that may be difficult to get off.

Most women will be reassured by their results. Those who are not face difficult choices: to have more tests, to continue pregnancy knowing their baby may have a problem, or to opt for termination. Such decisions are never easy to make.

Special tests

Broadly speaking, invasive tests like amniocentesis, chorionic villus sampling (CVS) and fetal blood sampling carry small risks but they do diagnose with a good measure of certainty the presence of chromosomal, genetic and metabolic defects. Procedures such as ultrasound scans and blood tests that do not involve penetrating the uterus carry fewer risks to the baby, but give less information.

Hospitals protocols regarding how and when tests are performed vary. Most women are offered an ultrasound scan, although routine scans do not always check for abnormalities. In some areas women over 35 or with a family history of a disability are offered amniocentesis. In others, all women are offered a blood test followed by amniocentesis if the results suggest that the baby might have a disability. If a test is not available locally you could arrange referral to a centre that provides it. If you are considered low risk a test may only be offered privately.

The more experienced a hospital is at providing tests and interpreting results the better. Recently introduced tests may be less reliable and carry more risks. Ask your doctor for up-to-date local information.

Blood tests select pregnancies where the baby may be at higher risk of certain defects so that the mother can be offered further tests. The AFP test analyses alphafetoprotein levels to assess the risk of neural tube defects such as spina bifida. The double, triple and triple-plus (quadruple) tests combine various markers with your age to give a predicted risk for neural tube defects and chromosome abnormalities such as Down's syndrome.

The triple-plus test is performed from 13 weeks; others from about 15-22 weeks. Results are available in a week or two. Ten per cent of women score below one in 250 and will be offered amniocentesis.

Blood tests can cause unnecessary anxiety. They are not very reliable – 60 per cent (triple) and about 80 per cent (triple-plus). Only 10 per cent of women with raised AFP levels will be carrying a baby with a defect.

Ultrasound scans: A dating scan (12-14 weeks) is brief and can check for major abnormalities of the baby's spine, limbs or organs, identify more than one baby, locate the placenta and confirm your dates (see page 62) to decide the timing of blood tests for fetal abnormalities.

A nuchal scan (10-13 weeks) checks for major abnormalities and measures a fluid-filled space behind the baby's neck to predict (together with your age) the risk of a chromosome defect such as Down's syndrome. It offers reassurance or further tests and termination if necessary earlier in pregnancy than blood tests, an important advantage for many women, but it's not widely available. Your doctor can refer you to a hospital which has the necessary sophisticated equipment, although you may have to pay privately for this type of scan.

If a nuchal scan suggests a normal or reduced risk you may be advised to have an anomaly scan to exclude defects not linked with chromosome abnormalities.

An anomaly scan (16-22 weeks, or 30-plus weeks for minor defects) is longer and more detailed than a dating scan. It checks for defects that might not be apparent on an early scan, but it cannot detect metabolic or chromosomal abnormalities unless there are associated physical signs.

‘ *I enjoyed my antenatal care, apart from waiting around at my first visit to the hospital. I wanted my baby to be healthy so I took all the advice offered, but of course I had moments of wondering what I'd do if she wasn't!*

I decided not to have tests after talking to my partner, my GP and friends who'd had them. I didn't think the evidence would tell me enough to base a decision on, and felt that I wouldn't be given anything I couldn't cope with. That was more important than numbers on a bit of paper saying I was low risk or whatever. ’ JOANNE

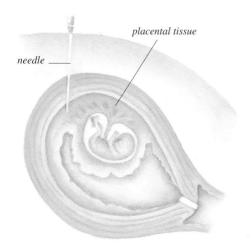

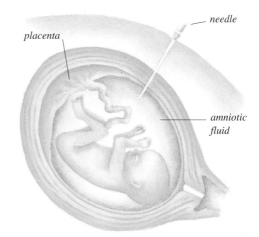

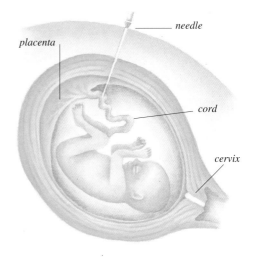

Above: Chorionic Villus Sampling (CVS). Cells are taken from the edge of the placenta at about 11-13 weeks.
Above right: Amniocentesis. A sample of amniotic fluid is withdrawn at about 16-18 weeks.
Right: Fetal blood sampling. A sample of the baby's blood is withdrawn from the cord (or from the baby's heart or liver) after 18 weeks.

When you have a scan your abdomen is lubricated with gel and a transducer bounces high frequency waves off your baby to build up a picture on a monitor screen. An abdominal scan in early pregnancy can involve the discomfort of a full bladder to push your uterus into view, so you may be offered a transvaginal scan, which gives a better image when your uterus is low in your pelvis. The transducer is a thin probe used inside the vagina.

A transvaginal scan can be used to investigate miscarriage, monitor bleeding or an IVF pregnancy, or detect an ectopic pregnancy (one that implants outside the uterus). It can only detect major physical abnormalities early in pregnancy.

A Doppler scan is performed through the abdomen using a different type of ultrasound. Doppler is the change in sound heard when a train rushes towards you, passes you and then disappears. It can help to determine how well the placenta is functioning, identify problems such as poor growth and

‘ If you decide to have tests you need to talk it through with your partner so that you're both sure what you would do if there was a problem. Our experience ended happily with the birth of a perfect baby, but my pregnancy was stressful.

My triple test suggested a risk of Down's syndrome so I had an amniocentesis. This showed an abnormality and I went to London for fetal blood sampling. Although we were given the all clear my husband and I were still afraid that something was wrong. We didn't admit it to each other until afterwards, but I couldn't look forward to the birth in case something happened. ’ ANNETTE

monitor a high risk pregnancy. The blood flow in the placenta is assessed by bouncing sound off cells as they rush through your blood vessels.

Scans appear to be safe and it's exciting to see your baby on the screen. Nobody knows if there are long term risks to future generations, however, so some people feel they should only be used when essential. You're not obliged to have a scan; if you're uncertain ask for more information.

Amniocentesis: Amniocentesis is performed at about 16-18 weeks to detect abnormalities such as Down's syndrome, cystic fibrosis and Tay Sach's disease. Guided by a scan, a fine, hollow needle is passed through your abdomen and a sample of amniotic fluid is taken from around your baby. Cells are cultured so results take between three and five weeks to come through. You may wish to ask your baby's sex; if you're told that it's a girl there is a slight chance that the female cells cultured could be yours, not your baby's.

Occasionally amniocentesis causes infection. There is a one per cent risk of miscarriage and a one per cent risk that the test will need to be repeated, with the same risk of miscarriage. Three per cent of babies have breathing problems after birth, but these are usually temporary and mild.

Chorionic villus sampling (CVS): This detects similar abnormalities to amniocentesis. A sample of the chorionic villi (the tissue that will later develop into the placenta) is taken through the vagina or the abdomen at about 11-13 weeks. Results take a few days. There may be at least one per cent risk of miscarriage, up to two per cent risk of false positive results (changes in the cells of the chorionic villi that are not present in your baby), and one per cent chance that the test may need repeating. Recently there have been concerns about the test affecting the baby. The skills of the laboratory technician and the doctor who carries out the test are significant in maximizing reliability and safety. A doctor needs to perform about 75 tests to learn the technique.

Fetal blood sampling: This tests for a wide range of defects plus diseases such as rubella and toxoplasmosis. A needle is inserted through your abdomen and a sample of the baby's blood is taken from his liver, heart or umbilical cord. The test is usually performed after 18 weeks when the baby's blood vessels are big enough.

It is not widely available and is only done to confirm a diagnosis suspected after other tests. The results are available in about two days, depending on the problem. The miscarriage risk is two to four per cent, or less if the doctor performs over 30 tests a year.

Deciding about tests

Fetal testing produces dilemmas that previous generations never had to face. The burden of responsibility may feel impossibly heavy to bear when you realize that the tests themselves carry potential risks as well as benefits, and the decisions are down to you.

Whether you opt for testing depends on how you weigh up the risks and benefits. For instance, at the age of 40 the risks of amniocentesis causing a miscarriage or detecting a major chromosomal defect are equal: one in a hundred. If you are under 40 the risk of miscarriage is greater than the likelihood of detecting a problem. If you are over 40 it's the other way round.

You might also want to consider factors such as how easily you conceive, how important *this* baby is to you and how you feel about having an affected child. If you were 38 years old and worried about having a baby with Down's syndrome, detecting this might outweigh the risk of a miscarriage. On the other hand, a woman of 42 who had trouble conceiving and has fewer chances of conceiving again might feel the risk of losing a baby through an invasive test is too high.

Many people with a disability are saddened by the fear their condition arouses in others. But fear is not always rational. It depends on your view of the world, your emotional and financial resources, your experience of children with a disability and the effects you feel such a child would have on you and your family.

Some reasons for having tests:
- You simply could not cope with a disabled baby. Tests may reassure you or give you the option of termination.
- You already have a child with a disability or a family history of a defect, and want to know if this baby is affected.
- You feel that having tests means you have done everything possible to avoid having a child with a disability.
- You feel the potential drawbacks are a small price to pay for the information or reassurance tests could provide.

Some reasons for not having tests:
- You feel that they would not give you accurate enough information on which to base decisions.
- You are not unduly anxious and want to enjoy your pregnancy without the worry tests might cause.
- You prefer to accept what comes and would find out about a disability and cope if it happened.

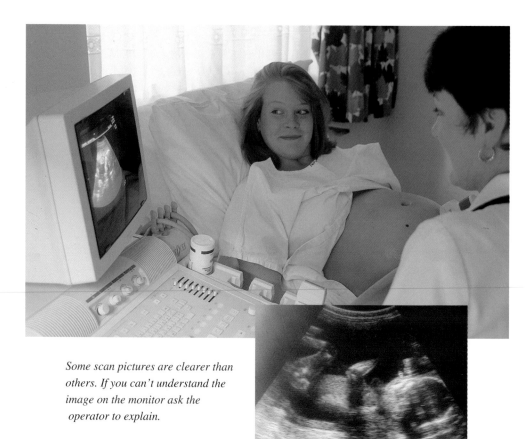

Some scan pictures are clearer than others. If you can't understand the image on the monitor ask the operator to explain.

The following summary may help you decide, with your family and your doctor, the test that is right for you.

Blood test: Blood tests carry no risks but they may increase anxiety. Ten per cent of women are offered amniocentesis, so think twice if you don't want to risk an invasive test. If you are considered high risk but want to avoid amniocentesis a blood test might reassure you. If you are not offered a blood test you could ask to pay privately. The triple-plus test is more reliable than the triple test.

Amniocentesis: If you want a definite diagnosis waiting for blood test results would delay this, so consider going straight for amniocentesis.

CVS: An option if you want a definite diagnosis early in pregnancy and a centre near you offers it.

Ultrasound scans: Brief routine scans do not check for all physical defects, but an anomaly scan at 20 weeks might reassure you. A first trimester scan to measure the dark space behind the baby's neck might help you decide whether to have further tests.

Waiting for results

Waiting for results may be more stressful than you anticipate. Wondering if your baby has a defect brings unexpected and distressing emotions, and if further tests are suggested most women expect the worst so waiting is especially stressful. You never think you'll face this situation so it's always a shock, and your confidence may be so shaken that you never feel completely reassured until your baby is born.

Remember that more than half the women who are offered further tests will be told that all is well; and that around half of all abnormalities are mild or moderate defects that can be treated.

Facing an adverse result: Many women intend to have a termination if there's a problem, but what seemed the obvious choice when there was a strong possibility it would not be necessary can be much harder when your pregnancy is showing and you can feel your baby moving.

You may worry about ending a pregnancy needlessly because the test was wrong, or the baby was only mildly affected. This is something you will never know so it's best to assume the test is correct. Termination is not, of course, the only option. You could continue your pregnancy even though your baby might not live or might be disabled. Another possibility you could consider is fostering or adoption.

Don't be pressured into making quick judgements; thinking about things for a few days will make little difference. The decision has to be one that you can live with. It isn't easy and you will need support.

Discuss the results with your GP or a genetic specialist, and your family. It may help to talk to parents who have faced similar decisions, or to someone with the same disability. Organizations that can put you in touch with someone, give you information or support you whatever your decision are listed in the Appendix.

Coping with termination: Although it is distressing to think about it, knowing what may happen can make termination less daunting. You will be admitted to the gynaecology or maternity ward, and will probably be given a single room. If the pregnancy is less than 14 weeks, the neck of the uterus is usually dilated and the fetus is removed under general anaesthetic. Between 14 and 18 weeks obstetricians have different policies, some favouring dilatation and evacuation and others feeling that induced labour is safer.

After 18 weeks it is considered safer to induce labour using prostaglandin pessaries or a drip (see page 146). Because the uterus is not ready for labour it can be longer and more painful, but your partner or a friend can be with you and pain relief will be available. The thought of going through labour may be profoundly upsetting, but this really is safer for you.

Termination inevitably causes great sadness. It's hard to take such a responsibility, but uncertainty is part of life and you can only make a decision with the knowledge you have at the time. If you have done your best you have to assume your choice was the right one. Discuss how you feel with a good listener. Your midwife or a sympathetic friend may help if your partner feels unable to talk about it because of his own distress.

Give yourself time to come to terms with feelings of grief or guilt. Emotional pain cannot be anaesthetized; it has to be faced and lived through. Taking positive steps to come to terms with it will help you to move forward more confidently to a new pregnancy.

QUESTIONS AND ANSWERS

Q: Going by my last period, my baby is due on 17 May. A scan at 12 weeks said I am due on 22 May but another at 20 weeks gave 14 May as my due date. A midwife said they judge when a baby is due from the scan dates, but which ones?

A: Scans date a pregnancy accurately to within a few days at 7-12 weeks. From 13-20 weeks they are slightly less accurate (within a week) and after 20 weeks they are steadily less reliable. The earlier scan date is probably the one to go on. Your baby is likely to arrive within a week either side of May 22. Having said this, babies sometimes ignore what they are supposed to do and arrive when they feel like it!

Q: When I was scanned at 14 weeks I was told that my placenta is low and I'll need another scan later on to see if it has moved. If not I may need a Caesarean section. Why is this?

A: Usually the placenta implants in the upper wall, well out of the way of the cervix, or neck of the uterus. If it was low down it might begin to detach when the cervix opens. Depending on the degree, a Caesarean section might be the safest option. A placenta that lies completely over the cervix (*placenta praevia*) would prevent the baby from emerging safely, so a Caesarean birth would certainly be planned.

The placenta doesn't physically change position, but early in pregnancy it's hard to tell if it has implanted in the lower area of the uterus or what will become the upper part. This can be checked by another scan later on, when the uterus is bigger. The majority are found to be absolutely fine.

Q: I'm three months pregnant and my doctor says I've put on half the total weight gain I'm allowed already. Should I go on a diet?

A: In early pregnancy women who suffer nausea and vomiting sometimes put on no weight. Others gain weight rapidly, laying down fat stores on thighs and buttocks that are used up when breastfeeding. Doctors often suggest a total gain of 11-20kg (25-45lb) is reasonable. A large-framed woman would be towards the upper end and a petite woman at the lower end.

These are guidelines and there are wide variations. Excess weight increases the risk of minor problems such as varicose veins and backache and may contribute to more serious problems.

The quality of the food you eat is probably more important than the quantity. Eat according to your appetite, and no more. Don't diet, except on medical advice, as using up your fat stores would only provide your baby with calories and babies also need a steady supply of nutrients to grow healthily.

Q: My sister prevented stretch marks by rubbing oil into her stomach every day, but a friend who also did so said it made no difference. What should I do?

A: Stretch marks appear on your stomach, thighs or breasts. They look like purplish streaks under the skin and are caused by the lower layers stretching. Women who gain weight rapidly tend to have more of them but it also depends on skin type. Rubbing in oil or special creams doesn't prevent them, although it may make your skin feel more comfortable. If your sister has no stretch marks you may have inherited skin with good elasticity. About 90 per cent of women develop at least a few, and some women get a lot. Occasionally a rash develops, but your GP can prescribe something for it. Stretch marks gradually fade to cream or silvery grey. Look on them as a badge of motherhood!

Q: I have a small frame and my midwife says my baby is a good size. I'm worried about having a difficult birth. Should I eat less so that the baby will be smaller?

A: When your midwife says your baby is a 'good size' she may mean exactly right for you, or she may simply be making conversation! It can be remarkably hard to judge a baby's size before birth. Anxiety often makes women give doctors' and midwives' pronouncements unjustified significance.

The sort of birth you have depends on the size of your pelvic cavity (not your overall frame so don't worry about your height or shoe size), the amount of the hormone relaxin circulating to increase its dimensions, and the position of the baby. A small woman with a good-sized pelvic cavity or plenty of relaxin circulating could give birth to a big baby more easily than a large woman whose baby was in an awkward position.

Try to eat nutritious food according to your appetite as a healthy mother is more likely to have a normal birth. If you eat slightly less than your body requires your own health will suffer as your baby is served first; if you eat much less your baby will fail to grow. This is undesirable and could make the birth more complicated rather than easier.

5

Mid-Pregnancy

(MONTHS 4–6)

' I felt my baby flutter today!
Suddenly I'm alive and full of energy.
Everywhere the world seems filled with
pregnant bumps. I never really noticed
how many there are around before
I had one myself! '

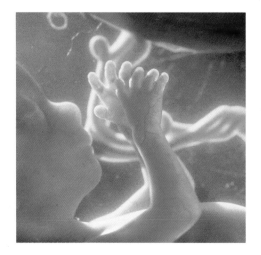

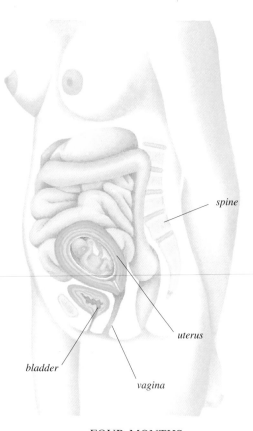

spine

uterus

bladder

vagina

FOUR MONTHS

Above: *This fetus is about four months. You can see the umbilical cord by the hands.*
Right: *Fourth month: Your uterus has expanded into your abdominal cavity and soon you'll feel the baby's movements.*
Fifth month: There's less room for your intestines and stomach as your uterus takes up the space.
Sixth month: Your baby still has room to turn somersaults in your uterus.

HOW YOUR BABY DEVELOPS

In the fourth month your baby and the placenta are each about the length of your first finger. 'Placenta' means cake in Latin, reflecting both its shape and its nourishing function.

The blood vessels in the umbilical cord carry food and waste products between you and your baby. Their walls are like a mesh fence, excluding large molecules while allowing small molecules and gases to filter through. So anaesthetics and some infections can pass from mother to baby and certain drugs can be used to treat the baby via the mother. Like a water-filled garden hose the cord rarely becomes knotted as it uncurls if the baby's movements tangle it.

By 16 weeks your baby is as long as your hand and as heavy as an apple. He floats in about a teacupful of amniotic fluid. His eyes, ears and nose are well formed and his fingernails and genitals can now be identified. At the end of the fifth month he measures about 30cm (12in) and weighs 450g (1lb). Now

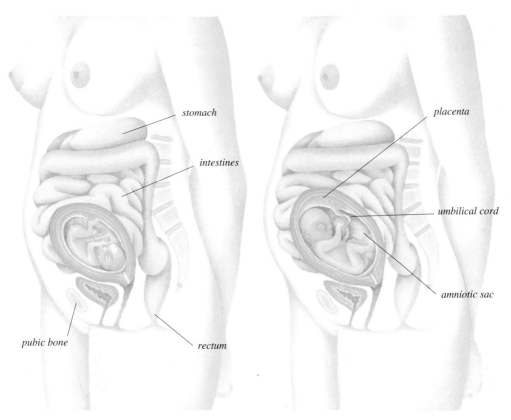

stomach

intestines

placenta

umbilical cord

amniotic sac

pubic bone

rectum

FIVE MONTHS

SIX MONTHS

he has eyelashes and pale pink nipples and the buds of his permanent teeth are forming. Your baby opens his eyes and looks around. His grip develops and he makes breathing movements with his chest. Although still too immature to function on his own, all his bodily systems are beginning to work.

HOW YOU MAY FEEL

By about 16 weeks the exhaustion, sickness and see-saw emotions you may have been experiencing usually settle down. It's a great morale booster to feel pregnant rather than ill! A first pregnancy often barely shows for five or six months, but with later pregnancies you may lose your waist by the fourth month. Most women enjoy looking pregnant, but some are mildly embarrassed or feel that instead of looking pregnant they simply look fat!

For the next few weeks you may feel relaxed and fulfilled, although you could also experience apprehension about the future, and a feeling that you

COMMON MID-PREGNANCY SYMPTOMS

◆ *Hair and skin problems similar to those experienced before a period, caused by increased secretion of oils.*

◆ *Red, itchy patches or dark pigmentation on your skin, brittle nails, or a heightened sense of smell.*

◆ *An ache at one or both sides of your abdomen, caused by the fibrous ligaments that anchor the uterus in your body stretching as your baby grows.*

◆ *Increased vaginal secretions and a tendency to overheat more easily because of the extra blood circulating.*

◆ *Vivid dreams as your sleep is disturbed by your baby's movements and you wake up more frequently.*

cannot quite keep your usual grip on life! Fortunately, these moments of self-doubt often occur between periods when you feel utterly confident and almost euphoric.

Many women feel and look healthy, with thicker hair and a clear skin, but others wonder when the flower of womanhood will start to bloom! As the growing uterus takes up space in your abdomen, moving your intestines and stomach aside to make room, you may begin to experience annoying discomforts. If they are troublesome talk to your doctor or try a self-help remedy (see page 72). The symptoms listed at the top of this page usually disappear soon after the birth.

RELATIONSHIP WITH YOUR PARTNER

Your partner also has to adjust to parenthood, which will affect him as profoundly as it affects you. As your pregnancy progresses he may become more actively involved, encouraging your efforts to get fit, or helping to gather information and make decisions about the birth. He may re-think his attitude to work or life in general, make changes in his commitments, notice small jobs around the home that have been ignored for months, or enthusiastically decide that you should move house before the birth.

However, some men react by withdrawing to ground where they feel more confident; for example, taking on extra work or spending more time with their friends. If your partner resists taking an active interest don't pressure him. He may change his mind in time.

Pregnancy is a time of transition for both partners but, while you have your expanding girth to focus attention on you, your partner has no physical signs to mark him out in any way. It's easy to overlook his needs, especially if like many men he finds it hard to talk about feelings.

About one man in 10 suffers mild anxiety symptoms, such as toothache, stomach ache, loss of appetite or sickness. This is called the 'couvade' and in some cultures it is expected and ritualized because it re-focuses attention towards the father and helps him to handle change. Many fathers become less anxious as the pregnancy advances and they begin to adjust to their new role.

Making love

Some couples want to make love more often during pregnancy and others find their libido declines. The most common experience is that sexual desire fluctuates, often increasing in mid-pregnancy and declining nearer the birth. You may be more aware of your sexuality during the fifth and sixth months, when your blood supply and vaginal secretions are increased. Enthusiasm is catching and can lead to a more satisfying sex life than ever. The physical and emotional changes of pregnancy affect desire and pleasure positively and negatively. Body image can be a real issue for some couples. Some women dislike having a rounded body and need reassurance that they are still attractive. Some men find the voluptuous shapes and stronger smells of pregnancy turn them off. Equally, many couples find these factors a novel delight.

Your partner may become anxious about the baby, but intercourse that is comfortable and enjoyable for you is not harmful, although you may need to choose positions that do not cause pressure on your abdomen or deep penetration. If your pregnancy is unstable your doctor might suggest abstention. Orgasm may cause colostrum (a creamy substance) to leak from your breasts, or mild, harmless contractions, but it does not normally cause miscarriage or premature labour. Oral sex is safe and can be a substitute for intercourse if you both find it enjoyable.

The quality of a relationship is built not on prowess in bed but on communication, love and understanding. Your sexual needs and your partner's may alter as pregnancy progresses. Be patient and talk about any difficulties. You will find that making these adjustments infinitely strengthens your love life.

FEELING THE BABY MOVE

For most women, feeling the baby move for the first time is a red letter day. It can happen any time between about 14 and 25 weeks. Babies are particularly active between 24 and 28 weeks. Later, they have distinct periods of rest and activity and the kicks feel stronger, a daily reminder that they are fine. If you have not felt movement for a while try sending a 'thought message' to your baby – you may get a reassuring kick in reply. A series of rhythmic knocks means your baby has hiccups!

Typically, women begin to feel movements at about 18 weeks for a first baby and somewhat earlier for subsequent babies, but they describe the sensation of those first kicks differently:

'It felt soft and fluttery, like a butterfly kiss on your cheek. I wasn't sure if I was imagining it at first.'

'I thought a fly had landed on my tummy. When I looked there was nothing there, but I felt it again and knew immediately what it was.'

'It was like somebody knocking or bumping against my stomach but from the inside. It became more definite over a week or two.'

'The nearest I can describe it is a rolling or lurching sensation. I thought it was wind at first!'

Getting to know your baby

You may think that bonding is something that only happens after the birth, but for most women the process starts long before this. Thinking about your baby's welfare, worrying that he will be alright, or imagining your future life together is evidence of the bond between you.

Finding out about your baby's likes and dislikes can be great fun. He may respond to certain types of music, or to his father's voice. He may stop kicking when you massage your abdomen, sing to him or sway your body; or he may decide that it's playtime as soon as you sit or lie down!

When he's in the mood he may play 'games' with you, pushing your hand away when you gently press the bulge of a foot or a hand. The more you get to know your baby before he's born the more familiar he will feel when you hold him in your arms.

STAYING WELL

Considering the changes your body undergoes in pregnancy a certain amount of discomfort is to be expected. Doctors rarely treat common symptoms such as cramp and backache unless they are extremely troublesome, because they are caused by the very things that help to maintain a healthy pregnancy – your hormones, extra blood supply and increasing weight. This doesn't mean that you have to suffer silently. Many minor problems can be avoided by common sense or alleviated by self-help remedies.

Remember to look after your body! Get some fresh air and exercise every day and make sufficient rest a priority. Eat regularly and drink plenty of fluids. These simple measures will help you to cope with the extra demands of pregnancy and may prevent a range of symptoms, from mild headaches to backache and constipation. If you still have a problem, check with your GP that it's nothing serious, then try a self-help remedy or alternative therapy.

‘ Feeling movements makes up for everything else in pregnancy. At first I thought of the baby as a fish-like creature, but now I think of her as a little person. I feel very protective and grateful for each kick as I know she's alright. She won't kick for my partner, though. As soon as he puts his hand on my tummy she goes quite still and quiet! ’ DEE

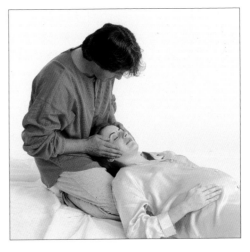

Massage Techniques

Sit or kneel while your partner massages your shoulders. He presses his thumbs on either side of your spine, working in small circles around the line of your shoulder blades.

Alternatively, lie on your back, resting your head in your partner's lap while he sits or kneels. He gently strokes along your jaw, your cheeks and your forehead.

You could also kneel or lie on your side while your partner slowly and firmly strokes his palms down your back, hand over hand. This can be comforting in early labour.

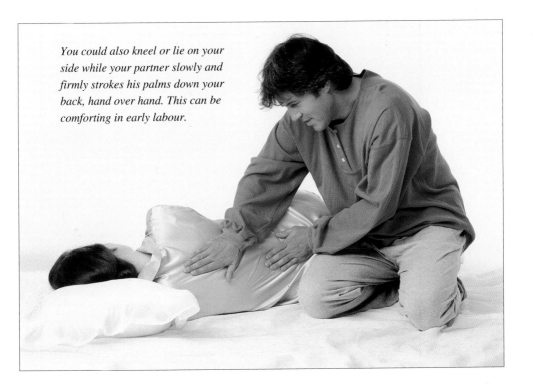

How to help yourself

Try the following self-help remedies for these common pregnancy problems:

Cramp: Painful muscle spasm, often in your leg or foot.

Self-help: Pull your foot upwards instead of pointing your toes when you stretch on waking up. To improve your circulation, roll an empty milk bottle vigorously under your bare foot every night before going to bed. Aromatherapy massage may help. Try increasing your intake of calcium, (in milk and cheese, for example) or cut down if you eat a lot of any food, such as dairy produce or bananas.

Fainting: Feeling light headed or dizzy may be caused by lowered blood pressure or low blood sugar levels.

Self-help: Lie on your side or prop yourself up with pillows (see page 101). Keep a healthy snack handy to maintain your blood sugar levels. Dress in layers and carry a battery fan, mineral water or a spray to refresh yourself. To forestall dizziness, press down on the balls of your feet – the guardsman's trick. If you feel faint sit with your head between your knees or lie down.

Varicose veins: Soft, blue knotted cords in the legs, caused by extra blood passing through veins with relaxed walls.

Self-help: Put your feet up whenever possible, but shift your weight from foot to foot if you have to stand. Avoid crossing your legs, sitting on a hard chair edge, wearing tight knicker elastic, knee highs or hold-up stockings. Keep support tights under your pillow and put them on before getting up. If you forget, raise your legs and hips for ten minutes to drain blood towards your heart before putting them on.

Constipation: Hormones and your growing uterus slow down the passage of waste from the body.

Self-help: Drink more fluids and eat more fruit, vegetables or fibre-rich foods such as bran or oats. Prune juice or dried prunes are natural laxatives. If iron tablets make you constipated ask your GP to prescribe a different brand. Always go to the toilet when you need to – raise your feet on a stool or upturned bucket and relax your pelvic floor (see page 45).

Piles (haemorrhoids): Swollen veins in the rectum or around the anus, that may bleed or be itchy and painful.

Self-help: Avoid straining on the toilet. Drink plenty of fluids and do pelvic floor exercises (see page 45) to improve your blood circulation. Avoid hot baths which make the blood vessels dilate; warm baths may be soothing. Ice packs, a proprietary cream or a pad soaked in witch hazel lotion from the chemist may give temporary relief. Increasing your intake of vitamins C, E and B6 may help.

Stress incontinence: When you cough or laugh you 'leak' some urine, or you need to go to the toilet when your bladder is empty.

Self-help: Do pelvic floor exercises (see page 45). Never try to hold on if you know your bladder is full. If you feel the urge when you know your bladder is empty gently tighten your pelvic floor and fix your mind on something else until the sensation subsides – in a few days things should improve.

Heartburn: A burning pain in your chest, or a sour taste in your mouth. Pressure on the relaxed stomach valve allows acid from partly digested food to 'burn' your oesophagus.

Self-help: Eat little and often, drink separately so that your stomach is not too full, and avoid spicy and fatty foods. At the first sign of heartburn, take something alkaline such as a sip of milk to neutralize the acid in your oesophagus and prevent a sore patch developing. Don't exercise or bend before a meal has had time to be digested. Raise your head and shoulders on pillows in bed. Ask your GP or pharmacist for an antacid preparation.

Itchiness: Your skin may itch, especially in the stomach area, because bile salts are not metabolized so well during pregnancy.

Self-help: Drink plenty of water to help flush out your system. Calamine lotion or half a cupful of bicarbonate of soda in a warm bath may soothe itching. Use aqueous cream or emulsifying ointment (from the chemist) instead of soap which can be drying.

Alternative therapies

These can be helpful to treat pregnancy discomforts and make you feel good. Some of them can be harmful during pregnancy so it's very important that you only go to a qualified practitioner. Your Regional Health Information Service (see Appendix) can advise you. Declare your pregnancy from the start even if you think it's obvious! Here are some therapies:

Acupuncture: Fine sterile needles are inserted at certain points to balance the flow of energy in the body. This can stimulate your body to produce endorphins (pain relieving substances), and help relieve problems such as nausea or fluid retention.

Aromatherapy: Essential oils or plant extracts are massaged into the body. Treatment may seem to be a pleasantly scented massage that gives a feeling of well-being, but it can affect your nervous system and hormones. To be safe, only consult someone who is fully qualified.

Homeopathy: Based on the principle 'like treats like', minute amounts of substances that produce the symptom are given, to stimulate the body's own defences. It can alleviate nausea and digestive problems for example, and also prepare your body for the birth and help speed recovery.

Medical Herbalism: This ancient healing art uses the entire leaf, bark or root of a plant instead of extracting an active ingredient from it. It's gentle, but treatments can be just as powerful as conventional drugs and need similar caution. Morning sickness and anaemia often respond well.

Osteopathy: A widely accepted therapy that treats skeletal and muscle problems using leverage and manipulation. There is a special clinic (see Appendix) to treat problems in pregnancy.

Exercise in pregnancy

Good circulation and suppleness will make pregnancy more comfortable. Any form of exercise that helps develop stamina and suppleness is beneficial. For example, you could swim regularly, or combine exercise, fresh air and recreation by taking a brisk walk for half an hour two or three times a week.

These stretching exercises make you more aware of your body and reduce stiffness. Hormone-softened ligaments can be overstrained, so warm up gently first and stretch slowly, holding a pose for a few seconds up to a few minutes. Repeat each exercise about six times, and do not overdo things.

Some exercises can be adapted; for example, if you get uncomfortable or lightheaded lying on the floor do the exercise on page 77 standing against a wall: with your knees bent, tighten your abdominal muscles and pull your back firmly against the wall, holding it for a few seconds.

Above: Inner Thighs
Sit for a few minutes each day with your back straight and the soles of your feet together. Rest your forearms on your knees and let them relax downwards without forcing or bouncing them.

Left: Back and Thighs
Sit with your back straight and legs apart. Lean gently forwards, pushing your heels away. Feel your back, thighs and calves stretch. Relax and rotate your ankles to improve your circulation.

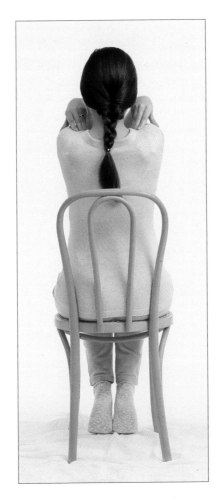

Right and below:
Neck and Upper Back
Sit up straight with your
hands on your shoulders.
Sweep your elbows
round in wide circles.
Feel the stretch
loosening any stiffness.

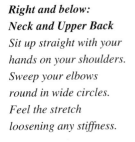

It's worth doing upper
body exercises such as
these if you use a
wheelchair. You may be
able to adapt other
exercises from a book,
or ask a physiotherapist
for advice.

EXERCISE IN PREGNANCY

◆ *If you have any doubts about suitable exercise ask your GP's advice.*

◆ *Join a pregnancy exercise class where you'll meet other mums-to-be and may form friendships to enjoy after your baby is born. Ask at your local health club, leisure centre, swimming pool, hospital or health clinic.*

◆ *If you have a disability talk to the class teacher first to make sure that the location is suitable and she can provide appropriate exercises.*

◆ *If you join a general exercise class make sure the instructor knows that you are pregnant and can advise you.*

◆ *Be wary of taking up a new sport in pregnancy, and of any competitive sports or activities that could prevent you from listening to your own body.*

◆ *Stop any exercise that 'feels wrong', hurts, or leaves you exhausted rather than refreshed.*

Pelvic Rock
Right: *Stand with your feet apart and your knees slightly bent. Tighten your buttock muscles and tuck your 'tail' under.*
Far right: *Release your buttocks and swing your pelvis gently back with your body upright and your knees in the same position throughout.*

Rock your pelvis back and forth to loosen it and help prevent backache. When you feel comfortable with this, move your pelvis from side to side like a belly dancer (not illustrated).

Abdominal Exercise (*see page 74*)
1. Lie on the floor with your arms a little way from your body and your knees hip width apart and bent.

2. Flatten your back to the floor – notice the difference between pictures 1 and 2.

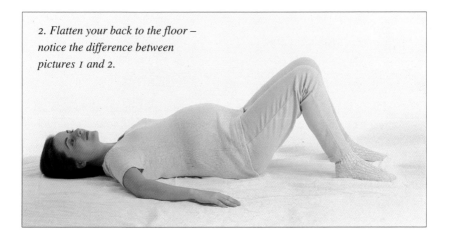

3. Very slowly slide your feet along the floor while keeping your back pressed firmly down. As soon as it begins to arch bend your knees and try again.

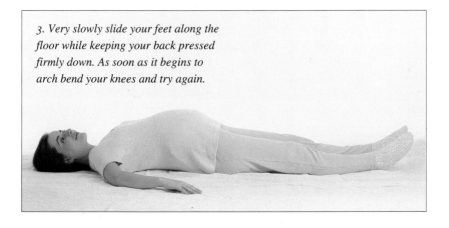

PREGNANCY AND WORK

In mid-pregnancy you usually have more energy, so working is easier; but it's still tiring, so don't expect too much of yourself. Most women stop work when maternity pay and leave become available about 11 weeks before the baby is due. Depending on certain regulations, your health and the demands of your job, you may want to stop sooner. If you want to work for longer your employer may require a letter from your doctor saying that you are fit.

You may count the days until you can stop work, or you may dread leaving. Either way, most women have mixed feelings when they stop work. While you are adjusting to life as a lady of leisure, take time to make friends in your neighbourhood. It can be harder to make the effort after the birth.

A good balance between work, recreation and rest will help you to enjoy your pregnancy. Try these tips:

- Conserve energy whenever you can and use every spare moment to consciously relax. Don't rush around in your lunch hour. Instead, try resting at your desk or in the car, or put your feet up in your firm's rest room.
- Put your social life on 'slow' for a bit and get regular early nights.
- Rearrange your work hours to avoid travel during rush hour. Ask politely for a seat on public transport.
- Don't leave things like decorating the nursery too late. You may not feel energetic by the time you get maternity leave.

MATERNITY CLOTHES

The golden rule for maternity wear is comfort, so avoid tight waistbands, skirts that ride up or very high heels that throw your pelvis out of balance and cause backache.

If you are too large for your regular clothes but feel awkward wearing maternity clothes, raid your partner's wardrobe for bigger shirts and sweaters, or buy clothes a size or two larger than usual that you can wear later on. You will not be your normal size for several weeks after the birth but most women do not want to continue wearing maternity clothes.

In the past there has been a lack of smart, affordable business clothes but this problem has been tackled by a number of small firms. Look for addresses in the small advertisements in *Practical Parenting* or your local paper. The NCT (see Appendix) sell a comfortable range of lingerie and maternity swimwear.

' I'm used to being active and it's frustrating not being able to do as much as usual. I run out of steam in the afternoon so at lunch time I lie down in the company medical room.

My husband and I have our main meal in the canteen so that we don't have to cook in the evening. We have salad or put a pizza under the grill for supper and I eat with my feet up in front of the TV. It gives me a real boost of energy. ' SALLY

USEFUL MATERNITY WEAR

◆ *For work, buy a good quality maternity skirt that will not lose its shape. Wear it with a variety of loose tops.*

◆ *For leisure wear, comfortable trousers can be worn with jersey tops and large T-shirts.*

◆ *Extra weight and swollen feet can ruin shoes. Buy one or two pairs to wear throughout pregnancy and discard them afterwards.*

◆ *If you intend to breastfeed buy loose, front-opening nightwear or use a big T-shirt. Your bust will be larger at the end of pregnancy and in the early weeks of breastfeeding.*

◆ *A serape, cape or poncho makes a comfortable outer garment in winter, or try to borrow a coat from a friend.*

◆ *For special occasions check your local paper and yellow pages for dress hire firms that include maternity wear. When choosing an outfit for a wedding, remember that the size and fit of your dress is more important than the style. A specialist bridal shop can offer you good advice.*

ANTENATAL CLASSES

Nothing can guarantee you an easy birth but if you go to antenatal classes you'll know what may happen and you'll be able to talk about pregnancy without feeling that your friends and family are stifling yawns! Classes vary in size, formality and the range of topics covered. You usually attend them later in pregnancy but good ones get booked up early.

NHS classes may be run by a midwife or shared between staff including health visitors and physiotherapists. They are free and can be excellent, although some hospitals give them low priority and a lot depends on the staff involved. A labour-ward tour may be included but you don't need to attend the classes to join it. NCT and other private classes usually go into more detail about birth. They are held at the teacher's home or a local hall for a charge, although this may be reduced in certain cases. Groups are small, the approach is informal and the teachers are usually knowledgeable and supportive.

Ask your midwife and your friends to recommend a class or check the notice board at the hospital or

' I was so ill for the first four months of pregnancy that I couldn't exercise and ended up feeling very sorry for myself. As soon as I was better I joined a pregnancy exercise class and met some super people on my wavelength.

We talk about anything, from how we're all secretly nervous about the birth to getting stranded in those incredible sex positions they show you in the books! I've learned that you don't have to be virtuous all the time. Sometimes we all meet up for a healthy swim and end up in a café eating cream buns instead! ' GINA

◆ *Attend monthly antenatal checkups. Write down questions to ask the midwife in case you forget.*

◆ *Improve your fitness – go for brisk walks, swim or join a pregnancy exercise class.*

◆ *Book antenatal classes now, and start to think about the sort of birth you hope to have (see page 84).*

◆ *Plan a holiday at home or abroad before you become too large to enjoy it, and before you face restrictions on air travel (see next page).*

◆ *Write to your employer at least 21 days before leaving work to retain your rights. Check qualifying dates for benefits (see page 46).*

◆ *Send for catalogues and check out baby equipment now – you may feel too tired to trek round the shops in late pregnancy.*

◆ *Make enquiries about alternative therapies (see page 73) for pregnancy discomforts and to help you feel good.*

clinic. The NCT and the Active Birth Centre (see Appendix) can give addresses of their trained teachers.

Here are some guidelines on choosing a class:

- A small, discussion-based class may suit you if you want to ask lots of questions and make your own decisions.
- If you are nervous about giving birth, ask friends to recommend a teacher who helps parents to feel relaxed and confident.
- Look for a large class where you can merge in, or arrange an individual class with an NCT or independent teacher if you prefer not to discuss birth with virtual strangers.
- Check the class is geared to fathers if your partner wants to be involved. Some classes treat men as onlookers, divide you into separate groups or only invite men to one or two sessions.
- Look for a women-only class if you are on your own.
- Ask whether alternative approaches will be covered if you want a natural birth. Some classes assume everyone will have drugs.
- It can be easier to share experiences with other parents and perhaps make lasting friendships in smaller groups.
- Ask whether classes tend to continue after the birth. You'll meet women who live nearby at classes run by your local midwife. On the other hand if you travel some distance to a class that friends have recommended you're likely to meet people who share your outlook on life.

QUESTIONS AND ANSWERS

Q: I am a lone parent and wish I had somebody to share my pregnancy and birth. I don't want to rely on my family, although they are very supportive. Where else could I get support?

A: Women often share the ups and downs of pregnancy and support each other, as some partners are not interested in the details of pregnancy or don't want to attend the birth. You may be able to develop a rewarding relationship with your midwife (see page 27), and you'll meet other women at antenatal classes. It may be easier to make friendships at exercise classes, or small birth preparation classes rather than at larger ones. The NCT (see Appendix) also organizes 'Bumps and Babes' sessions in some areas, where you can get to meet other mothers. If your family is supportive, letting them share your pregnancy can give pleasure to everyone. Organizations such as Gingerbread and the National Council for One Parent Families (see Appendix) can also give you practical and emotional support.

Q: We plan to go on holiday before our baby arrives. How can I make travelling easier, and how late in pregnancy can I fly with a scheduled airline?

A: Mid-pregnancy is a good time to go on holiday, and planning will make getting there and back less stressful. However you travel, wear loose, comfortable clothes and take plenty of snacks and mineral water.

In the car a cushion to place in the small of your back or to sit on may help. Your seat-belt should fit below your bump and across your chest, not under your arm. Sitting still for long periods makes you stiff, so allow extra time to stop every couple of hours and stretch your legs.

If you travel by plane, try to book a front or aisle seat so that you have more leg room and can walk about and visit the toilet more easily. Most airlines require a doctor's letter confirming you are fit to travel from 28 to 36 weeks, after which they will only carry you in an emergency. Individual airlines may vary, so check this. Remember to take your notes with you, just in case you need a doctor during your holiday!

Q: My brain cells are disappearing as fast as my waist expands! Why do I forget and lose things and what can I do about it?

A: Hormones cause some upheaval and part of your mind becomes taken up with the changes you are experiencing. Tiredness may also affect your ability to concentrate. The best solution is to accept it with good humour, rest more and use strategies to handle the overload. Start each day by listing things to do, putting a tick by the essentials and a query by the rest. Keep it on your pinboard or in your bag. A checklist by the door will remind you of vital things like closing windows or locking up. Tie your keys to your handbag with a long ribbon. Write reminders in your diary or on the back of your hand, or put tiny, coloured stickers where you will see them to jog your memory about appointments. If you streamline your life it will be much easier to cope.

6

Plans and Choices

‘ *You don't have to make choices. You can go along with what other people decide. But I love the challenge of learning about birth and I'd rather decide for myself what suits me. It's not so different from planning a special holiday.* ’

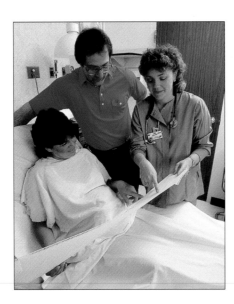

The midwife is explaining what the output from a fetal heart monitor means. You can share decisions about your treatment with her and your partner.

YOUR CHOICES FOR BIRTH

There are two, equally safe, basic approaches to care in labour. The first advocates intervention before a problem occurs in the hope of preventing it. The second favours watching carefully, but not intervening unless a problem actually arises. For example, if your labour was normal, but slow, a midwife who favoured the first approach might want to speed it up using a drip, in case you became too tired to push effectively. One who preferred the second approach might want to reassure you that everything was normal and help you to conserve energy for pushing.

If a complication occurs technology will be used to help, but if everything is normal there is no evidence that it makes birth safer. Intervention is a matter of judgement, which depends partly on the philosophy of the staff. Some feel that intervening prevents a difficult or dangerous situation arising. Others argue equally strongly that it can make further intervention necessary and actually cause problems that might not otherwise have arisen.

You may feel more confident giving birth using technology or you may feel that nature knows best.

Birth in hospital

The majority of births take place in hospital. In every labour a midwife will carry out routine checks such as listening to your baby's heartbeat and measuring your blood pressure. Beyond this hospitals have different approaches to labour. Some expect their staff to follow so many protocols that it considerably reduces your options; others are much more open to individual choices.

For a 'high-tech' birth you stay in bed throughout labour, with a hormone drip to control the contractions, a fetal monitor to record your baby's heartbeat and perhaps an epidural (see page 122) to numb sensation. One intervention sometimes leads to others, so read Chapter 10 to decide if this approach is right for you.

With a 'low-tech' approach there is no active intervention so long as you and your baby are fine. You don't have to stay in bed but could walk about, use a rocking chair, kneel on a mattress on the floor or lean over a bean bag to get comfortable. You could cope with contractions using relaxation and breathing techniques, but pain relief is always on hand if you need it.

' I decided not to give birth in my local hospital because it doesn't offer epidurals on request. I accept that there are some disadvantages to them but I don't see any point in suffering unnecessarily. If you wouldn't have a filling at the dentist without an injection, why give birth in pain?

I phoned a larger hospital twenty miles away to find out their approach, and then asked to be referred there. It's completely geared up to using technology and I feel secure knowing that everything will be monitored very closely. It also has excellent facilities in its special care baby unit, just in case. ' MEGAN

Many hospitals have a mixed approach: basically low-tech but with protocols regarding, for example, when a drip should be set up to speed up labour, or how long you could push before having an assisted delivery. These rules are often set by the consultant.

In most hospitals you can opt to stay for between six hours and a few days after your baby's birth. Even with a first baby some mothers go home within hours, and most leave within a day or two. Your midwife will visit you at home to check on your health and advise you on feeding and baby care.

The length of stay in hospital is an individual decision, depending on how you feel and whether it's your first baby or you have other children at home. If you plan an early discharge make sure you have help at home so that you can concentrate on your baby at first.

The staff at the hospital

Midwives' uniforms vary so the best way to find out who people are is to ask, or look at the name badges. Make a mental note of the colour of the belt, shape of the cap or whatever distinguishes the ranks at your hospital. If everything is normal you won't need a doctor's services, but there is always at least one on duty whom you could ask to see. Check the name badge, which will normally have a doctor's status on it. Here are some of the people you may see in hospital:

Midwifery sister: She may look after you during labour or postnatally. She also supervises the other midwives on the ward, so talk to her if you have a problem during your stay.

Staff midwife: She is qualified to care for you during pregnancy, normal

TO DECIDE WHICH APPROACH WILL SUIT YOU BEST

Tick the statements that you agree with:
- ◆ *I don't mind being wired to machinery in labour. (a)*
- ◆ *People who choose to have babies at home must be mad! (a)*
- ◆ *I prefer to move around and choose comfortable positions. (b)*
- ◆ *Labour is a natural event for most women. (b)*
- ◆ *I want my baby's heartbeat monitored by machine throughout the birth just in case anything goes wrong. (a)*
- ◆ *Relaxing in familiar surroundings should make labour easier. (b)*
- ◆ *Doctors and midwives usually know what's best for you. (a)*
- ◆ *I prefer no intervention as long as my baby is alright. (b)*
- ◆ *I want to avoid drugs if possible, as they have side effects. (b)*
- ◆ *Knock me out, please! I'd rather not feel a thing in labour. (a)*

The more 'a' statements you ticked the more likely that you'll feel reassured using birth technology. If you ticked mostly 'b' statements you may prefer a natural approach. Staff in large hospitals may be more geared to using technology than those in small hospitals or midwifery units. Home births are least likely to involve intervention in labour.

---

labour and delivery. After the birth she helps you to feed and care for your new baby.

Student midwife: A qualified nurse or direct entrant training to be a midwife. Depending on how far she has got she may observe your labour, perform examinations or deliver your baby. She will be under the supervision of a qualified midwife. You can refuse to have a student care for you although many women enjoy it as the midwives often explain everything in more detail when a student is around.

Other staff: Auxiliary nurses are unqualified but help with tasks such as serving meals. Nursery nurses are trained to look after babies in the nursery.

Obstetric physiotherapists have specialized in pregnancy and birth, and teach postnatal exercises or help with problems like backache.

Consultant obstetrician: A specialist in the medical problems of pregnancy and birth. He rarely attends a normal delivery but may be called in if there is a problem his registrar cannot deal with.

Senior registrar or Registrar: Specialists in obstetrics who usually deal with routine problems like a straightforward forceps delivery or Caesarean birth. The registrar is still training, although he often has considerable experience.

Senior house officer, or House officer: He or she has not specialized in obstetrics but might, for example, set up a drip if you need one. He is likely to be the first doctor called for any problem.

Student doctor: He or she is undergoing initial training so will be closely supervised. You can refuse care by a student if you wish.
Anaesthetist: You'll see him or her if you've decided to have an epidural or need a Caesarean birth.
Paediatrician: A specialist in baby problems, who will also check your baby to make sure that she's healthy before you leave hospital.
Breastfeeding counsellor: A mother who has breastfed her own children and who has trained to help other women. Not all hospitals have them.

Birth in a midwifery unit

Midwifery units are run by community midwives. They can be separate institutions or attached to a hospital, and appeal to women who prefer a 'low-tech' approach. They are not, as is sometimes thought, reserved for women having second babies, women who live in certain areas, or for any other pre-determined reason.

Phone the midwifery unit when you think you're in labour, as you would if you were having your baby in a hospital. A community midwife will supervise your labour and deliver your baby. If a complication occurs you will be moved to a consultant unit in hospital.

Home birth

Home birth is as safe as hospital birth for the majority of women, and it reduces risks such as infection and the negative effects of drugs and interventions. Even if you are over 35 years of age, small in stature, having your first baby or have a history of problems in pregnancy or labour you can still have a home birth. Some medical conditions, such as heart trouble, which could be stressed by labour, might make this an unwise choice; but each case must be treated individually.

About a month before you are due your midwife will bring a sealed delivery pack of things she'll need at the birth, and discuss arrangements like having a clear space where she can put her supplies. When labour starts she'll assess you. If it's still early she may make other calls, but once labour is established she'll stay with you, contacting your GP if he wants to be there. She'll have pethidine, gas and oxygen and baby resuscitation equipment with her, although many women don't need them. She'll deliver your baby and stitch you if necessary. If a problem arises she'll transfer you to hospital. After the

Some people prefer not to think about the birth in advance and just take things as they come, but I feel more confident if I've thought everything through.

I'm going to have my baby at my parents' house, where I usually stay while my husband is away. The midwife seems very happy about it, and my mother will look after my two year old daughter. When she was born my labour was quite short – only six hours – so if this labour is faster as second ones sometimes are I'd worry about getting to hospital. WENDY

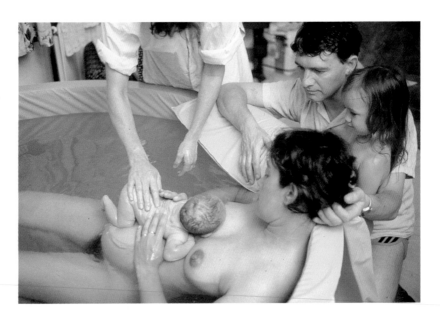

birth she'll visit frequently at first, then daily for about a week. You will be given a phone number to contact her for advice.

Home birth is usually a positive choice reflecting confidence in your ability to give birth, your midwife's skills and your family's support. You do need help – there's no holiday at home, no midwives to take over if you want a rest! Making everything ready before the birth takes effort and you'll need someone to keep the household running. To find out more about home birth contact AIMS (see Appendix) or visit the website www.homebirth.org.uk.

' I knew nothing about water birth until I was 33 weeks pregnant, when a friend mentioned it. It sounded just right as I want as little intervention and as much privacy as possible during labour.

The midwives left us to find out about it for ourselves so I borrowed books from the library. My partner was supportive but he insisted that I have the baby in hospital.

I've hired an oval pool so that I can stretch out, or brace myself across it. When my contractions start we'll go to the hospital and my partner will put up the pool. It's been such fun planning the birth that I'm really looking forward to labour! ' RACHEL

Water birth

Labouring in water can help you feel relaxed and make it easier to cope with the pain. Some hospitals have a pool installed, or you can hire a birth pool. But water isn't the answer to every problem! It can help labour to progress but it cannot reduce dangerously high blood pressure, or deal with severe pain as effectively as an epidural. If a problem arises intervention may still be needed.

Water birth usually means using water to relieve pain and reduce the need for intervention during labour.

Left: Using a birth pool can be an effective way of relieving pain in labour.
Right: You may find it easier to relax in the familiar surroundings of your own home.

Some babies are born underwater because the birth is very fast, but most mothers leave the pool before delivery. It is thought to be very safe if guidelines about water temperature and things like the use of aromatherapy oils, how far dilated you must be before you enter the pool, and when you must leave it are followed.

Most practical difficulties can be overcome, although you may have to persevere to find someone supportive. Women have had water births with twins or a breech baby, when they normally use a wheelchair or after a previous Caesarean section. They have been arranged at a week's notice and have taken place in caravans and mobile homes. For more information, look for a book at your library or book shop, or ask your midwife or the Supervisor of Midwives at your hospital. If you want to talk to someone who has had a water birth, the NCT, AIMS (see Appendix) or one of the companies that hire birth pools (see small advertisements in *Practical Parenting*) may be able to put you in touch.

If you cannot arrange a water birth don't forget the bath! It may be too small to allow free movement but the water could still help to relieve pain.

Getting the birth you want

The easiest way to get the sort of birth that's right for you is to choose where to have your baby with care. Listen to your GP's advice, read Chapter 10 on help in labour and discuss all the possibilities. When you and your partner have weighed everything up, you're entitled to have your baby wherever you feel is right. Ask your GP or midwife to arrange it.

If you decide to have your baby in hospital canvass your midwife and friends who have recently had a baby for their views about different hospitals. One institution might be so accustomed to using birth technology that you'd find it hard if you wanted a natural birth, but another might not offer epidurals on request if you prefer this. You can phone a hospital antenatal clinic directly to find out what they offer. The staff should have time to discuss their approach straight away or to arrange for you to visit.

Think about asking some of the following questions.

For a high-tech birth:

- Can my baby be monitored electronically throughout my labour?
- Can I have an elective epidural even if I go into labour at night or during the weekend?
- How long would I be left before a drip was set up to increase the strength of my contractions?
- Would the technology be available even if the unit was busy?

For a low-tech birth:

- Provided the baby and I are both alright, how long can I go through labour without intervention?
- How will the staff help me to have a natural labour?
- What is the episiotomy rate here, and will the staff help me to deliver my baby without an episiotomy (see page 151) or tear?
- Can I use whatever position I like for the delivery?

CHOOSING NURSERY EQUIPMENT

Choosing baby clothes and decorating a nursery is fun, but don't buy everything before your baby arrives. You may receive gifts or change your mind in the light of experience. Here's a guide to the bare necessities you'll need for the early weeks:

Four vests: Wrap-over styles are easy to put on but the ties can be fiddly. Envelope necks fit well but pulling them over the baby's head takes a little practice. Bodysuits don't ride up but they may be outgrown more quickly.

Four stretchsuits/nightgowns: Stretchsuits are neat and easy to care for; nightgowns may make nappy changing easier at first.

Two cardigans/matinee jackets: Loose sleeves make dressing easy.

Two shawls: wrap your baby snugly in a cotton shawl or cot sheet to sleep at first. Draping a warm shawl over the car seat is easier than putting a snowsuit on your baby in the early weeks.

Snowsuit, hat, mittens (for a winter baby): A snowsuit with zips down both legs or right under the nappy and wide armholes makes dressing easier. Hats with ties stay on better.

Nappies: Disposable ones are more convenient. Buy small packs until you know what suits you then shop around to find the cheapest supplier and buy them in bulk. Re-usable terry squares or shaped nappies are environment friendly but need sanitizing powder. Terries need liners and pants, too. Some areas have a nappy washing service.

Changing equipment: You'll need a changing table or a changing mat to put on the floor, or on a table or chest of drawers at the right height. Cotton wool rolls are cheaper than balls. Buy small sizes of nappy cream until you find what suits you and your baby's skin.

Car safety seat: Birth to nine months seats with handles are easy to carry around. Two-way models (birth to four years) can be heavy and cumbersome in the early weeks. Some car seats do not fit in all cars, so check that the model you choose fits your vehicle.

Carrycot/Moses basket: A carrycot could be used as a pram; Moses baskets can be lighter and easier to carry around.

Pram/buggy: Choose from traditional or collapsible types and try pushing, folding and lifting different models. You could delay buying a pram or buggy by using a baby sling at first.

Four cot/pram sheets and two blankets: Look for easy-care labels. A shawl could double as a blanket, and vice versa.

Bath: A basin or washing up bowl will be fine at first. A simple plastic bath (with or without a stand) is heavy to lift with water in; one that rests on the big bath may be outgrown quickly.

Six bottles and sterilizing equipment (for bottlefeeding): Wide-necked bottles are easier to fill but may be more expensive. To sterilize them, cold water with sterilizing tablets or liquid is cheapest; electric steam sterilizers are convenient and use no chemicals; microwave sterilizers are compact.

Breast pads (for breastfeeding): Shaped pads are more expensive but may be more comfortable and stay in place better.

BREAST OR BOTTLEFEEDING?

Many parents believe, incorrectly, that formula milks are so sophisticated that there is little difference between them and breast milk. Breast milk contains hormones and enzymes that are not in formula milks because nobody knows what purpose they serve, plus substances to help fight bacterial and viral infections and combat childhood illnesses. It has all the right nutrients in the right amounts for your baby to grow healthily.

Breast milk adjusts to compensate if a baby is premature and alters as your baby grows and her needs change. It even dilutes in hot weather to satisfy a baby's thirst. There can be no doubt that breast is best for your baby.

Whether you breast or bottlefeed, the most important thing is a happy, rewarding feeding relationship with your baby. If you can't breastfeed or choose for various reasons to bottlefeed, there are compensations. It can be daunting to feel that your baby is completely dependent on you, and other people can take over when you bottlefeed. Babies often settle and sleep for longer because formula milk forms curds in the stomach so they feel more satisfied. If your baby is still hungry after a feed you can offer her more formula milk, whereas it takes a day or two of frequent feeding to increase your breast milk supply.

DISABLED PARENTING

Disabled parents' needs are as varied as their disabilities, but pregnancy can seem especially daunting if your GP or midwife has little practical experience of your particular disability. Disability, Pregnancy & Parenthood international (DPPi) is an information service for disabled parents, prospective parents and professionals. The Disabled Parents Network, run by and for

parents with disabilities, offers support and works for improvements in services. These organizations (see Appendix) can help you to access various resources, including specialist equipment and services.

You may feel it's hard to plan ahead when you don't know the problems you are likely to face, but all parents discover how to handle pregnancy, birth and childcare by trial and error. Small children seem to adapt easily to a parent's disability, perhaps because disabled parents spend more time over each task and talk to their baby more, so that a co-operative relationship develops.

Looking after a baby is a challenge. Together you and your child will find ways to overcome your disability.

PREPARING A TODDLER

Parents who are delighted to be having another baby want their other child to feel the same. But small children have little idea of time so announcing the arrival of a baby six months ahead is like talking about Father Christmas in June! Usually, the younger the child the closer you can leave it to the birth before telling her.

Get your child used to the general idea of families first. Point out babies, read stories and talk about her friends' brothers and sisters so that she begins to understand what will happen.

Make changes in her life, such as starting playschool, well in advance. If she is moving to a new bedroom let her settle in before setting the cot up in her old room! In the last month she may enjoy helping to wash baby clothes or clean the pram. Get her used to a routine that will make life easier when you have less time after the baby arrives.

QUESTIONS AND ANSWERS

Q: I don't think I'll get the sort of birth I want at the hospital my GP has sent me to. My first baby is due in three weeks. Is it too late to have a home birth?

A: You're entitled to change your mind and be referred to a different hospital or a midwifery unit, or to choose a home birth at any time. Talk to your GP. If he or she feels home birth is risky in your case listen to the reasons. Making a decision means taking responsibility for the outcome so be sure in your own mind about what you want.

However, don't be put off by initial opposition. It often melts away when you show you've thought something through and are determined. You don't need your GP's agreement to have a home birth. If your own midwife is unsympathetic and you don't know another one to approach direct, write to the Supervisor of Community Midwives at your local hospital keeping copies of your letters. She must ensure you're provided with a midwife who'll give you total care and any necessary back-up.

Legally, health authorities are not obliged to provide a home birth service, but mothers are not obliged to go into hospital to have a baby. It's something of a grey area at present, but AIMS (see Appendix) will help if you have any difficulties.

Q: What should I look for when choosing a nursing bra?

A: It's best to delay buying nursing bras until your baby's head has engaged (see page 52). When the head is high your ribs expand to allow more space, so a bra that fits well may be loose around the ribcage after the birth.

A nursing bra should be comfortable and substantial enough to play an effective supporting role. Look for a broad band to give support under the cups. The bra should fit without gaping, but with space to slip your hand between the top of the cup and your breast, to give room for expansion after the birth. Stretch straps are too bouncy when breastfeeding and elastic loses shape with repeated washing. Cotton rich fabric allows your skin to breathe. Zips or front openings are a matter of taste, but avoid seams that press and mark your skin as this could lead to pressure problems during breastfeeding.

Q: How much equipment do new babies really need? We are not well off and I'm worried about overspending our budget.

A: Not as much as many people imagine, and there are ways to economize. Look through catalogues and collect information, but delay spending until you really need something. You may find you can borrow equipment from friends or relatives, or improvise after your baby arrives.

Most large towns have shops that sell nearly-new clothes and equipment but do look up *Which* reports on safety standards before you buy. Economy is often a necessity, but if your heart really longs for something rather extravagant, consider the lift it could give you in return for economizing sensibly the rest of the time. Treat yourself if possible. Babies are fun as well!

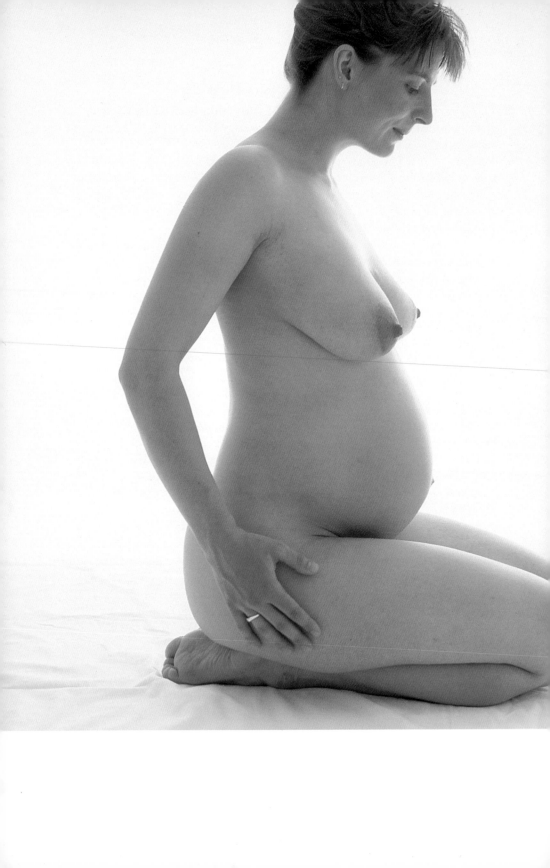

7

Late Pregnancy

(MONTHS 7–9)

' The last few weeks, and the finish is almost in sight. I feel a mixture of terror, excitement, boredom and elation. The days drag, yet I want to hang on and savour every last bit of them. Once they are over life will never be the same again. '

Seventh month: This baby is already lying head down, but about 25 per cent of babies will be breech at this stage.

Eighth month: Compare this picture with the one on page 36 to see how much space your baby takes up, moving internal organs to make room.

Ninth month: Your baby stores fat under his skin in the last month so he looks much rounder and plumper.

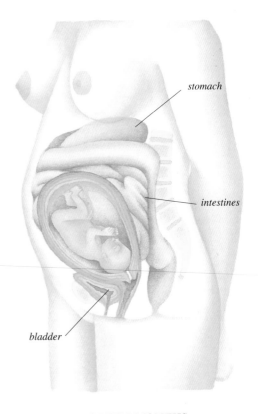

stomach

intestines

bladder

SEVEN MONTHS

HOW YOUR BABY DEVELOPS

In the last three months of pregnancy your baby's breathing and swallowing rhythms become increasingly well regulated. Cartilage develops to give shape to his ears, his eyelids open, his fingernails grow and the soft dark body hair (lanugo) disappears. Fat stores build up to provide energy and regulate his temperature.

Your baby receives antibodies to common bugs and childhood illnesses such as chickenpox through the placenta, which also produces gamma globulin to help both of you to fight infection. Up to 1 litre (1¼ pints) of constantly renewed amniotic fluid filters out waste products from the uterus and his skin is protected with creamy vernix to stop it getting waterlogged.

At 28 weeks the average baby measures about 35cm (14in) and weighs nearly 1kg (2lb). Each week for the next month he grows roughly 1cm (½in) and puts on 225g (½lb), although this growth pattern gradually diminishes and almost stops a week or so before birth. Hormone levels in the placenta

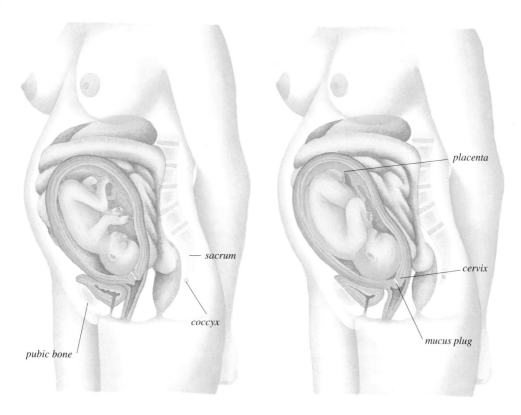

EIGHT MONTHS

NINE MONTHS

change, the uterus is fully stretched and the baby has little room to move. It's time to start the short journey into a new and independent life!

The majority of babies born after 32 weeks survive nowadays, and delivery after 37 weeks is considered normal. By this time the baby's lungs have matured and surfactant, a soap-like substance in the amniotic fluid, makes breathing easier by preventing the lung surfaces from sticking together. After 40 weeks a baby is well equipped to enter the world, although he will still need loving care for months and years ahead.

HOW YOU MAY FEEL

Most women slow down a little, but if you are fit and experience no complications, late pregnancy can be very enjoyable. You may feel at your happiest and most relaxed. A large bump usually elicits well-intentioned support and kindliness from other people, not to mention relieving you of unwelcome social obligations!

‘ *My pregnancy has changed our lives in little ways. I haven't stopped doing anything, but I've pulled over from the fast lane and I amble along in the slow lane. My husband has given up his share of the duvet and sleeps right on the edge of the bed because I've taken over the rest.*

He has to keep a sense of humour and think for both of us. Last week the ceiling of a room we were decorating needed painting and he was going out. I asked him to get the stepladder for me before he went. He refused, and came home with a ball of wool and a pair of knitting needles! With three weeks to go I reluctantly took the hint. ’ KAREN

Many women have mixed feelings about giving up work; some count the days until they leave, while others dread the loss of income, stimulus and companionship. Every change in life has its good and bad aspects. You will be able to rest more, but you may find that time passes slowly without the rhythm of work and you may become bored with your pregnancy. The last few weeks can seem to stretch ahead interminably if you are already uncomfortable and heavy. See the next page and page 70 for suggestions on how to stay well.

You may feel increasingly worried about your baby's health and feel vulnerable to casual, throwaway comments, especially from health professionals. You may be panicky about birth and motherhood as they draw inescapably nearer, or you may swing wildly from depression to euphoria. By the ninth month this is usually overtaken by a positive longing to see your baby and to have your body to yourself again.

To create and give birth to a new human being is very special, but the last few weeks can be uncomfortable. As your baby grows your uterus takes up space under your lungs which can leave you short of breath. When your baby's head engages (see page 52) you'll breathe more easily, but will probably need to go to the toilet more often! Your uterus may cause pain under your ribs, or an itchy or tight, stretched feeling in the skin over your bump. Some women feel a sharp pain when the baby butts their bladder.

By now, most babies have definite waking periods with stronger kicks and movements. Some seem less active while others knock a book off your lap or wake you up at night. You may have difficulty sleeping because your pelvis aches. The hormones that soften your ligaments to make the birth easier may also contribute to cramp, varicose veins, piles and heartburn (see pages 72-3).

Your breasts will enlarge and they may leak colostrum, a creamy fluid present in your breasts before milk is produced. Some women experience nasal congestion, nose or gum bleeds, thrush or a copious but inoffensive vaginal discharge. Others find their ankles start to swell (see page 102) or they suffer from carpal tunnel syndrome, where fluid compresses the nerves in the wrist causing tingling or numbness. Your GP may suggest an orthopaedic wrist support and the NCT (see Appendix) have a helpful leaflet about this problem. These symptoms of late pregnancy can be tiresome, but do see your doctor if they seem excessive.

You may feel your tummy become firm for about 30 seconds as Braxton Hicks contractions tone up your uterus. These practice contractions may be barely noticeable, or so strong (especially if it is not your first baby) that you have to stop and breathe gently over them as though you were in labour. If you're fed up with your appearance a new hairstyle or a good cut could give your morale a boost, and save time later on.

RELATIONSHIP WITH YOUR PARTNER

Your relationship with your partner will change during pregnancy, especially if this is your first baby. Discuss the future, so that you can find common ground that allows each of you to get something of what you want from your partnership. When a baby arrives a cosy twosome does not change magically into a cosy threesome! You will both be concerned about your baby's welfare but will also have individual needs to be fulfilled by negotiation.

It's normal and healthy for a woman to focus on her changing body and the birth, but not to the exclusion of all else. If you are too self-absorbed it can be tedious for your partner. He will support you in many little ways, so try to respond to his needs too. If he attends classes or listens to 'baby talk' for your sake, show equal interest in something that primarily concerns him.

When you are adding to your family, or your partner has children from a previous relationship, he may show less interest in your pregnancy. This can be disappointing if it's your first baby, so tell him how you feel. Some men need reminding to give extra help in late pregnancy, although many fathers willingly take on responsibility for other children. On the other hand, if this is your partner's first baby, give him the chance to enjoy being a first-time father by going to antenatal classes with him, even if you don't feel the need.

Taking pleasure in your partner's company helps to fan the flames of love. Try to find activities that you both enjoy, can do together and can keep up after your baby arrives. Family life is challenging; pregnancy is an opportunity to deepen your understanding of each other's needs and strengthen the bond between you.

STAYING WELL

The extra weight, softening hormones and gymnastic ability of your baby can make late pregnancy uncomfortable. You will feel better if you use your body well and conserve energy. Maintaining good posture (see page 44) prevents unnecessary muscle tension and painful strains to softened ligaments.

It can be frustrating to tire quickly, especially if you have work to do, but you'll help yourself if you listen to your body and rest before you become over-tired. Fifteen minutes of complete relaxation is worth an hour of half-resting with your mind whizzing around things you feel you should be doing instead!

COPING WITH LATE PREGNANCY

◆ *Never stand when you could sit down, or sit when you could lie down.*
Make sure you stand, sit or lie without twisting your body.
◆ *A v-shaped pillow can provide some comfortable support when you are*
sitting in a chair or propped up in bed.
◆ *To relax completely for five minutes, sit comfortably with your*
shoulders down and hands palm uppermost in your lap. Concentrate on
the sensation in one hand and imagine it gradually growing warmer.
◆ *For a quick pick-me-up, mash a banana and blend it with a glass of*
milk, a little honey and two tablespoons of natural yoghurt.
◆ *Try to make some friends locally, to stand you in good stead after*
your baby is born. Exercise and antenatal classes are good places to meet
other pregnant women.
◆ *If your pregnancy seems endless and you feel low, lift your spirits with*
an outing, or treat yourself to a massage or a special luxury to keep up
your morale.

Relaxing and sleeping

Most women sleep less soundly at the end of pregnancy. You might be woken by night sweats, but more often it is the baby's movements and the call of nature! Have a glass of water beside the bed as your body needs extra fluid during pregnancy and dehydration can cause slight headaches.

If you and your partner sleep badly because you are restless, perhaps he could take to the spare bed occasionally to get an unbroken night. A packet of biscuits, a thermos of cocoa or a good book, within reach, may help if you can't get back to sleep once you have woken. On the positive side, at least insomnia gets your body prepared for night feeds after your baby arrives!

When you are really exhausted you will sleep soundly in any position, but if you are having difficulty relaxing or sleeping you may find some of the positions illustrated opposite comfortable.

ANTENATAL CHECKS

Most women see more of their midwife after 28 weeks, but in between visits you can contact her to ask questions, seek advice or discuss anything that worries you. If it is necessary to keep a closer eye on you or your baby you will have as many antenatal visits as required.

The checks will be familiar by now, but the midwife will also determine your baby's position (although this can change), make sure that he is growing well and look out for potential problems such as swelling or pre-eclampsia (see page 102).

Relaxing and Sleeping *Try lying on your side with a pillow between your knees to reduce the strain on your ligaments. You may like to put another pillow under your bump.*

Prop yourself up using a bean bag or two pillows under your knees to take the strain off your lower back. This position can help you to avoid heartburn.

Sit in a chair with a v-shaped pillow supporting your head. You could put another pillow on a small stool to support your legs.

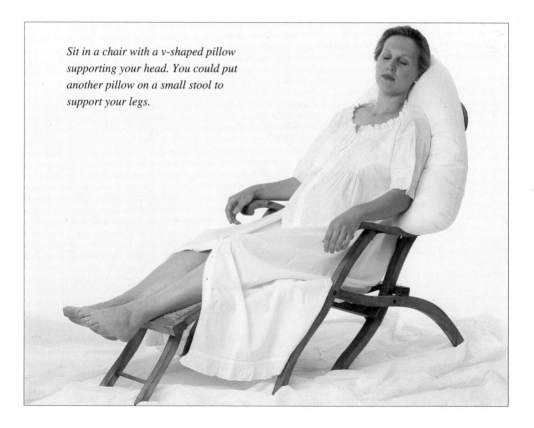

Your midwife may measure between your pubic bone and the top of your uterus (the fundus) to see if your baby is growing well. This has been shown to help identify babies who could benefit from being scanned, but it's only a crude measurement and it produces many false alarms.

A kick chart is sometimes given towards the end of pregnancy to check that the placenta is working well. You record your baby's kicks over a given period and after a few days a pattern emerges so that you know what is 'normal' for you. Your midwife will explain what to do, but tell her if it makes you anxious instead of reassuring you.

It's always worrying if your midwife wants you to have further checks, but most babies of mothers who are well nourished, healthy and don't smoke turn out to be fine. Just occasionally these simple checks pick up a hidden problem at an early stage.

Swelling

At least three-quarters of women suffer from fluid retention at some time in pregnancy. Your legs or ankles may swell in hot weather or at the end of the day. You may wake up to find your fingers tingling or your rings feel tight. If you cannot get your shoes on or your hands or face become puffy, contact your midwife or GP.

Don't restrict your intake of liquids or salt unless you are told to. Wear support tights and sit with your feet up whenever possible. If your fingers swell, wriggle them to help ease discomfort; gently wind string around your finger from the tip so that a ring will slip off when you unwind it.

Mild swelling can result from the normal fluid increase of pregnancy. If a hollow remains when you press the skin for 30 seconds and let go, you have oedema. This is not dangerous in itself, but it can be a symptom of pre-eclampsia which needs medical attention, so consult your GP.

Pre-eclampsia

This illness affects both the mother and baby and is cured by the delivery of the baby and placenta. Early in a normal pregnancy your arteries adapt to accommodate an increasing blood supply so that your baby gets more food and oxygen as he grows. For an unknown reason, possibly genetic plus an environmental trigger, in about one in 10 pregnancies the blood vessels fail to adapt. The placenta gets insufficient blood, the baby doesn't grow well, the mother's blood pressure rises and she may suffer symptoms such as oedema and impaired kidney function.

In most cases pre-eclampsia does no lasting harm. Worry and stress do not cause it; rest and relaxation do not cure it. In very mild cases, extra rest may help and your blood pressure might be checked daily at home.

However, for one in a 100 first pregnancies and fewer subsequent ones, the illness is serious enough to lead to convulsions or even coma unless it is treated. You will be monitored in hospital so that symptoms such as high blood pressure can be treated with drugs. Depending on the severity of the illness you may go into labour spontaneously and have a normal delivery, or you might be induced or delivered by Caesarean section.

Pre-eclampsia is usually suspected if you have at least two out of three classic symptoms: raised blood pressure, oedema and protein in your urine. Repeated scans may show your baby is not growing well, or abnormalities may show up in a blood test. In rare cases where the illness comes on suddenly there may be pain in the upper abdomen, vomiting, visual disturbances or a very severe headache. Contact your GP about such symptoms, although they don't necessarily mean you have pre-eclampsia.

Poor growth

Research shows that many things affect a baby's growth right from conception, perhaps even laying the framework for future health. A baby may fail to grow properly if his mother is ill, smokes or has an unhealthy lifestyle, or if the placenta fails to supply all his needs. The placenta reaches maturity somewhere between 32 and 34 weeks and then gradually becomes less efficient, although most will sustain all a baby's needs for more than 42 weeks.

One of the objectives of good antenatal care is to look for signs of undernourishment. If a baby is smaller than expected for the stage of pregnancy you have reached, ultrasound scans (see page 56), repeated at intervals, can help to determine whether he is growing normally or is genuinely malnourished.

Poor growth is more common in first pregnancies, and fifth or later ones. Many individual factors probably contribute to it, but it is unlikely to happen if your weight is normal, you are well nourished, and you don't smoke. If you attend regular antenatal checks any problem associated with poor growth, such as anaemia or kidney disease, can be treated early.

If poor growth is diagnosed you may go into hospital for bed rest or medication to improve placental blood flow. In extreme cases your baby would be delivered early. Although prevention and treatment of poor growth are preferable, even when they are unsuccessful such babies often eventually catch up.

It is often hard to know why an individual baby fails to grow properly, but it is never too late to improve your diet, get more rest or tackle a smoking, drugs or alcohol problem.

‘ To be perfectly honest, I'm fed up with pregnancy. I can't sleep properly or eat a decent meal or walk more than a few yards before sitting down to rest. My ankles swell each evening and I haven't felt like going out for weeks.

I know it's well-intentioned, but I've found it hard to adjust to being 'public property'. Sometimes people I hardly know come up and pat my bump and it's hard not to resent it. Pregnancy is not my favourite time of life. I can't wait for the baby to arrive. ’ SIOBHAN

YOUR BABY'S POSITION

Somewhere between 34 and 40 weeks most babies turn head down and settle deeply in the pelvis. But babies are individuals: some wait for extra softening hormones produced at the beginning of labour before they engage and others just stay bottom down. Once a baby is head down and fully engaged he rarely changes position.

If you feel a firm area down one side of your tummy it may be your baby's back. Ask your midwife if your baby is lying in an anterior position. This is a good lie: with his back to your tummy he can tuck his chin on his chest, fit neatly into your pelvis and turn slightly to emerge at the birth.

If he lies with his back towards to your back (posterior), his chin may not tuck in so well and he has further to rotate to pass under your pubic arch, which could make the birth longer. Try kneeling on all fours as often as possible so that gravity helps his spine, which is heaviest, to move round. It sometimes helps to gyrate your hips whichever way feels most comfortable, to encourage him to rotate.

A baby who lies bottom down and refuses to budge by the recommended turn-by date may simply be a late starter. Sit up straight to give your baby more room. Keep a bottle of baby lotion in the fridge to soothe the sore patch where his head lies. Try the remedies for heartburn (see page 73) if this is proving a problem.

If your baby does not turn head down spontaneously by 34 weeks you could encourage him using the methods described on page 106. Your doctor might also try, especially if it is not your first baby. You will be asked to lie on your back with your knees up and relax while the doctor massages your tummy, helping your baby to slip round. This is called external version; no force is used and the attempt will stop if your baby clearly does not want to move.

After 36 weeks it's sensible to discuss breech birth (see page 160) with the midwife in case your baby doesn't turn. Only three per cent of babies remain in a breech position at birth.

Your baby's position has quite a lot to do with how your labour goes. If he lies well curled up and with his spine to one side of your tummy, your labour may be easier. But remember that being well prepared can also make your labour easier. Learning to relax and being realistic about labour (see page 132) will help you to cope if your baby adopts a less favourable position.

' *Being pregnant again is great! I haven't had time to worry about every little thing and I've enjoyed sharing it with Emily, my two year old, who loves babies. She's very knowing so we had to tell her quite early because everyone else knew, but she has no idea of time and I'm sure she thinks we're making it all up! Now I'm almost there I can't wait to see her face when she finds out we're not.*

We bought bunk beds for her bedroom and left her cot up. The first night she slept in it. Then she decided she was a big girl and wanted to sleep in the bed, so we went to buy a duvet and she chose the cover. Now she happily tells people the cot is for her baby. ' ZOE

PRESENTATIONS FOR BIRTH

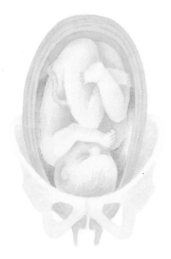

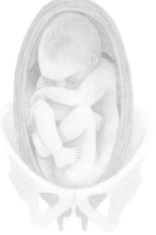

Above: Right occipito posterior (ROP) where the baby faces the mother's abdominal wall.

Above: Left occipito anterior (LOA) is the most common presentation. The baby faces the mother's spine.

Below: Frank breech where the thighs are flexed but the legs are pointed upwards. The arms are around the legs.

Below: Footling breech where the thighs are only slightly flexed and baby's foot is born first.

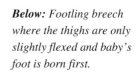

Above: Full breech presentation where the thighs are flexed against the body and the knees are bent.

◆ *Find out if your employer needs a letter from your GP if you want to continue working after you become eligible for maternity leave.*

◆ *Go to an experienced fitter for nursing bras (see page 93).*

◆ *Hire maternity wear for any special occasions. Look in your local paper or Yellow Pages for advertisements.*

◆ *Pack your suitcase (see page 116) about six weeks before your due date. Buy or hire a car seat (see page 91) to bring your baby home in.*

◆ *If you have a toddler, make arrangements (with back-up) for his care while you are in labour. Buy a small present for him, ready for his first meeting with his sister or brother.*

◆ *Write your birthplan (see page 118). There's still time to alter your booking if you want to have your baby somewhere else.*

◆ *Arrange to hire a TENS machine (see page 122) if your hospital or midwife cannot lend you one. Hire a radiopager to ensure you can contact your partner when you go into labour. Look in Yellow Pages or the small advertisements in* Practical Parenting.

◆ *Arrange outings for after your 'date' as you might go overdue!*

◆ *Record a message on your answering machine if you need a rest from too many phone calls before and after the birth.*

QUESTIONS AND ANSWERS

Q: I am 35 weeks pregnant and my baby is lying in a breech position. Can I do anything to encourage him to turn?

A: You could certainly try to encourage your baby to turn using positions or alternative therapies, although babies are individuals and some prefer being bottom down.

Put a bean bag or a pile of pillows on the floor and make a hollow in them for your bump. Lie on your front with your bottom higher than your hips for about 20 minutes. Relax and try to 'will' your baby round. After a while (not always at the first attempt) your baby may float free of your pelvis and do a somersault. Get up slowly (you may feel rather shaken) and walk around or squat to help fix your baby's head in your pelvis. Alternatively you could lie back with your hips raised on pillows and your knees bent and roll gently from side to side for 10 minutes three times a day. Stop if you feel light-headed or uncomfortable.

An acupuncturist might suggest applying pressure, acupuncture needles or heat from a singed herb (moxibustion) to a point on the outer edge of the little toe to help your baby to turn. A homeopath might recommend a single dose of Pulsatilla at high potency. If you want to try alternative therapies (see page 73), do consult a qualified practitioner.

After considering your history – for example, how firm your muscles are and the position of your placenta – your doctor may try to turn your baby by massaging your abdomen at 37-38 weeks. External cephalic version (ECV) is successful in about 70 per cent of cases and has been shown to reduce the Caesarean rate for breech babies by about half.

Q: Last week a van driver failed to give way to me on a roundabout and almost hit the side of my car. I was unhurt but very shaken and later that day my baby kicked wildly for two hours. Could the accident have harmed him, and should I stop driving?

A: There's no reason to stop driving short distances right up to delivery day, provided you feel fine, fit behind the steering wheel and can comfortably fasten your seat belt. You should not drive yourself to hospital when you are in labour, and you may find long journeys tiring in late pregnancy whether you are the driver or a passenger (see page 81).

A baby may react with a period of greater than normal activity after any sudden shock, such as an accident or receiving bad news. Rest for a few hours to give your body a chance to recover, and if you are worried for any reason contact your GP or midwife.

Q: I'm 34 weeks pregnant and my midwife says that my baby's head has engaged. I thought this happened at 36 weeks, so does it mean that my baby will be born early?

A: It suggests that your baby is lying in a favourable position and your pelvis is roomy. First babies engage on average at 36 weeks, but later babies may not do so until you're in labour. Once your baby has engaged he has resolved the question of whether your pelvis is big enough for this. Every baby has to engage at some stage in order to be born normally, but it doesn't predict when you will go into labour. The timing depends on the size of your pelvis, how firm your abdominal muscles are, the amount of hormones flowing and your baby's position.

Q: My teenage daughters from my husband's first marriage want to be present at the birth. We have asked my mother-in-law to look after our three year old son, who adores his Gran. How can I prepare my step-daughters for the birth and make sure that my son does not feel left out?

A: Your daughters might like to look at books or a video with you, and they should be aware of the realities of birth. Tell them they can leave at any time if they wish, and explain circumstances when they might not be able to be there. Make sure that your midwife is happy for them to be present, so that they will feel welcome.

If a day spent with Gran's undivided attention is a treat for your son, he is unlikely to feel left out. He will not be at the birth but he can still be part of the celebration. Suggest that your mother-in-law might like to help him draw on balloons with thick felt tips and decorate a card for the baby. Pack a small surprise in his suitcase for him to find – and don't forget one for Gran, too!

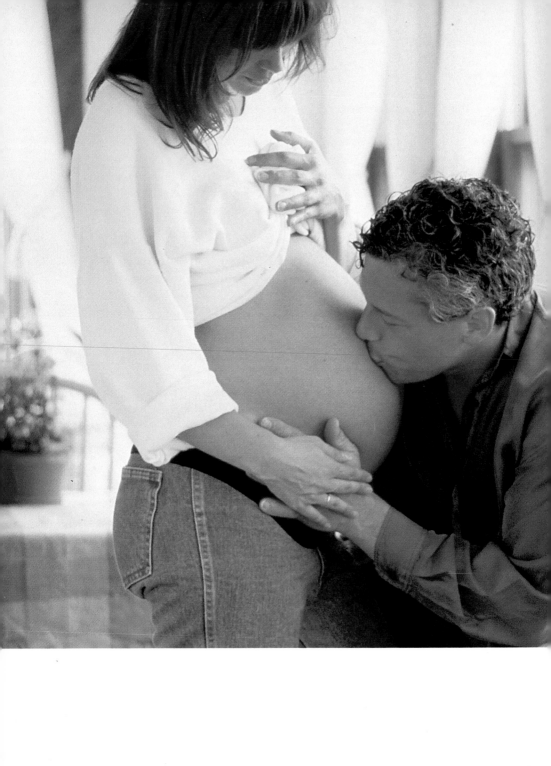

8

Preparing for the Birth

' There's so much to think about when a baby is born. It's not just learning to relax and help yourself to handle the birth; it's all the practical little details like remembering to pay the gas bill and feed the cat! '

WHAT MAKES LABOUR EASIER?

Labour is easier if you have space to relax, and privacy so that you can let go of your inhibitions and flow with the rhythm of the contractions. Intrusions, or distractions such as moving from one place to another, may disturb this rhythm. Darkness or subdued lighting can help you to use instinct rather than rational thought. You need to feel safe and at ease in the place where you give birth, and with the people who care for you. Otherwise, the delicate mechanisms of the natural birth process may be upset.

Preparing for the birth will help to make your labour easier by giving you confidence in your body and trust in your instincts so that you cope in the way that feels right to you at the time.

TOUR OF THE LABOUR SUITE

Most hospitals provide tours of the labour suite, often at evenings or week-ends so that partners can attend. Phone the hospital to check details, or ask at your next antenatal visit. Here are some things you could find out:

- What facilities are available? Is there a mattress for the floor, a bean bag, rocking chair or large bath? What are the arrangements for refreshment and what are the car parking regulations?
- What use could you make of the furniture in the room you'll be in during labour? A cupboard might be the right height to lean on; moving the bed might give you more space, for example.
- How do the staff feel about monitoring (see page 148), episiotomies (see page 151) or delivery positions (see pages 114-15)? Are there hospital policies regulating them, and can these be varied?
- Where should you go at night? Hospital security procedures may mean the door you normally use is locked.

RELAXATION AND BREATHING FOR LABOUR

Labour is a physical task, like running a marathon. If you run stiffly the race is harder. When your uterus contracts strongly other muscles tend to join in, but if you relax it works more effectively and your body's natural pain killing hormones flow. During labour you'll need to keep checking so that you can release tension before it engulfs you. Pull your shoulders down and let them go, part your lips to loosen your jaw, turn your hands palm upwards.

'I ignored the birth at first. Now I've started to face up to it and it seems like a huge wall. I'm like a yo-yo, one minute whining that I'll never cope and the next minute feeling that labour's no problem and it'll be all right on the night! I'm going to antenatal classes and on a tour of the labour suite. Once I've got labour in proportion I know I'll be fine.' SARA

Relaxation and breathing are intertwined – if you relax deeply your breathing will adjust to the best level for you. Some women prefer to concentrate on breathing control to help them relax and give them something to think about. Use slow, gentle breathing, pausing slightly between breaths and letting your breathing rise to your middle or upper chest during the contractions if it's more comfortable. Your body will tell you what feels best. Always concentrate on the 'out' breath to avoid hyperventilation, but if you do start to feel light-headed, cup your hands over your face and breathe into them slowly until the sensation passes.

Breathing for labour

Ask your partner to help you practise breathing for labour until you feel confident using different areas of your chest.

Right: Full chest: Relax consciously and aim your breathing towards the warmth of your partner's hands, so that he feels a slight movement below your waist. During labour use full chest breathing unless your contractions make mid or upper chest breathing easier.
Below: Mid chest: Breathe so that your bra gets tighter and your partner feels the movement with this hands.
Below right: Upper chest: Breathe lightly with little huffs, using the top part of your chest.

POSITIONS FOR LABOUR

The mechanics of giving birth suggest that some positions will work better than others in certain circumstances.

As your uterus contracts it rises up and forwards, so leaning in this direction lets the contractions work with gravity. Lying back makes them work against it. If you're upright your baby's head presses against your cervix, speeding up dilation. Positions where your thighs are flexed and wide apart will stretch the ligaments that join the three bones of your pelvis, thereby giving your baby extra room.

When your body is horizontal, gravity takes your baby away from your cervix and towards your spine, abdomen or side, depending on your position.

Sit reversed on a chair padded with a pillow. Relax onto another pillow placed on the chair back.

Stand, leaning onto your partner, the wall or a piece of furniture during contractions.

Sit with your knees apart, leaning onto your partner.

Some women find their contractions are more effective when they lie down because they are able to relax better; others find that lying down eases the pain of a very fast labour.

Adopting positions that use gravity and open your pelvis, such as the ones illustrated below, often makes labour easier. You could use pillows to reduce pressure on your knees or thighs. The positions suggested for relaxation on page 101 may also be comfortable.

There are no hard and fast rules – women are different and what works for one may not help another. Don't feel that you ought to use certain positions because they're supposed to be best. Just experiment to find those in which you can relax well.

Sit on the padded rim of a bucket. Plant your feet squarely so that you can rock or move your body freely.

Spread your knees to make space for your bump and lean forwards onto your hands.

Kneel on something soft and lean onto your partner's lap or the bed.

Stand to deliver while your partner holds you under the arms. He could lean against a wall and bend his knees to protect his back.

Stand or semi-squat, supported by your partner and a midwife. They should bend their knees as they take your weight.

POSITIONS FOR DELIVERY

Many women deliver on their backs because no one suggests anything else. This isn't ideal because your baby moves against gravity and puts extra pressure on the perineum (the delicate tissue around the birth canal) as it thins out. To move from your back to your knees, ask your partner to stand beside the bed to help you. Slide the outer border of one foot towards your bottom. Push on the bed with your arm to raise your body. Roll over to kneel facing the side of the bed, with your arms around your partner's neck. The midwife will help you deliver from behind.

Pushing is easier in upright positions because gravity helps and your tail bone swings back, giving your baby more room to move. If the birth is rapid you could move onto your side. Women who stand to give birth often report less damage to the perineum. It's up to you to choose your position. You will not know what's right until the time, but try out these positions in advance.

Lie on your side with your knees bent. Your partner supports your upper leg during contractions.

Kneel on the bed leaning onto the headboard, pillows or a bean bag. This position helps to prevent a tear.

Squat and lean into your partner's lap with your feet flat and your arms over his knees.

YOUR LABOUR BAG

Your hospital will provide a list of things to bring in, but here are some practical suggestions from mothers for what to take:

◆ *Light clothing, as hospitals are very warm.*

◆ *Travel or paper fan or mineral water spray to keep cool.*

◆ *Crushed ice in a thermos flask (to suck); cool box with mineral water or fruit juice.*

◆ *Flannel or natural sponge to moisten lips; lip salve.*

◆ *Squashy ice pack, pack of frozen peas or wooden back massager to ease backache; oil or talc for massage.*

◆ *Cassette recorder, music or story tapes, headphones; jigsaw, games, books to pass the time.*

◆ *Treats to keep your spirits up; snacks for your partner; peppermint teabags for wind (especially after a Caesarean).*

◆ *Cushion, bean bag, small stool or bucket to sit on.*

◆ *Socks for cold feet.*

◆ *Poster or calendar to focus on; camera; money for the phone.*

YOUR PARTNER'S FEELINGS ABOUT LABOUR

Most men are excited at the thought of being present at the birth, but they may be worried about not knowing what to do, or perhaps fainting at the sight of blood. Films and videos often give a false impression of labour because, like TV holiday programmes where the sun always shines, they are selective in what they present. The birth of your own baby is usually less dramatic but much more emotional and exciting. If your partner is anxious it will help if he attends antenatal classes with you.

YOUR BIRTH PARTNER

Your birth partner could be anyone close to you, although it's usually your baby's father. Midwives have more than one woman to look after, so his role is to make your labour easier by offering comfort, encouragement and loving concern. Even if your birth partner does nothing except stay close to you, you'll value his (or her) presence. However, sensitive support, freely given at the right moment, is an added bonus since it raises your pain threshold and makes it easier for you to cope.

‘ *I've never been afraid of giving birth. I'm more worried about losing control and not being able to make my own decisions. Right from the beginning I read everything I could about birth. I've learned to be more flexible because now I understand why things happen that can't be avoided.* ’ ANNE-MARIE

Here are some suggestions for birth partners:

- Take care of her physical needs. Help her change position, keep her cool, put crushed ice in the water she sips, change the music tapes and generally give her your attention. Never appear to be bored, or more interested in the newspaper or the labour machinery than in her!

- Keep her morale up if labour is long and her energy flags. Think of labour as a series of short intervals, not one long stretch of time. In the early stages, you could read funny anecdotes or poetry to her, play 'I Spy', choose your baby's name, walk round the corridors with her, or produce an unexpected treat.

- Create a positive atmosphere, however her labour goes. She cannot relax if you are tense, so assume an air of calm like a swan gliding on the surface while paddling fast underneath!

- Help her to relax. Watch for tight face muscles or clenched teeth. Keep reminding her to relax her shoulders. Some women can't bear to be touched during labour; others like their shoulders massaged or their hair stroked. When the contractions are strong, redouble your efforts to keep her relaxed.

- Help her to focus on something other than the contractions. Describe a place you both know so that she can imagine it; stroke her palm, or name groups of muscles so that she can relax them one by one. Most women find idle chatter distracting but counting can be helpful: look into her eyes and count slowly aloud from the beginning of the contraction until it's over.

- Act as a physical support. Put your arms around her so that she can lean on you, if necessary, during contractions. Let her drape herself over you when she's kneeling, or sit on the floor using you as a sort of armchair. If she asks for support when she's pushing protect your back by bending your knees.

- Act as her spokesman. Interpret her wishes to the staff, and vice versa. She'll rely on you when the contractions are strong and may appear not to hear anyone else. Be sensitive to her wishes. She may genuinely change her mind about some things, like accepting pain relief.

- Remind her to breathe gently, emphasizing the 'out' breath. Tension causes changes in breathing rhythm and rate, so concentrating on quiet breathing will help her relax.

- Massage her back, mop her brow, praise her efforts. Encouragement is more helpful than sympathy when a woman is trying hard to cope without any drugs. Stay supportive even if she gets cross with you – she really wants you there! After the birth reassure her that she has coped well.

MAKING A BIRTHPLAN

Most women form a general idea about the sort of birth they hope to have by reading books on the subject and talking to other parents, relatives and friends, their partner or GP, midwife or antenatal teacher. Regardless of what other people think, you have to balance out what *you* see as the advantages and disadvantages of the different approaches to labour (see page 84).

Some women prefer the experts to take charge and make most of the decisions, believing that they know best. If this leads to the sort of birth that suits you there's no problem. However, many parents are disappointed because decisions made by other people turn out to be wrong for them. Ideally, you'd discuss your wishes with your midwife beforehand, but it's not always possible in busy hospitals. The midwife you see during pregnancy may not look after you in labour.

A birthplan makes you think about what's important to you. It can make you more realistic about labour, or even prompt you to change your hospital booking (see page 93), as you come to realize that certain things in childbirth go together. For example, it may be easier to achieve a natural birth in a low-tech hospital or at home, as the staff in a high-tech hospital may see the need to use technology – speeding up labour with drugs for instance – where a midwife at a home birth might not consider that it's necessary.

A birthplan conveys your wishes to the staff even if you're too busy coping with contractions to discuss them. Your hospital may provide a form or you could use the birthplan available from the Maternity Alliance (see Appendix). Alternatively, you could simply write a letter that can be attached to your notes, briefly describing the approach that suits you best and specifying three or four things that are really important to you. A birthplan isn't cast in concrete – you can always change your mind later.

There are many ways of giving birth safely. Your midwife will make sure that what you choose is safe, so in the end it comes down to what makes you feel happy and confident, and only you can decide that!

PAIN IN LABOUR

The amount of pain you experience in labour is determined by physical factors such as the shape of your pelvis and the position of your baby, and psychological factors such as fear. You may describe contractions as strong sensation, or you may find them agonizing.

Some women feel daunted by the thought of pain and have an epidural at the earliest opportunity; others accept severe pain in preference to using any drugs. Being realistic, and able to relax and be positive, raises your pain threshold, and women who attend antenatal classes use fewer drugs for pain relief. They either feel less pain or handle it better. Pain in labour needn't be overwhelming – *you* decide how much you're prepared to tolerate.

BIRTH PLANNER

◆ *Companions in labour: do you want a friend or relative instead of or in addition to your partner, to share support if labour is long? Do you want your partner to stay throughout labour or to leave during certain procedures? Can he stay for a Caesarean birth?*

◆ *Your stay in hospital: do you want to know the midwife who delivers you, do you prefer to be examined by a female doctor, or do you have special needs because of a disability, a language difficulty, your religion or diet? Do you mind students being present during labour and delivery? Enemas are rarely offered but you can ask for one if your bowel is full.*

◆ *Positions for labour and delivery (see pages 112-15): upright positions work with gravity; they tend to speed labour up and help you push, but you may get tired. Lying down lets you rest but may prolong labour.*

◆ *Pain relief: pethidine and epidurals help severe pain but may have some side effects and it may be hard to move about or change position. Gas and air, TENS, and self-help methods do not affect your baby but are only effective for moderate pain. If you prefer not to use drugs you could ask the staff for help and support.*

◆ *Speeding up labour: breaking the waters (see page 147) may shorten labour, although it may be more intense and require more pain relief. If it fails a hormone drip (see page 146-7) may be needed. This also shortens labour but your baby may become distressed so you'll be continuously monitored and movement may be restricted. If this fails you might need a Caesarean section.*

◆ *Monitoring the baby by machine (see page 148): having a continuous record of your baby's heartbeat may give you confidence, but the trace can be hard to interpret, leading to unnecessary anxiety or intervention. Belt monitors restrict your movement; scalp electrodes allow more movement but are also invasive.*

◆ *Episiotomy or tear (see page 151): an episiotomy could be bigger than a tear but neater to repair. Women who express a strong desire not to have either are more likely to achieve their wish!*

◆ *Delivery of placenta (see page 138): Leaving the cord to pulsate may mean up to an hour's wait for the placenta, but the baby gets extra blood and a gentler transition to independent breathing. Having an injection reduces bleeding and brings the placenta away quickly but the cord must be cut immediately. Say if you prefer a 'gentle birth' (see page 137).*

◆ *After the birth: do you prefer to hold your baby immediately or after she's been cleaned and wrapped up? Do you want to breastfeed immediately? Would you like to have a bath with your partner and baby shortly after the birth.*

Self-help methods of pain relief

Most people learn to handle moderate pain in everyday life, for example by simply ignoring a headache or using a hot water bottle for stomach ache. *Distraction, temperature changes, movement* and *touch* are thought to work by stimulating larger nerve bundles which, like shutting gates, intercept pain messages as they travel along fine nerves to the brain. When your body gets used to the stimulus you feel pain again as the gates swing open but changing the stimulus shuts them again. This principle can help you cope with labour pain. Try these self-help methods:

Problem: In early labour your contractions hurt and you feel apprehensive.

Self-help: *Distraction:* watch TV or a video, beat your partner at Scrabble, or sort through the family photos.

Problem: Your abdomen aches during or between contractions.

Self-help: *Touch:* massage under your bump with a relaxed hand; *warmth:* use a hot water bottle wrapped in a towel; *movement:* change position and rock your pelvis gently.

Problem: You have constant backache, peaking at each contraction.

Self-help: *Change the temperature:* press your back to the central heating radiator padded with a towel, use a flannel wrung out in iced water, or a packet of frozen peas wrapped in a towel; *touch:* ask your partner to massage your back.

Problem: Contractions are overwhelmingly strong.

Self-help: *Focussing:* ask your partner to count slowly through each contraction with you; *movement:* rotate your pelvis gently, change your position, rock your body, make yourself walk to the toilet.

Backache Massage *Your partner places his hands either side of your spine keeping his elbows straight while he applies pressure.*

Alternatively, you may find it comfortable to stand with your feet apart, leaning onto the bed or another piece of furniture.

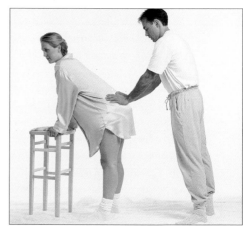

Backache massage in labour

Firm massage or pressure can help if you feel the contractions in your back. Your partner should use body weight, not muscle power, so that he can keep it up for as long as necessary. Use talc or oil to prevent soreness and tell him the best position – usually it's about halfway between the base of your spine and your waist. Practise beforehand the techniques on page 120 and below.

Your partner supports himself on his hands and presses the balls of his feet against your spine.

Sit or lie with the base of your spine against your partner's, while he leans gently back to apply pressure.

Your partner supports his elbow on his hip bone, leaning gently forwards. It may be easier if his body is at an angle.

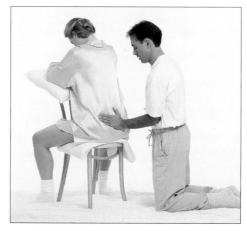

121

Other methods of pain relief

Each method of pain relief has advantages and disadvantages. For example, gas and air has little effect on your baby but may only relieve moderate pain. Pethidine and epidurals are effective for severe pain, but against this you have to balance their potential side effects. Think about it beforehand, but choose the most appropriate method of relief available at the time.

Epidural: A pain relieving drug is passed through a fine tube into the space around your spinal cord, eliminating sensation in your tummy. It can be topped up as needed. You may have a drip to accelerate labour and counter-act low blood pressure, a monitor for your baby's heartbeat and a catheter in your bladder. About half of all women who have epidurals need an episiotomy and an assisted delivery (see pages 149-51). Occasionally women who have an epidural get severe headaches or long-term backache afterwards. However, an epidural is the most effective method of relief for severe pain.

Mobile epidural: See page 124.

Pethidine: This is given by injection, once or more during labour. If you are small, a vegetarian or someone who rarely takes medicines or alcohol, a small dose may be adequate. You'll stay in bed as it makes you drowsy; most women say it distances the pain rather than taking it away. Women react differently and some suffer nausea or vomiting, but another drug can stop this. If you have pethidine too close to delivery your baby may need an antidote or be sleepy, so that breastfeeding is difficult at first. Against this, pethidine is a muscle relaxant and helps relieve severe pain.

Gas and air (Entonox): You inhale a mixture of nitrous oxide and oxygen through a face mask or mouth piece. It makes you feel light-headed, rather like having three sherries on an empty stomach. If you don't like the sensation just stop taking it! The secret of using it successfully lies in timing. Take deep breaths at the start of a contraction so that it takes effect at its height. If you wait until the contraction hurts it's too late; you'll get pain relief between contractions, not during them.

TENS: Transcutaneous electrical nerve stimulation consists of a battery-powered device with electrodes that are taped to specific areas of your back. At low frequencies it helps release endorphins, your body's natural pain-killers, while at higher levels it stops pain messages reaching the brain. The frequency can be increased as your contractions become stronger. Some women say TENS feels tingly, like fine sand paper rubbed on your skin. Practise beforehand to get used to the sensa-

'It's surprising how much you can decide for yourself in labour. I want to move around so I hope I don't need pethidine or an epidural. I don't fancy a crowd of students coming in to gawp at the last minute, but they have to learn so I wrote on my birthplan that I prefer a student to be there the whole time. The most important thing is to have my baby with me after the birth, not taken off to some nursery, because as I'm partially deaf I'd worry about not hearing her if she cries. ' JUSTINE

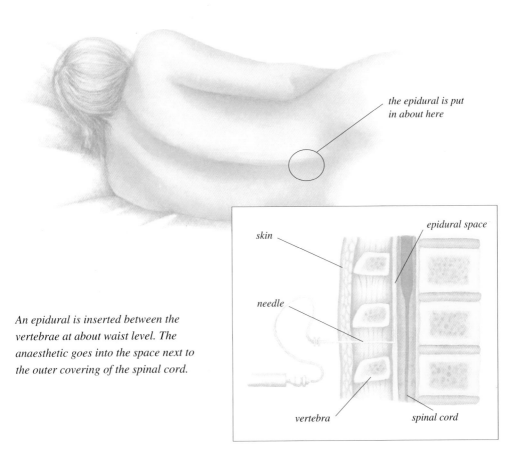

*the epidural is put
in about here*

skin

epidural space

needle

*An epidural is inserted between the
vertebrae at about waist level. The
anaesthetic goes into the space next to
the outer covering of the spinal cord.*

vertebra

spinal cord

tion, but if you don't like it you can take it off. You can't have a bath, but your partner can massage you without removing the electrodes. The hospital may lend you a machine, or you can arrange to hire one.

Acupuncture, Electro-acupuncture and Acupressure: Needles, electrical stimulation and pressure (respectively) can reduce pain when applied to specific points in the body. In labour you may be able to use electro-acupuncture or acupressure yourself. Acupuncture requires the presence of a specialist, and treatment may begin before the birth.

Hypnosis: Most antenatal classes teach some form of relaxation technique. The hypnotist takes this to a deeper level and helps you to narrow your attention until you are ready to accept the suggestion that you will feel no pain during labour. The hypnotherapist may be present during labour, or you may learn self-hypnosis or auto-suggestion. Several sessions are needed, starting some weeks before the birth. Hypnosis may work by altering your emotional response to pain. Only about 25 per cent of women can be fully hypnotized, but others may find some help from the technique.

HOME PLANNER

◆ *Arrange for someone to feed any pets at home while you're in labour.*

◆ *Remember to stock up the freezer, buy tins/packets for the early days.*

◆ *Stock up on household basics like detergent, biscuits for visitors, extra food, soap etc if relatives are staying.*

◆ *Buy batteries for a cassette recorder, film for a camera, thank-you notes and small surprises to keep toddlers occupied.*

◆ *Pack a bag if your toddler is going away; write a diary of her day to help whoever looks after her.*

◆ *List phone numbers – midwife, GP, hospital, partner, friends, neighbours, relatives – on a pinboard and write down all offers of help!*

QUESTIONS AND ANSWERS

Q: My friend had a mobile epidural and walked about instead of lying in bed during labour. Will I be able to have one?

A: Discuss this with your midwife because it depends on your hospital. Some anaesthetists use a combination of drugs injected into the epidural space around the spinal cord and the sub-arachnoid space where cerebro-spinal fluid circulates. Smaller doses can be used, so you retain feeling in your legs and are less likely to need a catheter to empty your bladder.

You may not get complete mobility, but most women can move in bed more easily, sit in a chair or stand with support. Some feel light-headed or their legs turn to jelly, so you should have someone with you all the time. You are less likely to need an assisted delivery but there is a slightly higher chance of problems with low blood pressure.

Q: I assumed my husband would be with me at the birth but to my dismay he has suddenly refused. I feel rejected and worried about coping alone. How can I persuade him to change his mind?

A: Twenty-five years ago few fathers were present when their children were born. Today most men are there, a revolution that is bound to suit some people better than others.

If he refused because he's anxious about his role, finding out how to help you may be the answer. But some men simply don't want to witness labour and delivery and this attitude isn't a betrayal. Relationships work in different ways and there's more to being a good husband or father than attending the birth!

You won't be alone when your baby is born. Your midwife will provide some help and companionship as part of her professional duties. Single mothers or women whose partners work away often ask a close relative or girlfriend to be their birth partner. Why not consider this? It's a privilege for the person you choose and it can also be great fun. She can attend antenatal classes with you and share your experience in a way that complements your husband's involvement. If he feels there is no pressure on him you may find your husband's feelings change and he wants to be more actively involved, perhaps staying for the early part of your labour. You might even end up with two birth partners working together!

Q: I am determined to avoid stitches after the birth and have heard that massaging the tissue around the vagina can help. How should I do this?

A: Nobody can guarantee that you won't need stitches because it depends to some extent on factors like your baby's position and whether the delivery needs assistance. However, you can help to avoid damage to your perineum (the tissue between the vagina and anus) by gently massaging it.

In the last few weeks of pregnancy massage vitamin E or wheatgerm oil (these are particularly suitable although any pure vegetable oil would do) into your perineum for about five minutes each day. Immediately after your bath is a good time. When it's completely absorbed, gently stretch the tissue with your fingers until you feel a slight burning sensation.

In time you'll find your perineum stretches further before you feel this sensation, proving that it's becoming more supple and less likely to be damaged during the birth. When you are in labour, ask your midwife to help you to avoid the need for any stitches, or write this on your birthplan (see page 118).

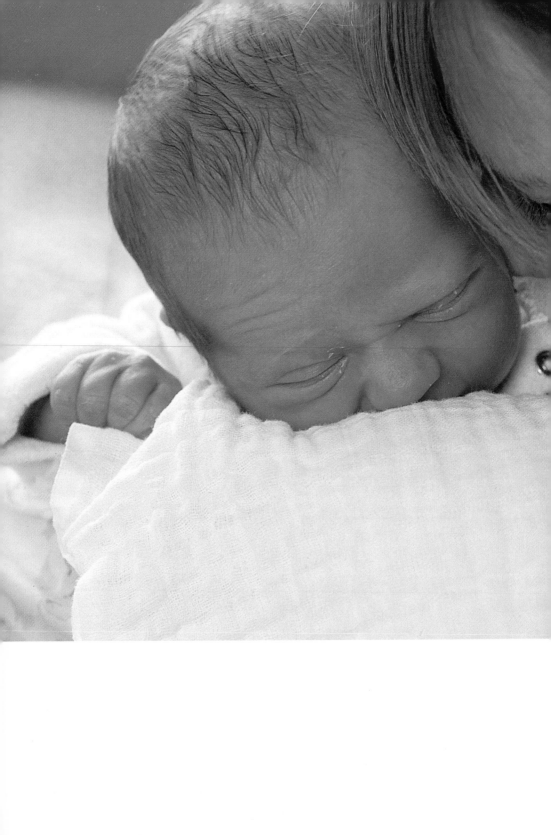

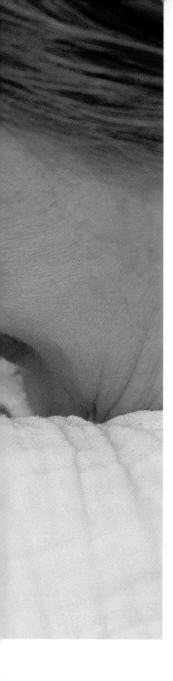

9

Labour and Birth

' When my contractions started it felt like being launched into space for the first time. I bubbled with excitement and elation and couldn't wait to see my baby but at the same time I was terrified! After all the theory and the preparations I had to jump and trust that I could fly. '

WHEN WILL THE BABY ARRIVE?

About 85 per cent of babies are born within two weeks either side of their due date. When this date is calculated from the first day of your last period, some 10 per cent (mostly first babies) go two weeks overdue. When it is estimated by ultrasound scan only about two per cent arrive two weeks late.

The timing of labour may be inherited from your baby's father, as some women go into labour consistently early with one partner but become overdue with a new partner. His family may be a better guide to whether your baby will be born on time than your own family, although babies do mature at different rates and tend to come when they're ready!

If you notice signs of labour starting three weeks or more before your due date, seek help straight away. Many babies come early without problems, but some will need specialist help. If you have several weeks to go the hospital may try to delay your labour to give your baby more time to mature. Take your notes with you when you stay away from home and contact the nearest hospital if labour does start.

If you go a week or more overdue it can be stressful, and after two weeks the hospital may want you to be induced (see page 146). Receiving concerned phone calls and comments from friends or relatives when your due date passes with no signs of labour may make you feel inadequate, like a performing seal who can't perform! On the other hand, the last few days before your baby's birth could be a very special time for you and your partner. Arrange treats or outings to look forward to together instead of just sitting around waiting for contractions.

WHAT CONTRACTIONS FEEL LIKE

If you tense your leg, the muscles in your thigh contract and become hard. When you relax they soften again. You tighten your leg muscles voluntarily but hormones make your uterus contract involuntarily to open your cervix. Your baby's head (or bottom) then holds it open and the next contraction stretches it slightly more. As more hormones are secreted during labour the contractions become stronger, dilating your cervix more effectively.

Did you wonder what the baby's movements would feel like when you were first pregnant, only to find the sensation strangely familiar when you felt it? You may notice the same about your contractions, although women clearly do feel the sensations differently as the following quotes show.

'At first the contractions felt like period pains down at the bottom of my tummy. Then they intensified into a hot sort of cramping sensation. My whole body went rigid with each one.'

'Nobody told me that you sometimes feel the contractions all in your back so it came as a shock. I kept waiting for something to happen in my tummy, but it never did.'

'The sensation started in my back and radiated round to my tummy and down my legs. It felt like the ache you get if you have cramp. I could still feel it when the contraction was over.'

'My contractions felt as if someone was hugging me too tightly so that I couldn't breathe. They weren't very painful but there was this tremendous sensation of pressure that almost overwhelmed me.'

BEFORE LABOUR STARTS

The first stage of labour lasts from when your cervix begins to open until you're fully dilated, ready to push. Before dilating your cervix softens and thins out. Some women experience diarrhoea, or have a 'show' of blood-streaked jelly – enough to cover the top joint of your thumb. This is the mucus plug that seals the cervix and it means that your cervix is softening. If there's fresh bleeding tell your midwife or hospital, but otherwise do nothing. You might not feel contractions for some hours, or even days.

Sometimes the 'waters' leak and you keep finding that your pants are damp; or the waters may break (see page 141). Phone your midwife or the hospital for advice – they will probably want to check you. Even if you have no contractions for several hours they may become strong quite quickly once they start.

Many women have regular contractions as the cervix thins and the baby's head moves deeper into the pelvis. You may feel niggly pains that come and go over several days, or you may have painful tightenings that continue for hours, or even a day. The length and strength of the contractions is usually more significant than the interval between them. If they last 30-40 seconds and you feel normal enough to chat or drink a cup of tea in between them it's unlikely that you're about to give birth, even if they are five minutes apart. Doing something different may make these contractions disappear for a while. Have a bath or go out for a walk if you've been resting, or lie down if you've been up and about.

The 'pre-labour' phase before true labour begins can be tedious. So much the better if you can ignore it for as long as possible. Try the following ways of passing the time:

- Ask a friend to keep you company.
- Hire some videos (and a video recorder if necessary).
- Go for a walk or window shopping.
- Start doing a large jigsaw, reading a new novel, making an outfit for the baby.
- Clean out a cupboard, re-cover the ironing board, bake a cake.
- Address birth announcement cards, write letters or phone friends.
- At night have a bath, a milky drink, a couple of paracetamol tablets, if necessary, and try to sleep to conserve energy.

TIME FOR HOSPITAL OR HELP?

If you have fresh bleeding or your waters break your midwife will probably want to check you out, so phone her or the hospital straight away. With contractions, it's a matter of how you feel. If you're happy and confident that's fine, but don't hesitate to phone if you're worried about anything or just need reassurance that all's well. Ask your community midwife to visit you or phone the labour ward yourself. An experienced midwife can usually tell if you're in labour by just talking to you.

EARLY LABOUR

To decide whether you're really in labour, compare your contractions with the ones you have been having. As they build up in length and strength you'll be more certain that true labour has started. Strong contractions last about 40-60 seconds, come regularly and definitely feel as though they mean business. Some women are elated knowing they're in labour while others get butterflies, as though they have got stage fright.

If you're going to hospital for the birth phone to let them know that you're coming in. Get your partner or a friend to drive you there. When you arrive a midwife will take your details and do the routine checks that you're familiar with from antenatal visits. She may examine you internally to check if your cervix is dilating. If it's still thinning you'll be reassured and sent home or put in an antenatal ward. Don't let this upset you, contractions can sometimes feel more purposeful than they are, even if it's not your first baby.

If you're in labour you'll probably be given a single room and offered a bath or shower. It is not normal practice now to offer an enema unless you ask for one. An electronic fetal monitor may be put on your tummy for half an hour to get a 'base reading' of your baby's normal heartbeat. You and your birth partner will then be left together, with a buzzer to summon help if you need it, and a midwife will pop in from time to time to see how you're getting on. Every three to four hours she may examine you to check dilation. If progress is slow she may suggest breaking your waters or setting up a hormone drip to strengthen the contractions (see page 147). Try not to get disheartened if early labour is rather long-winded.

Here are some ways to pass the time:
- Sort through the family photograph album, look at travel brochures and plan a real or imaginary holiday.
- Give yourself a treat – smooth a luxury cream onto your face, eat Belgian chocolates or use some special massage oil.
- Play story tapes or music, ask your partner to read to you or to give you a shoulder or foot massage.
- Try out different positions for labour (see page 112), remembering that stronger contractions help you make more progress.

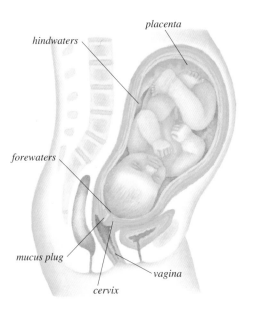

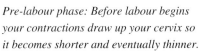

hindwaters

placenta

forewaters

mucus plug

vagina

cervix

Pre-labour phase: Before labour begins
your contractions draw up your cervix so
it becomes shorter and eventually thinner.

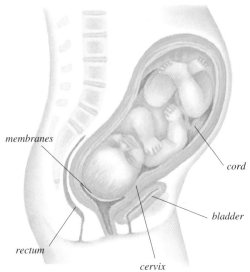

membranes

cord

bladder

rectum

cervix

First stage of labour: Your uterus tips forwards with each contraction as your cervix
opens to let your baby into the birth canal.

ACTIVE LABOUR

As your cervix dilates your contractions will become even longer, stronger
and closer together. They may last 60-90 seconds and come every two to four
minutes. You'll be making good progress, but you'll probably need to concentrate hard on relaxing both during and between them. You may feel calm and
very peaceful; or you may feel weary and anxious to get the birth over.

In the final stages of dilation, or 'transition', there's often almost no space
between contractions. Some women feel angry or panicky, or find themselves
weeping tears of frustration or despair; others feel deeply calm, confident, and
so detached that they actually doze off between contractions.

Your midwife will continue to listen to your baby's heartbeat and make sure
you're alright, and she'll offer pain
relief if necessary (see pages 122-3).
It can be hard to cope with the
intensity of active labour, but
you're nearing your goal and it's
worth remembering that the
stronger the contractions the
sooner you'll reach it.

*' I couldn't decide if I was in labour so we
went to hospital when I thought travelling
would be uncomfortable if we left it any
longer. I had backache all the time, but my
partner gave me lots of emotional support. I
needed his strength and was glad that he was
very firm with me. '* ANGELA

‘ *I didn't realize that labour could go on for over 20 hours. It was much longer and more tiring than I'd expected, but less painful. I only needed gas and air at the end. I tried every position in the book, and some that weren't.*

My husband massaged my back and played music tapes for me, but most of all he kept my spirits up. When I was pushing I kept thinking I was going to mess the bed and so I held back when I should have gone for it. But the moment the midwife put Louisa in my arms for the first time it was magical. I forgot all about labour and felt like a star. ’ MONIQUE

Be realistic about labour

It's claimed that there are about 150 contractions in the 'average' first labour, while a second or third baby takes about half that number. A text-book first labour lasts about 12 hours, including the delivery but not the pre-labour phase when the cervix is thinning out. So the average rate at which the cervix dilates is 1cm per hour.

Of course, this tells you very little about *your* labour, because women are individuals and are not so conveniently predictable! Some labours start and stop over several days. Some babies take their time to turn to a better position. Some women take many hours to dilate to 4cm and then the uterus gets the hang of it and finishes in less than an hour.

Whether it's your first baby or your fifth, you don't know beforehand what your labour will be like, so be realistic. Some women have an easy time. Others, including well-prepared or experienced women, find themselves struggling for reasons outside anyone's control. Keeping calm and relaxed always helps, but it does not guarantee labour will be normal. Nor is a normal labour necessarily an easy labour.

Accept your labour for what it is, not for what you would like it to be! Midwives can offer help if you need it, so be flexible. Labour will be a positive experience if you feel you made the right decisions in the circumstances.

Most problems in labour are unpleasant rather than dramatic, but nobody can prepare you for a real emergency. It happens rarely and you just have to cope as best you can and rely on the hospital team for help.

COPING WITH CONTRACTIONS

◆ *Relax with a sigh at the start and end of each contraction.*
◆ *Breathe slowly and gently, emphasizing the out breath.*
◆ *Keep checking that your shoulders and jaw are loose.*
◆ *Rest your palms upwards.*
◆ *A deep, warm bath may help you to relax.*
◆ *Using imagery may help. For example, think of feeling heavy and soft, or imagine riding over the contractions on a surf board.*
◆ *Ask your partner to count aloud to help you to pace yourself through each contraction.*

Long labour

About 80 per cent of first labours are over within 12 hours, without any intervention. A slow labour, although it can be normal, is hard to handle. It can be exhausting and your morale may plummet when there's little progress, but it can also be much gentler and more enjoyable than a very fast labour. These suggestions may help you to cope better:

- Try to deal with each contraction without thinking about those in the past or still to come.
- Walking or squatting often stimulates contractions. Have short rest periods lying down, then get upright and moving again.
- Have several deep, warm baths.
- Go to the toilet every hour to keep your bladder empty.
- Ask for guaranteed privacy for half an hour if hovering staff make you feel tense. Kissing, cuddling and breast stimulation can help to release contracting hormones.
- Send your partner out for 10 minutes of fresh air every hour. He needs energy to keep your morale up.

Backache labour

If your baby faces your tummy rather than your back it's harder for him to pass under your pubic arch during the birth because the shape of his head makes it like an egg trying to fit sideways into an egg cup. About 10 per cent of babies start labour in this position. The contractions turn them gradually into a better position for the birth. This rotation is progress even if you are not dilating, but labour may be longer and pressure may cause severe backache.

Try out these helpful remedies:

- Kneel on all fours, gently rocking your pelvis.
- Massage or have your partner or friend put firm pressure on your back during contractions (see pages 120-1). Some women prefer feather light massage.
- Hot or cold compresses, renewed frequently.
- An epidural if nothing else helps.

Very fast labour

It may seem like a good idea to get labour over and done with in a few hours, but if your cervix opens three times as fast as most women's, your contractions may also seem to be three times as strong! In a very quick labour there may be barely time to catch your breath before the next contraction is upon you. On the other hand, a short labour is usually straightforward.

Some women are disappointed that they were not more in control but felt swept along in a raging torrent unable to do anything but bob about like a cork. You may feel shocked and shaky after such an experience, although you will probably also feel pleased that your labour did not last any longer!

Left: Pushing is hard work but it can also be very satisfying as you are actively helping your baby to be born.

Below: This mother is upright, supported between her partner's knees. As her baby's head emerges the midwife gently guides it to prevent a tear.

THE BIRTH

The second stage of labour lasts from when your cervix is fully dilated until your baby is born. Pushing contractions are shorter and less frequent. They feel different from those that open your cervix. You may think you need to go to the toilet, you may feel a downward movement in your abdomen and pelvic floor, or find yourself making deep sounds in your throat. Your knees may feel weak, or buckle so that you need support.

Press the buzzer if your midwife isn't there. She'll check that your cervix is fully dilated. If you push when there is a rim of cervix in front of the baby's head it could swell like a bruised lip and take longer to dilate. To prevent

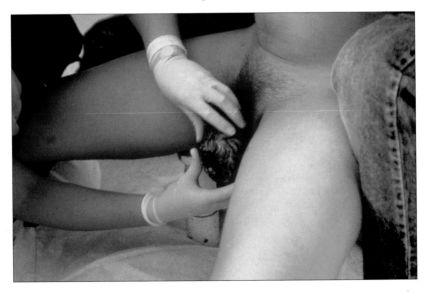

this, use gas and air, or breathe slowly and blow out sharply on each out breath, as though you were blowing a feather off your nose. When you are fully dilated you may need to push immediately or there may be a pause when you can rest. Get into an upright position so that gravity will help your baby move down the birth canal until you get an urge to push.

Your midwife will put on a plastic apron. If you are in hospital she'll bring her trolley of equipment, or move you to a delivery room. She'll stay with you during the birth, guiding you and making sure that your baby is coping well.

Many women find that the pushing action is a welcome relief after the tumult of final dilation, although this depends on the baby's position and

Above: The mother helps to deliver her baby and the midwife supports his head as it turns to let his body slip out easily.

Right: A wonderful reward for all that effort! The mother cuddles her newborn baby for the first time, her face full of love.

135

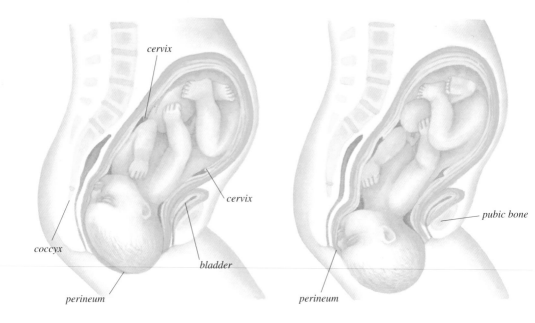

cervix

cervix

coccyx

bladder

perineum

pubic bone

perineum

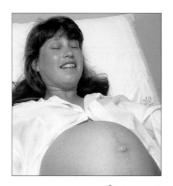

Your baby's head follows the curve of your pelvis, moving your coccyx (tailbone) aside. Notice how thin the perineum is – your midwife may ask you to pant instead of pushing at this point.

Your baby's head flexes up underneath your pubic arch and emerges, releasing pressure on your coccyx and perineum. At this point the back of your baby's head is towards your front and you'll be able to feel his hair.

whether the pelvis is roomy. It can be hard work and you may feel too exhausted to be bothered; alternatively you may feel full of energy, excitement and joy.

Ask beforehand for a midwife who is happy to deliver you in any position. If you choose an upright position, gravity will help your baby to descend, but if the birth seems fast or you've already delivered a baby quickly, you could try lying on your side to slow it down. Ask your midwife to help you to deliver your baby's head without a tear, and listen to her instructions.

Your baby's head will turn to fit under your pubic arch and you may feel a burning sensation as the perineum (tissue around the vagina) stretches. The midwife will support your baby's head to protect your perineum and tell you when to stop pushing and pant instead. She'll perform an episiotomy if

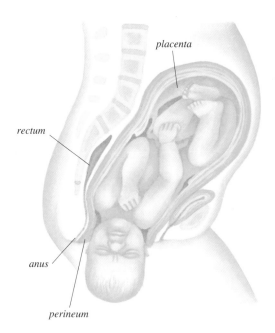

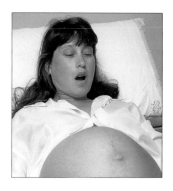

Your baby turns to face your thigh, so that his shoulders fit more easily through your pubic arch and pelvic floor. When his shoulders are born his body tumbles out.

needed. About 25 per cent of women suffer no damage at all or only have a very small tear in the perineum.

You may have an injection to bring the placenta away quickly (see page 155). Your baby's shoulders will turn to fit under your pubic arch and his body will tumble out, to be placed on your tummy or in your arms. He can be cleaned and wrapped up first if you prefer.

Gentle birth

Have you ever thought about what birth feels like for your baby? He's squeezed through your bony pelvis, thrust from warmth and security into space, bright lights and unmuffled sounds.

If the birth is normal, you and your midwife could help make it a gentler experience for your baby.

- Ask your midwife to deliver your baby onto your tummy or into your arms and leave the cord to pulsate before cutting it (see page 138).
- You can provide a particularly soft wrap to keep your baby warm while you cradle him after the birth.
- Ask if the lights can be dimmed and unnecessary noise avoided.
- Bath your baby in warm water soon after the birth.
- If the birth has to be assisted, make up for any distress suffered by you or your baby by being especially gentle and loving with him afterwards.

HELPING WITH THE BIRTH

To actively help the birth of your baby:
- *Choose the position that feels best at the time.*
- *Think of the entrance to your vagina and direct your pushes down there. Involuntary grunts are normal and can be helpful.*
- *Open out your birth canal and 'give' birth. Some women hold back for fear of emptying their bowels, a sensation that's caused by the pressure of the baby's head.*
- *Listen to your midwife. She'll guide you and tell you when to stop pushing so that she can ease your baby out gently.*

Your newborn baby

When you see babies with perfectly shaped heads and silk soft skin in film or television dramas, they are usually a few hours or days old! Some truly newborn babies look like that, but others look purple, blue or grey and covered with vernix, a substance that stops the skin becoming waterlogged in the uterus. You may or may not think your baby is beautiful!

Some babies have puffy eyes, blue hands and feet or fine black hair (lanugo) on their bodies. Others have lumps and bumps from the pressure of your pelvis, or streaks of blood from a tear or episiotomy. Don't be alarmed, many babies look vulnerable and birth bruised at first. All this changes quite quickly and in a few hours or days he'll look as perfect as any cherub!

After the birth

The third and final stage of labour is the delivery of the placenta. If you had an injection (see page 155) the midwife will clamp and cut the cord immediately; otherwise she'll wait until it stops pulsating. Your partner can cut the cord if he wishes. Some babies are put on a sloping table to have their airways cleared or are given a whiff of oxygen to help them breathe.

Identity bracelets will be attached to your baby's wrist and ankle and you can cuddle and breastfeed him if you wish.

You may well feel a tremendous elation, a rush of love for this new person and pride in your achievement. You may feel wide awake and full of energy; but it's equally normal to feel curiously detached, rather disappointed in your baby and simply

'*Labour wasn't at all what I'd expected. I had a show but then nothing else happened for several days. I had contractions every night and then they'd die away again. After a week of this I couldn't stand it any longer and went to stay at my Mum's house. That night I felt a bit strange. By the time we got to hospital the contractions were so strong that I couldn't walk and they had to bring a wheelchair to take me to the ward. After three quick pushes Kiara was born. I'd go through a birth any day. I can't believe I was so lucky!* ' DENISE

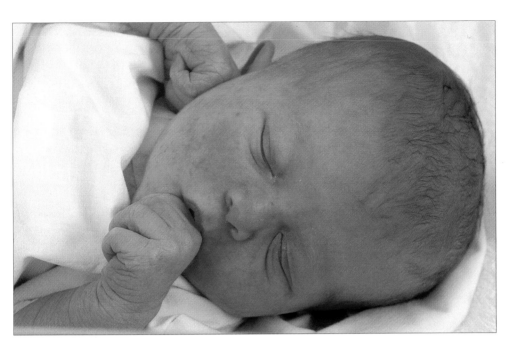

relieved that the birth is over. Don't judge your initial reaction harshly, just accept it for what it is.

You'll be asked to push again to bring the placenta away, although you might not want to! It feels like delivering a blancmange after the firmness of a baby's head. A midwife or doctor will stitch you if necessary, and you can wash or have a bath and put on a clean nightgown. Later, your baby will be weighed, measured and checked by a paediatrician. You and your partner will be offered tea or coffee and left alone to get to know your new arrival.

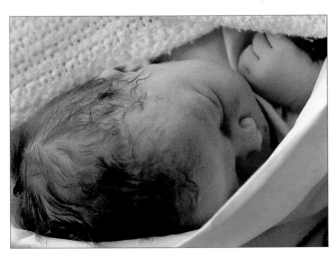

Above: *This baby has wrinkled skin and slightly puffy eyes. In a few days he'll fill out and the swelling will subside. His skin is blotchy which is very common in newborn babies.*

Left: *This newborn has an elongated head. It moulded to this shape to pass more easily through the mother's pelvis, but in a few days it will become round again.*

139

Some hospitals give every baby vitamin K, either orally or by injection, to help prevent a rare disease where the baby's blood fails to clot and bleeding occurs. You may want to discuss this with your midwife before the birth so that you can make a considered decision. Ask the staff to explain the pros and cons of any treatment they suggest, because responsibility for making decisions on your baby's behalf lies with you.

After an hour or two you'll probably be transferred to a postnatal ward and your partner may go home. Hospital routines do vary but the staff will show you the ropes. By now you may be feeling calm and confident like the cat that got the cream; or wobbly and unsure of yourself, like a new girl at school. Remember there's plenty of help available and there's no 'right' or 'wrong' way of caring for a baby. Just give your feelings time to settle down!

The Apgar score

This is a standard method of ensuring that babies who need it receive special attention. One minute after the birth the midwife checks your baby's appearance (colour), pulse (heartbeat), grimace (reflex), activity (muscle tone) and respiration (breathing). Each measure is awarded nought to two points. A total score between seven and ten means your baby is fine. The assessment is repeated five minutes after the birth, and by then a low score has often improved. If the score is still under seven your baby will be watched carefully for a while, but even then most babies turn out to be fine.

Bonding

Babies have no idea of other people's needs and are very demanding. Bonding is the process of emotional attachment that makes parents put their child's needs first. You'll know it's happened when you feel a rush of love, or heart-stopping anxiety, as someone else picks up your child!

Bonding is easier if you can hold and feed your baby soon after the birth, but don't worry if you're separated for some reason. Like falling in love, you may bond instantly or over time. Sooner or later it happens to all parents!

BIRTH AT HOME

If you have your baby at home the birth will proceed much the same as in hospital. Call your midwife when you feel you need her help or reassurance. You'll be free to do what you please and she'll observe you, checking your blood pressure and your baby's heartbeat and examining you occasionally.

After the delivery you'll have a bath while she clears up and collects any washing for your partner to see to later. She'll dispose of the placenta, although some couples prefer to bury it in the garden and plant a tree in the baby's honour. When you're settled and everything is tidy your midwife will leave a phone number in case you need her; she'll return in a few hours.

QUESTIONS AND ANSWERS

Q: I'm prepared to accept pain in order to have a natural labour but I'm no superhero! How can I cope with the pain without using drugs?

A: Try lots of different positions until you find what's most comfortable. For example, kneel on something soft and lean onto a bean bag, or sit back to front on a chair and lean on a pillow placed over the back. Stand with your arms around your partner's neck; rock your body or circle your hips to ease any discomfort. Massage can help: lightly stroke the skin around and under your bump to take away surface tension, or ask your partner to press firmly on your lower back (see pages 120-1). Try sitting in a deep warm bath; some women find it helps if their partner pours cool water over their stomach or down their back during contractions!

Think of contractions as rushes of warmth and energy; or as exhilarating waves that build up, tumble over and recede. Some women imagine riding waves on a surf-board, or climbing a hill and sliding down the other side.

Keep your breathing slow and gentle, emphasizing the out breath and trying to let the contractions flow over you without resistance. Concentrate on relaxing so deeply that you feel as if you are inside a glass ball, aware of what is going on outside but not distracted by it. Remind yourself that the pain is caused not by injury but by muscles working hard to deliver your baby. There are lots of ways to cope and it will not go on for ever!

Q: I'd feel so embarrassed if my waters broke in public. Is it likely and if it happens what should I do?

A: Fewer than 15 per cent of labours start with the waters breaking, and it mostly happens at home where you spend most time. Even if it happens it's unlikely your baby will arrive immediately. If you are upright and your baby's head is engaged gravity makes it act like a cork in a bottle, preventing liquid from escaping.

Put a child's rubber sheet over your mattress for the last month or so of your pregnancy. When you're out, wear a couple of sanitary pads, or even a gel-filled incontinence pad (available from a chemist). You can be sure that if anybody noticed a gush in public (which is rare) they would either look the other way or be concerned to help you out.

Q: Must I wear a hospital gown in labour and can I eat anything? I'm worried about running out of energy if I have a long labour.

A: You may be offered a gown but you can wear what you like in labour. If you're admitted early and want to walk around to get your contractions going, keep your ordinary clothes on. When the contractions become so strong that you want to stay in your room, change into something cool and comfortable like a nightgown, a large T-shirt or one of your partner's shirts. Some women feel best wearing nothing; others feel inhibited if there is a lack of privacy.

In the past women were often only given sips of water or ice chips during labour. When you're in strong labour you may not want to eat. However, withholding food and drink does not guarantee an empty stomach should a general anaesthetic be necessary. If you are hungry have something light such as toast, soup, scrambled eggs, stewed fruit or plain biscuits. Many hospitals provide small meals of this sort to give you energy.

Q: I live an hour's drive from the hospital. My first labour took three hours. What should my husband do if we can't reach the hospital and are alone with our toddler?

A: Set off without delay when you think something is happening, but if there is no time, don't panic! If you are on your way to hospital and you can feel your baby coming your husband should pull over safely and stop the car. At home, he should stay with you, reassure you and use common sense.

Most babies deliver themselves and breathe very competently. They are wet and slippery when they are first born so need to be held firmly and kept warm. If your baby has mucus in his mouth your husband could wipe it away before giving him to you, still attached to the cord, to put to the breast. He could get a blanket to keep both of you warm, and phone for help if there was no time earlier. Your midwife or GP will come immediately to cut the cord and deliver the placenta. Quick births are usually straightforward and toddlers are rarely upset if you stay calm.

Q: I want to have a natural birth but I'm worried that the midwife might not let me. I don't want to be difficult but how can I make sure that I will be allowed to cope with labour my own way?

A: Provided everything is going normally your midwife will probably be happy to go along with your wishes and you should be able to do whatever feels comfortable for you at the time.

Communication can be a problem when you're under stress, so write a birth plan (see page 118), discuss it with your midwife at your next antenatal visit and have it attached to your notes.

Remind the staff that you're keen to have a natural labour when you phone to say you're coming into hospital. Midwives differ in their approach to birth just as mothers do and this gives the staff on duty a chance to assign you a midwife who feels the same as you.

Q: I have had several colds during pregnancy which interfered with my breathing and during a recent bout of 'flu I worried about the birth. What can I do if I go into labour feeling ill?

A: Minor illnesses like colds and 'flu are usually either suppressed during labour or labour is delayed until you have recovered. This also tends to happen with asthma or migraine attacks, sinus headaches and the like. That's not to say that women always feel at their best during labour, but the body seems to decide its priorities instead of overburdening you. If you feel run down or under stress it makes sense to try to improve your general health, perhaps by checking your diet or resting more, so that your body gets a chance to recover its full strength.

Q: I've been to classes and read a lot about labour but I'm not confident that I'll cope when it comes to the real thing. What happens if I can't relax and breathe properly, or if I make a huge fuss?

A: Women often worry that labour is too big a job for them to handle, only to find hidden strengths they never knew they had! Relaxation and gentle breathing will help you to cope with contractions, so they are worth learning. However, there are no rules such as 'you must relax all the way through ... you should not make a noise ... you have to breathe like this or that ...'! You'll automatically give your best, so forget about setting yourself targets. It's not a competition and nobody wins prizes for breathing brilliantly or suffering stoically. All you have to do is let it happen.

Giving birth is more like crossing a field full of molehills than climbing a mountain. You may not know how many there are and some may be harder to get over than others; but if labour is normal the task is not impossible. If it isn't, help is available. Take one contraction at a time, deal with it and let it go. Try to cope not according to any rules but in whatever way feels right and works best for you.

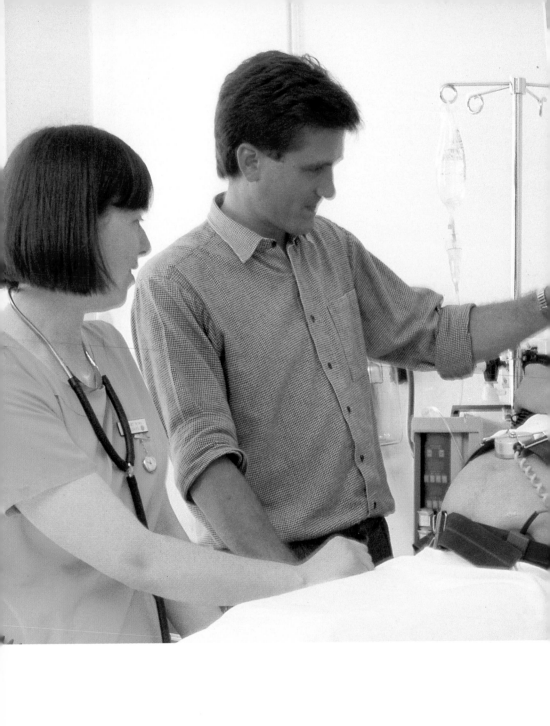

10

Help During and After the Birth

' *You never know what might happen at the birth. Doctors are like the lifeboat – you're glad they're there but you hope they won't be called out! I'm nervous, but I can relax knowing help is always at hand, although it probably won't be needed.* '

HELP IN LABOUR

If things don't go as smoothly as everyone hopes, intervention can make the birth easier or safer for you or your baby. It isn't something to be dreaded; it can provide a positive solution to a problem. Sometimes it is essential because you or your baby are at risk; in any rescue situation you should simply let the staff take control and tell you exactly what to do.

In other cases assistance is not essential but it might help. The decision depends on the professional judgement of the staff (see page 84), and on what *you* feel is best for you and your baby. You could leave it up to the staff, but if you want to share the decision you need to think about the issues.

Intervention usually comes in a 'package'. For example, if your labour is speeded up you will be monitored to make sure the baby copes well, so you may have less freedom to move about and seek comfortable positions; labour may be more painful so you might need more pain relief. If you or your baby are at risk you will want to accept help without question. Thinking about the pros and cons of the various elements of a 'package' will help if you want to share the decision when intervention is optional.

Induction

Labour may be started artificially if your baby is clearly at risk. For example, treatment might fail to improve pre-eclampsia (see page 102), or there might be concern because the baby's normal pattern of movements changes dramatically or she stops growing.

Induction might also be suggested when you are overdue, to reduce the risk of the placenta failing or of a more difficult delivery because your baby is bigger and her bones are less pliable.

You might *want* to be induced, but the procedure carries some risks so the decision should be made individually and only for a good reason.

Some doctors induce women routinely 10-14 days after their due date. Others allow three weeks, so if your baby is kicking happily you could ask whether this would be safe in your case. If you are given a date for induction try gently stimulating your breasts and nipples the day before to increase the release of oxytocin, the hormone that causes contractions. It may just get the labour started!

About one labour in six is induced. Hospital regimes differ, but typically if it's your first baby you'll be asked to go in the previous evening. You'll be examined and a prostin pessary, or some gel, will be inserted in your vagina to soften the neck of the uterus.

Prostin may start your labour easily so that it progresses normally. If not, you may be given further doses at intervals until your cervix starts to dilate. You may experience some colicky 'hormone' pains, especially with higher doses of prostin, and with second or later babies. These usually settle down after an hour or two and true labour contractions are easier to handle. With a second or later baby your cervix may be so thin and soft that it's not necessary to use pessaries or gel.

Your waters may be broken using an amnihook (rather like a plastic crochet hook) or an amnicot (a finger stall with a tiny plastic hook on the end). This shouldn't hurt as there are no nerves in the amniotic sac, but the internal examination may feel uncomfortable. Breaking your waters often establishes effective contractions but if not they will be stimulated using a hormone drip. This will be set up immediately if there is an urgent reason to induce you, such as pre-eclampsia. Where it's less urgent – you're simply overdue, for example – you may be left for a few hours to give labour a chance to establish itself naturally.

Induction does not affect most babies, but you'll be monitored throughout to make sure. If your baby is distressed, a tiny drop of blood may be taken from her scalp and analysed to double check her oxygen levels, and she'll be delivered quickly if necessary.

How painful you find induction depends on how easy it is to establish your contractions. If you're overdue, or have already had a baby, it may be no more than mildly uncomfortable. However, it can be painful if your uterus is not ready for labour. Comfort sometimes has to take second place to your own or your baby's safety, but pain relief will always be available if needed.

Speeding labour up

If your waters break but the contractions still fail to start, or start very slowly, your labour may be speeded up. The risk of infection, which could be serious for a baby, rises slowly after about 12 hours and more rapidly after 24 hours. A compromise has to be reached between leaving the contractions to start or strengthen spontaneously, which could take some hours, and ensuring that your baby is delivered without risking infection.

Sometimes contractions start and stop, or continue for many hours with little progress. Sometimes they are strong but fail to dilate your cervix, although they often become more effective as you relax. Slow labour is tedious but not abnormal in itself; every contraction helps you towards your goal. If your baby is fine you may prefer to accept this pattern of labour.

When labour is accelerated your waters are broken which usually strengthens your contractions. Your baby is monitored and a hormone drip is put into your arm to stimulate stronger contractions; this remains until after your baby is born. Your contractions may be more painful, but labour will be over sooner and you can have pain relief, if necessary. Unless speed is essential, you could ask if the drip can be started slowly and increased gradually to avoid overwhelming you.

Some hospitals offer 'active management' to guarantee that your labour will be over in 12 hours. Once you're in labour your waters are broken and internal examinations are performed every two hours or so to check progress. If

' The birth didn't go remotely as I'd hoped. I had pre-eclampsia so there were drugs to control my blood pressure, a drip to speed up labour and I wasn't allowed to push. They tried to deliver Sam by ventouse followed by forceps. I felt cheated. It was total technology when I wanted a natural birth! If I could do it all over again I'd still prepare in exactly the same way. I understood what was happening so I felt in control. Some decisions were hard to make, but others were very easy. It wasn't a good birth but I coped well and I certainly produced a lovely baby! ' DEBBIE

your cervix dilates slowly a drip is set up and increased until the contractions dilate your cervix at the rate of about 1cm an hour. Your baby is monitored in case she becomes distressed. Recent research suggests that this active management shortens labour by an average of one hour, but does not make an assisted delivery less likely.

Many women have mixed feelings about speeding labour up unless it is essential, so you may want to discuss it first with your midwife. Often it's possible to delay the decision for a few hours, to see how you get on. However, although a drip increases the risk that other intervention may be necessary it can also be a safe and speedy solution to a prolonged labour.

Monitoring the baby

During labour the midwife listens to your baby's heart rate through a hand-held or electronic stethoscope. The beat changes as the uterus contracts, returning to normal when the contraction ends and blood flows freely again. If a baby is short of oxygen her heartbeats increase or decrease too much, or return to normal too slowly after a contraction. This gives early warning of distress so that action can be taken straightaway.

An internal or external electronic fetal monitor can give a continuous record of your baby's response to contractions. Most hospitals record a 'base reading' of your baby's heart rate in early labour and fetal monitors are used routinely in 'high-tech' births. They are also used as a safeguard when there is intervention in labour such as a drip, and if there is any concern about your baby's heart rate.

An external monitor has two electrodes, held on your tummy with soft webbing belts. One picks up the strength of the contractions and the other records your baby's heartbeat. The information is fed into a machine with digital and auditory displays (which can be turned off if they worry you), and recorded as a trace. Your movement may be restricted because every time you move your baby also moves so the electrode may need to be repositioned. The monitor could be attached while you sit in a chair and moved each time you want to change position, but it obviously makes it harder to move freely.

An internal monitor provides similar information but an electrode is attached to your baby's scalp through your cervix. Scalp electrodes are less restrictive; if you had backache, for example, you could kneel to have your back massaged. However, many women feel they are intrusive to the baby.

Occasionally they cause minor scratches or hair fails to grow at the spot where the monitor was attached, although this will be unnoticeable when the baby's hair grows thickly.

The trace from a monitor needs skilled interpretation. If it is not absolutely clear whether your baby is distressed and action is required, you could ask for a second opinion. However, if there is a problem with your labour a fetal heart monitor can reassure you and improve safety for your baby.

Forceps or ventouse delivery

Ideally, your baby needs time to gently negotiate the contours of your pelvis, but no great delay during her delivery. Forceps or ventouse (vacuum extraction) can help to ensure that her birth is neither too fast nor too slow.

Forceps are shaped like spoons, curved to fit the birth canal, with different types according to the need. They are lubricated, inserted individually into the vagina and locked together at the handles like old-fashioned salad servers, so that they cradle the baby's head without harming it.

Ventouse or vacuum extraction equipment consists of a cup rather like a large bath plug that fits on the baby's head and a machine that creates suction to hold the cup securely in place.

Ventouse delivery is becoming more popular than forceps (which take up more space) but the decision depends on the actual circumstances and the experience of the doctor. The method he or she feels most confident using is likely to be the most successful.

Your baby might become distressed if the birth is too slow. Normally her head aligns with your pubic arch, moves down the birth canal with each pushing contraction and slips back a little between contractions. Some babies make no progress because they slip back too far after each contraction, or they try to pass under your pubic arch (which is shaped rather like a wishbone) at an angle. Using forceps or a ventouse, the doctor can gently turn your baby's head to fit the arch, or stop her from slipping back after each contraction. If you've been pushing for an hour or two without progress and are exhausted, it's a great relief when such assistance is offered!

Forceps or a ventouse can also help a baby to come out quickly. For example, a baby might be distressed because her cord was compressed or her mother's pelvis was a very tight fit. Adopting a different position or using extra effort might help, but if the distress continued an assisted delivery could solve the problem. A premature or breech baby might be delivered with forceps to guard against too rapid a birth, to protect the baby.

About one birth in ten is assisted, always by a doctor. Most doctors prefer you lying with your feet in stirrups, adjustable canvas slings attached to short poles at the foot of the bed. Your legs will be lifted into stirrups together, not one at a time which could strain your pelvic joints. Relax at the hips and ask the staff to adjust the slings if they are uncomfortable.

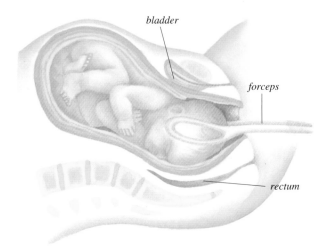

bladder

forceps

rectum

Forceps are curved to fit the pelvis. Without causing damage, they hold the baby's head securely so that the doctor can turn it slightly or stop it from slipping back into the birth canal.

Unless you already have an epidural in place you will be given an injection that numbs the nerves around the birth canal, so that you feel sensation but no pain. An episiotomy is usually performed to enlarge the opening to the birth canal and give the doctor extra room to deliver your baby.

When you feel a contraction or the staff say one is coming, you can help by pushing so that the forceps or ventouse then make it more effective. The doctor uses a slow and steady action, like taking the cork from a bottle of fine wine. A paediatrician will be there, but most babies need no help. You may see pressure marks from forceps or a swelling on your baby's head that

A ventouse or vacuum extractor looks like a shallow cup. It fits onto the crown of the baby's head and is held securely in place by suction. A forceps or ventouse delivery can make a difficult birth easier.

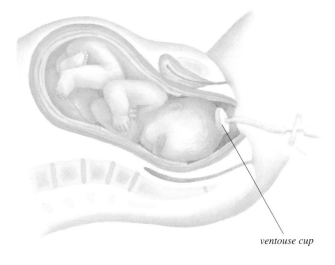

ventouse cup

matches the ventouse cup. These can look alarming at first, but they disappear within a day or two. Long-term problems are very rare because difficult assisted deliveries have been replaced by Caesarean sections. If your baby is irritable for a while as though she has a bit of a headache she will be comforted if you are especially gentle and loving in the early days.

' *I handled my contractions using nothing but breathing, but the delivery was difficult. Emily's head kept rocking to and fro under my pubic bone. I tried various positions but ended up with my feet in stirrups. The midwife mentioned getting the doctor, which motivated me to push like mad, but even so I had a ventouse delivery. It was very tense and confusing at the time, but as soon as Emily was born I was euphoric.* ' JANE

Some assisted deliveries are easy; the baby is simply lifted out, and you may feel little different afterwards from a mother who had a normal delivery. Sadly, others are very hard work for everyone concerned. This is sometimes unavoidable, and you may feel considerably bruised and sore afterwards. You will be grateful that your baby is safe but may also feel distressed at what happened (see page 153), even though it solved a problem and it was not your fault.

Episiotomy

This is a cut made in the outlet of the birth canal, to enlarge the opening and provide extra speed or extra space to deliver a baby safely. You might have one if your baby is breech, premature or in distress, or if you need an assisted delivery. A tear may be smaller and heal faster, but an episiotomy is preferable to a tear that damages the muscles that control your back passage; your midwife will judge this at the time.

An episiotomy is usually performed and stitched afterwards by whoever delivers your baby. Some staff perform more episiotomies than others. Hospitals that set a time limit on how long you can push, or don't encourage you to choose your delivery position, tend to have higher rates. If you use perineal massage (see page 125) and you tell your midwife that you are keen to avoid an episiotomy or a tear, you are less likely to have either.

Although an episiotomy sounds nasty, most women say that they were hardly aware of it at the time. Imagination is often far worse than reality! You may be given a local anaesthetic but in most cases the midwife or doctor waits until a contraction has reached its height. A short cut is made with round-ended scissors, and as the tissue is stretched by your baby's head it is naturally numb.

A local anaesthetic is usually given for stitching the wound, although some staff put the sutures in immediately after the placenta arrives, while the area is still numb, because they feel that the anaesthetic makes the tissues swell and this contributes to later discomfort. There is no need to suffer – just ask for more pain relief if you need it!

' *I had a drip because Thomas was badly positioned and the midwife wanted stronger contractions to help turn him. I pushed for about three hours because he hadn't turned enough. Having an episiotomy and a forceps delivery was a relief. You view everything differently if there's a problem. At that moment I didn't want choice, just a baby!*

Thomas went straightaway to the special care baby unit as he had inhaled something and they wanted to make sure his lungs were alright. He weighed 10 pounds, a giant compared to the tiny premature babies. He looked a fraud being there and he cried so loudly that I was embarrassed! But we were soon out and both were none the worse for wear. ' CAROL

Most women say that the pain of stitches came as a shock. Some discomfort is caused by bruising and swelling, which subsides in a day or two, but you'll feel very sore for a few days and the wound will take about a couple of weeks to heal (see page 175 for ways to cope). Be especially careful about hygiene to avoid any infection. Clean the bath before you use it as well as afterwards, and wipe toilet seats carefully. If your stitches are extremely painful tell your midwife. Stitches inserted after a difficult birth or that become infected can cause more severe pain that lasts much longer.

HELP AFTER THE BIRTH

When your placenta detaches from your uterus after the birth bleeding is inevitable. Heavy bleeding that is difficult to stop (postpartum haemorrhage) can be serious. However, it's not common and when treated promptly is rarely as dangerous as it used to be.

A haemorrhage might occur if the uterus failed to contract properly after the birth because it had been over-stretched by more than one baby, or if labour was prolonged and exhausting, or the mother was weakened by anaemia or illness. The uterus would be massaged and an injection of a drug such as syntocinon or syntometrine would be given to contract it.

An injection of syntometrine is often given routinely as your baby is being born, to reduce the likelihood of excessive bleeding (see page 155). For even faster action, the drug could be given straight into a vein. If the cause of bleeding is an injury to the cervix this would be repaired. Blood clotting agents, intravenous fluids or a transfusion could be given if necessary.

Occasionally, the placenta is not delivered normally after the birth because it is particularly firmly attached to the wall of the uterus. This can happen whether or not the mother has had an injection of syntocinon or syntometrine . A retained placenta is a potential source of heavy bleeding, so you would be taken to the theatre and given a general anaesthetic so that it could be removed successfully.

Any emergency, during labour or after delivery, is frightening for you and your birth partner. Nevertheless, if you have a postpartum haemorrhage the chances of successful treatment nowadays with no after effects are very high.

FEELINGS AFTER THE BIRTH

If you consider the fantastic feat nature performs during birth it's no surprise that a mother or baby sometimes needs a helping hand. It's a relief to come through a difficult situation safely and to know that your baby is alright. Many women can then put the experience in the past and enjoy their baby.

For some women, however, the memory of a birth causes great sadness. This is often linked with the insensitive treatment they've received, lack of support from the hospital team or feelings of powerlessness when events have been taken out of their hands. Some women blame themselves, or feel their body let them down. In reality it was probably nobody's fault – giving birth, especially for the first time, can be difficult sometimes. Flexibility is essential when coping with an unknown experience, but if you wanted a natural labour you will feel upset, even when you know that intervention was unavoidable. Occasionally both fathers and mothers can be haunted by feelings of anger and despair, almost to the point of obsession.

You may feel that it could have been different, that help wasn't needed, or that it should have come sooner. However, any decision has to be made with the information available at the time; judgement without the benefit of hindsight will be fallible. You may feel guilty if you can't come to terms with what happened. Other people often think a healthy baby is all that counts; of course this is important; but it's no compensation for a difficult birth.

Strong emotions are always better brought out into the open and not ignored or buried. You will feel grief at the loss of your expectations, but you have to accept what happened and how you feel about it. Sometimes there is no answer to the questions: 'why did this happen?' or 'why me?' How long it takes to heal, emotionally or physically, depends on the individual. In time you will be able to assign the past to its rightful place and move forward confidently to enjoy the future.

OVERCOMING A DIFFICULT BIRTH

Here are some of the ways parents have found helpful in coming to terms with a difficult experience:

◆ *Talk to your partner or sympathetic friends, until you don't need to talk any more. Find people who will listen to you, not just brush your worries aside or say that what matters is a healthy baby.*

◆ *If you were not able to discuss the birth with the staff involved, make an appointment to do so later. Write down all your questions in advance as it's easy to forget something at the time.*

◆ *Write down your experience, with comments about what made it better or worse. Send a copy to the hospital to help them handle similar situations in the future.*

HELP FOR YOUR BABY

Your baby will go to the special care baby unit (SCBU) if she needs extra attention after the birth. For example, she might be premature or very small; she might have breathing problems after a difficult delivery and need to be observed for a few hours. If she is ill or has a disability she might need some

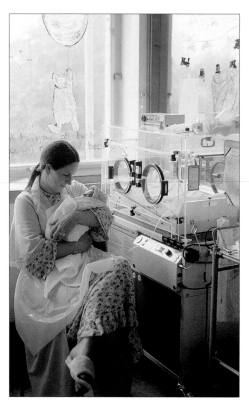

You can often stroke or cuddle your baby even if she has to spend some time in the special care baby unit.

treatment. You will be transferred with her, if necessary, to a centre that can deal with her particular problem.

The machinery and equipment in SCBU can be frightening at first and your baby will look tiny and frail, heightening your feeling of unreality and anxiety. But the tubes and winking lights provide extra security for her, and all the photos of past patients now doing extremely well indicates the success of most treatment.

SCBU is the best place for a baby with a problem. The wards are usually bright and attractive with staff who care deeply about babies and parents. You'll be taken to see your baby as soon as possible (although you may have to sleep in a different ward) and you'll be able to talk to the paediatrician. In some hospitals a polaroid photograph is taken of every baby who needs special care, so that the mother can have it beside her bed to look at between visits. Ask if this is possible; or if you own, or can borrow a video camera, your partner may be able to take a video of your baby so that you can see what she looks like and feel closer to her.

Breast milk is the best food for a baby, especially one in SCBU. Make your wishes known to the staff and ask for any help you need. Depending on the problem involved you may be able to breastfeed normally. If your baby has to be fed by tube you can express your milk. Don't be frightened to do what you can for her yourself, in partnership with the staff. It will help you to feel close to her. She will know she is loved if you touch her, stroke her and talk to her as much as possible.

QUESTIONS AND ANSWERS

Q: I really want to have a natural labour. How do the staff decide when to intervene and what help is needed?

A: A midwife's training and experience tell her when help is needed. For example, she feels your tummy to judge how your baby is lying. If she is unsure she can confirm it once your cervix has started to dilate because your baby's fontanelles (two diamond-shaped soft spots where the skull bones join) are different sizes. She takes your blood pressure and listens to your baby's heartbeat and judges whether they are normal, need watching, or warrant immediate attention.

If you or your baby were at risk a doctor would decide what action was necessary because midwives generally deal with normal labour. Your consent to treatment would be sought, except in a dire emergency where there is literally no time to spare.

Where intervention might or might not help your midwife may seek a second opinion from a colleague. She should also find out your wishes. Think about the issues beforehand and refer the staff to your birthplan (see page 118) so that you can share the decisions confidently.

Q: Will my partner be allowed to stay with me throughout labour, or will he have to leave the room during internal examinations or if I need a forceps delivery?

A: If your baby is born at home you can have anyone you wish with you in labour. In hospital your partner has no legal right to be present, although it is customary today for men to be welcomed. Most hospitals let you stay together throughout labour, including an assisted delivery or a Caesarean section performed under epidural. Some may ask your partner to leave for examinations, and many will not allow him to be there for a Caesarean section under general anaesthetic. If there is an emergency you will not want to query the rules, but in other circumstances exceptions have been made simply by talking nicely to the staff!

Q: Is it better to have an injection to bring the placenta away quickly, or to leave my baby's cord to pulsate after the birth?

A: To reduce the risk of heavy bleeding, many hospitals prefer to give an injection as soon as your baby's head or first shoulder is born, to contract your uterus quickly. The midwife clamps and cuts the cord immediately and makes sure your baby is breathing. She or a colleague then puts one hand on your tummy and gently pulls the cord to deliver the placenta within about ten minutes. There is some evidence that having the injection reduces the amount of bleeding after the birth.

When the cord is left to pulsate a jelly-like substance inside it swells up to cut off the blood flow. While this happens the baby gets oxygen and extra blood through the cord and there is less haste to encourage independent breathing. Some women prefer the more relaxed pace of such a delivery. If your labour has been completely natural (without drugs or other intervention), and your midwife is skilled and confident at delivering the placenta naturally, it is likely to be safe. Bleeding occasionally happens unexpectedly and rapidly, but if this occurs a drug to control it can be given, directly into a vein if necessary. However, without the injection you may have to wait considerably longer for the placenta to come away.

Further research is being carried out to find out more about the risks and benefits of these two approaches to delivering the placenta. In the meantime, discuss it with your midwife.

Q: My older brother has no sensation down one side of his face and my mother said it was caused by forceps when he was born. I'm afraid of this, so what should I do if I need a forceps delivery?

A: How easy it is for a throwaway comment to make such a lasting impression! Your mother's forceps delivery would have been necessary to solve a problem at the time, and unfortunately the way they were used at that time sometimes caused minor nerve damage. Twenty or thirty years ago forceps deliveries were performed in circumstances where today a Caesarean section would be performed as it is now safer.

Forceps are usually only used today for a simple 'lift out', when a baby is well down the birth canal. Talk to your midwife about your fears. She may suggest writing on your birth plan (see page 118) that you prefer a ventouse delivery if possible.

The best way not to need an assisted delivery is to be well prepared for labour. Learn to relax and handle labour without unnecessary stress and choose positions that work with rather than against gravity. However, anyone might need help if the baby is in an awkward position or labour is excessively long. Try to look on it positively; if you need an assisted delivery it will help you or your baby.

Q: My friend's baby had to go to the special care baby unit after he was born because he had inhaled something and his cord was wrapped twice around his neck. He's absolutely fine now but I'm worried about the same thing happening to me.

A: Your friend's baby probably inhaled meconium, the sterile, tarry substance that fills the fetus's intestines before birth. If a baby becomes distressed meconium is often released into the amniotic fluid. It can irritate the lungs and cause breathing problems if the baby inhales it, although in practice most babies don't.

Many babies with a long cord are born with it around their neck. The umbilical cord is said to be the part of the human body with the greatest variation – measuring from just a few inches to over 125cm (4ft), although the average is about 60cm (24in). The midwife checks for the cord during delivery, looping it over the baby's head or clamping and cutting it immediately to release it if necessary.

Often the baby seems untroubled by having the cord around his neck, even if there is more than one loop. This is probably because the blood pumping through the cord prevents it from pulling tight. However, some babies need extra oxygen or other care, and others are not interested in feeding immediately but prefer to wait a while, to get their breath back. Most babies do not need special care; your friend's baby may have gone to SCBU for a combination of factors, but the main thing is that he's fine now!

Q: I'm having my first baby at home with a midwife I really like. If I have to go to hospital because a problem arises will the staff blame me for wanting a home birth?

A: It won't be your fault if a problem arises! It could happen in any labour, but it's less likely if you're relaxed and confident. Presumably you chose to have your baby at home because you feel more at ease there, with a midwife you know and trust. These things are important for many women.

If you need help your midwife will take you to hospital and she'll probably stay with you until your baby is born. She'll know the staff and they'll be aware of your disappointment that the birth hasn't worked out the way you'd hoped. Everyone will work together to support you through a difficult time.

Afterwards you'll need time to come to terms with the experience – sometimes several weeks or months if it was very traumatic. It's unpleasant to be moved during labour but women who have experienced it say they are glad they spent part of their labour at home; most would have a home birth again.

11

Special Situations

‘ *As soon as the twins were born I forgot everything that had gone before. It didn't matter what labour was like. Their little heads rested on my chest and I was aware only of a feeling of great peace.* ’

TWINS OR MORE

There are twice as many multiple births today as there were a generation ago, and they are safer because most are diagnosed early by scan. With good care and attention over 90 per cent of twins are born healthy.

If you find out that you're expecting more than one baby make sure that you eat well. Small, frequent meals may be more comfortable in later months and some doctors will prescribe vitamins and minerals. You'll need extra rest, too, and may be advised to leave work early or to get help if you have other children. Pregnancy may be more uncomfortable but unless it's complicated you'll be treated much the same as anyone else, although you may have more antenatal checks.

Many twins are delivered vaginally without complications. Both babies will be continuously monitored and the second twin usually arrives within 20 minutes of the first. If a problem occurs an assisted delivery (see page 149) or a Caesarean section might be necessary even if the first baby has been born normally. Multiple births other than twins are usually by Caesarean section.

BREECH BABIES

Breech babies sit upright in the uterus rather than adopting a head-down position. About one baby in four is breech at 28 weeks, but only one in 40 at birth. Most have turned round by 36 weeks (see page 106).

A breech baby poses simple, mechanical problems at the birth. Usually a baby's head, his largest part, passes through the pelvis and birth canal first. He gets oxygen through his cord until his head and chest are born and he can breathe. The rest of his body, being smaller, slips out easily.

If his bottom emerges first his cord is compressed (reducing his oxygen supply) while his head passes through your pelvis. There must always be plenty of room for his head to follow his body easily as he relies on oxygen from his cord until his head is born and he can breathe. If your pelvis is roomy and your baby is small and well-positioned there is unlikely to be any delay during the delivery. Otherwise a Caesarean section is preferable to risking a vaginal delivery that might cause him distress.

Some doctors use X-rays or CT (computerised termography – a sophisticated X-ray) scans to help judge the chances of a trouble-free delivery. A pelvic diameter of 11cm might be considered adequate if your baby is small; a big baby would need

6 The staff at the hospital were laid back about a breech birth and made me feel really safe. I had an epidural for high blood pressure which would have been topped up if I needed a Caesarean, but there were no problems. It was a lovely birth.

They put a mirror where I could see to help me push and the registrar just ran his finger around Jessie's head as she was born. My boyfriend kept me calm and the staff made a fuss of me and told me what was happening so I trusted them fully. 9 LOUISE extra room. A scan may be performed before or during early labour to determine your baby's exact position, and you may be induced (see page 146) around your due date so that your baby's head is still soft enough to fit easily through your pelvis.

A baby's bottom does not fill the pelvis, so go straight to hospital if your waters break. There's a tiny risk that the cord will be washed down first and get squashed, leaving your baby short of oxygen.

‘ I wrote a birthplan before my Caesarean section, asking the staff to talk to me during the operation and to help me breastfeed immediately after the birth. The operation was complicated and I was very frightened, but even so the doctors stuck to my requests. Looking back, I wouldn't have changed anything. It was an intensely personal experience for me and my husband. We learned a lot about ourselves. ’ JENNIE

In hospital you will have blood taken for cross matching and a drip or a tube inserted for fluids, saving precious time in an emergency. Your baby may be monitored continuously (see page 148). Some breech babies pass meconium, the tarry substance from the gut. This is usually no cause for concern.

You may have more examinations to check dilation during a breech labour as your baby's bottom may slip through your partly dilated cervix, making you want to push too soon. Some doctors suggest an epidural to reduce this urge. Alternatively, you could use gas and air, kneel with your chin on your chest so that gravity takes your baby away from your cervix, or slowly and sharply blow out as you would candles on a cake, one by one in your imagination to stop yourself pushing too soon.

A breech delivery is usually performed by a registrar, with you lying back with your feet in stirrups. You may be given an episiotomy to create extra room. Some doctors use forceps to deliver the baby's head steadily while others cradle it in their hands to keep it well flexed. Then everything should proceed like any other birth.

CAESAREAN SECTION

On average, around 20 per cent of women have a Caesarean birth today. If you are under 25 your chances are around one in seven for your first baby and one in 30 for later babies. If you are over 35, the chance is double for your first baby and treble for later babies. Caesarean rates vary considerably between hospitals and doctors, but the Health Information Service or AIMS (see Appendix) can help you to find out the figures for your area. Over half of all Caesareans are classed as emergencies, performed because a problem arises during labour, but only about five per cent of problems occur without warning. Usually there's time to explain what's happening and to reassure you.

A Caesarean can ensure that your baby is born safely or you avoid excessive trauma so it isn't a second class sort of birth. It's major surgery, however, so

161

it's neither risk-free nor an easy option. Doctors sometimes disagree about whether the following indications make a Caesarean birth advisable, so you may wish to discuss it.

- You make little progress during labour. Your contractions may be long and strong but fail to dilate your cervix, or to move your baby's head down through your pelvis. They might be too weak to be effective, even with the added help of a hormone drip.
- Your baby and your pelvis are the wrong shape or size for each other (cephalopelvic disproportion). Your baby could be too large or your pelvic cavity too small or an unusual shape.
- Your baby becomes distressed and starts to pass meconium (waste products from his gut) into your waters or his heartbeat may be abnormal.
- Your baby is lying breech or transverse (horizontally); or his face instead of the crown of his head is coming first.
- Your placenta lies across the cervix (*placenta praevia*), or detaches from the wall of the uterus (*abruptio placentae*), causing bleeding; or the cord prolapses (slips down in front of the baby).
- You have a pre-existing problem, such as pre-eclampsia, low lying fibroids, diabetes, an active herpes infection, heart or kidney disease, or have had surgery to repair the vagina.
- Your baby is delicate or extra-precious. This might include premature or very small babies, and mothers who have had extensive fertility treatment or lost a previous baby.

Elective Caesarean

A pre-planned Caesarean avoids the risk of an emergency arising. It can be safer than a normal delivery as staff are more relaxed when they're not responding to a crisis; you can also plan ahead and organize your family. There are disadvantages, however:

- Recovery takes longer and women report more pain and infections than after a normal delivery.
- Caring for your baby may be more difficult at first.
- Studies have shown an increase in postnatal depression and long term health problems in women who have had a Caesarean birth.
- Scar tissue on your uterus reduces fertility and increases the risk of ectopic pregnancy (see page 29) and of placental problems in subsequent pregnancies.

A general or local anaesthetic

To avoid the small risk associated with general anaesthetic, most Caesareans are performed under epidural or spinal block. A spinal is similar to an

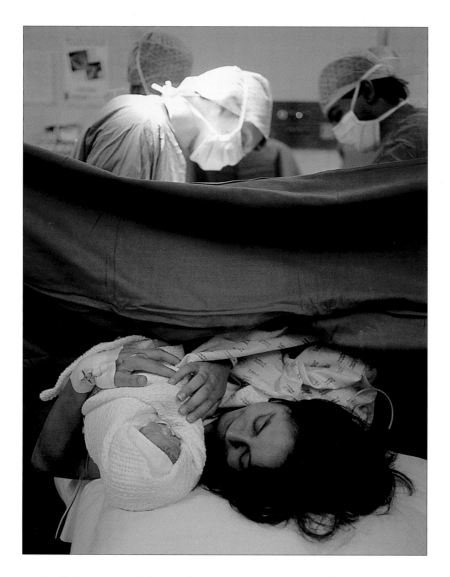

epidural but inserted lower down your back. It is quicker to set up so it can often be used in an emergency, instead of a general anaesthetic.

A Caesarean birth under epidural. The baby is given to the mother to cuddle while the wound is repaired.

Most mothers say that although they felt apprehensive about being awake during an operation, sharing the birth with their partner and the delight of having their baby lifted into their arms was well worth it.

A spinal block can't be topped up so if the operation takes longer than expected you'll be given a general anaesthetic. You can also have one in a dire emergency when there's no time to set up a spinal block or deepen an epidural to the level necessary for surgery, or if you feel at any time that you can't handle being awake.

If you have a general anaesthetic your partner will not be present, but you could ask if the staff could take photos and if he can wait outside the theatre so that your baby can be brought for him to cuddle while your wound is repaired. If he's there when you come round you'll see him and your baby first. Later, you could ask the staff to describe the birth to you.

A Caesarean birth

A registrar usually performs the operation and procedures are similar whether you have a general or local anaesthetic. Typically, for an elective Caesarean you go into hospital the day before so the staff can complete routine tasks like taking blood for cross matching. From midnight you usually have nothing to eat or drink. Before the operation you sign a consent form and have an antacid to neutralize your stomach contents in case you need a general anaesthetic. You also remove jewellery (a ring can be taped over), make up and nail polish so the anaesthetist can watch your colour during the operation.

The top part of your pubic hair is shaved and you have a bath or shower and put on a cotton gown. A drip for intravenous fluids is set up and a catheter inserted to keep your bladder empty. It may be uncomfortable but shouldn't be painful. Electrodes are taped to your chest to monitor your heart and pulse, and a blood pressure cuff is put on your arm. A diathermy plate, part of the equipment used to control bleeding, may be strapped to your leg. Just before the operation you breathe pure oxygen from a mask, for your baby's sake.

An epidural or spinal is set up in the usual way (see page 122). You may wear elastic stockings to help maintain your blood pressure. Your birth partner sits by your head wearing a gown, preferably with something cool underneath as the theatre is warm. A frame with sterile drapes is placed over your chest to block your view and the anaesthetist makes sure that your tummy is numb. You won't feel pain but there may be sensations such as the waters being sucked out or tugging as your baby emerges. Sounds such as taps flowing or instruments clattering can be masked if the staff chat to you, or you listen to music.

' My first Caesarean section was an emergency for failure to progress. An epidural left a "window" of sensation so I had a general anaesthetic. It left me feeling knocked out for a day or two but I got over the operation quicker than some friends got over normal births. After six weeks I was out playing tennis again. ' CLARE

If you have a general anaesthetic it's fed into your vein; a light one is used for the delivery followed by a deeper one for repairing the wound. As you drift off to sleep a narrow tube is passed into your windpipe and you may be aware of the midwife pressing gently on your throat to stop anything going down the wrong way.

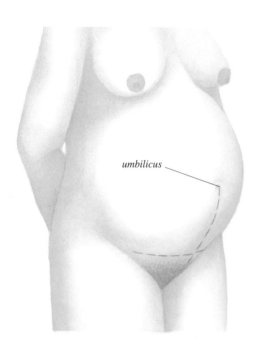

umbilicus

Vertical and 'bikini' cuts (shown) are more common these days. Occasionally a 'classical' cut is made to the side of the umbilicus.

Most babies are delivered through a 10-15cm (4-6in) 'bikini' cut near the pubic hair line. When hair grows back the scar barely shows. A vertical incision may be needed for triplets, a baby in an awkward position, or a dire emergency. Your abdominal muscles are gently parted and your baby is delivered in about 10 minutes. It takes about 45 minutes to close the wound, using individual stitches, a single 'running' stitch, or small metal clips.

A paediatrician is always present as some babies need temporary help to breathe, although this is less likely if you have had some contractions. If your baby needs to go to the SCBU (see page 154) you may be given a Polaroid photo of him. You will be taken to see him as soon as possible.

After the birth

If you were fit and healthy before the birth you're likely to recover quickly, although you'll feel a bit wobbly to begin with. General anaesthetics are much lighter these days so you may feel few or no after effects. After an epidural your legs may be numb for several hours. The drip and catheter will remain in place for up to 24 hours after the birth. If a drain was used to remove fluids from the wound it will come out after a day or two. Initially your wound may be covered by a plaster; the clips or stitches will usually come out in about five to seven days.

Pain varies from person to person and can be severe at first, but adequate pain relief will help speed your recovery. You may have suppositories to help reduce inflammation, plus an injection, an epidural top-up or patient controlled analgesia (PCA), where you give yourself pain relief (the machine prevents overdoses). Some women use a TENS machine, or the breathing techniques they learned for labour. In a couple of days paracetamol may be sufficient pain relief. Tell the staff if the pain does not diminish or gets worse, as this could indicate an infection that needs antibiotics.

Moving will be uncomfortable at first but try not to hold your scar except to cough or sneeze, and remind visitors that laughing hurts!

‘ Physically I was fine three weeks after my Caesarean, although I got very tired. But psychologically I lost confidence in my body. I couldn't take it for granted any more and was very fearful for about six months. Sex was difficult because I was afraid, and the longer I left it the more of a hurdle it became. I worried about little things and felt I was fussing, but I needed constant reassurance that everything was normal. ’ JENNIE

When you are allowed up, ease your body to the edge of the bed using your arms for support. Lean forward as you stand, taking the weight on your thighs. Walk tall instead of stooping – the stitches will not come apart.

An upright chair with arms is easiest to get into and out of and you may want someone with you when you take a shower or bath. Do as much as possible for yourself, but ask for any help you need and don't expect to do as much as someone who has had a normal delivery.

Caesarean babies are usually prettier looking than vaginally delivered babies as their heads have not been moulded through the pelvis, so that's a bonus! Bonding may happen immediately or it may take time – as with any delivery. Your partner can help you to move, lift your baby, breastfeed and so on, but most of all he can be understanding and supportive if you hit a low patch, as everyone does occasionally.

The first week after any birth is full of emotional ups and downs, with negative feelings mixed up with joy and love for the baby. You may be euphoric because you came through the operation safely, or dismayed that the birth was not what you expected. Your feelings may see-saw wildly, or you may feel very tearful.

Be kind to yourself! Cry if you want to. Rest as much as you can and be patient. A Caesarean birth is no easy option but care and support from staff and your partner will help you to recover both physically and emotionally.

AFTER THE BIRTH

You may find some of these items useful after a Caesarean birth:
- ◆ *Slip-on shoes and slippers – bending is painful at first.*
- ◆ *Small foot stool for getting off a high bed.*
- ◆ *Earplugs to get some sleep in hospital.*
- ◆ *Waist-high pants or boxer shorts that don't rub or irritate the scar.*
The NCT (see Appendix) sell comfortable stretch briefs.
- ◆ *Fennel or peppermint tea-bags to help combat wind.*
- ◆ *High-fibre bran cereal to help prevent constipation.*
- ◆ *Wet wipes beside the bed, to freshen up.*
- ◆ *A wire coat hanger to retrieve things that roll out of reach.*
- ◆ *A soft cushion to protect your scar from the seat belt during the journey home.*

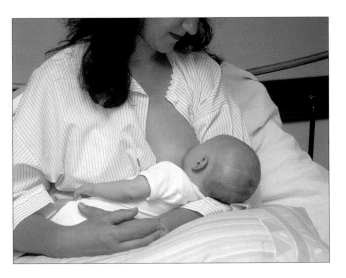

If you breastfeed your baby sitting up, make sure your back is well supported. Put a pillow over your scar and lay your baby on it, holding her close to your breast.

Breastfeeding after a Caesarean section

You'll be able to breastfeed your baby as soon as you feel ready. Anaesthetic drugs cause no problems and the milk usually comes in around the third or fourth day, although sometimes it takes a bit longer. If your baby is sick or premature you might need extra help, but any difficulties are more likely to be linked to the baby than to the birth.

Experiment to find a comfortable feeding position. It may be easiest to have your baby in bed. You'll have to cope with discomfort from your wound, but other women may have painful stitches after an episiotomy. Take it day by day. You may need to ask for help at every feed as you have had major surgery. If you are patient and positive you are almost certain to succeed.

You may feel much more comfortable if you breast-feed your baby in this position. Rest her head on a pillow and tuck her legs under your arms so that her weight doesn't press on your scar.

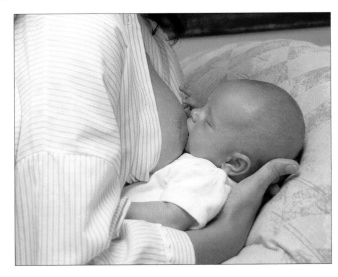

Going home

Most women leave hospital six to eight days after giving birth by Caesarean section. Going home can be unnerving and you may feel especially vulnerable at first. You'll recover faster if you take good care of yourself. Visitors can be tiring when you're recovering from an operation so ask them to come back when you're feeling stronger. There are some ideas for conserving energy below and also on page 177. You'll need extra practical help for several weeks, but by taking life easy most women get over the birth fairly rapidly.

Try to avoid any task that pulls on the scar for four to six weeks. This includes lifting, and driving as you may not be up to coping in an emergency.

The physiotherapist at the hospital will supply suitable postnatal exercises. Start them when you feel ready, but be guided by your body and make sure you don't overtire yourself.

The normal discharge (lochia) lasts from two to six weeks. Some women feel ready to make love after a couple of weeks and others not for several months. It depends on whether your wound has healed, how tired you are and so on. If you adjust your position to avoid pressure on the scar, gentle lovemaking can be more enjoyable than after a normal delivery followed by stitches, but if it hurts you might have a slight infection that needs treatment. If you have attempted intercourse before your postnatal check-up, any difficulties can be discussed with your GP. If not, you can see him or her for advice at any time.

CONSERVING ENERGY AFTER A CAESAREAN

◆ *Delegate as much as possible. If in doubt, don't do something straightaway, put it off until the next day or better still, the following week.*

◆ *Have somewhere for your baby to sleep and a set of nappy changing equipment upstairs and downstairs to save journeys. A table at the right height for nappy changing saves any bending.*

◆ *Have a thermos flask of tea and a snack beside you to keep up your strength, especially if you are breastfeeding.*

◆ *Write down all serious offers of help and suggest specific jobs like vacuuming or taking an older child to playgroup.*

◆ *Stock up your freezer, or buy takeaways or tins for easy meals at first. Check that you have basics such as washing powder, and list other items so that someone can shop for you.*

◆ *Wear loose clothing with large pockets to carry things.*

◆ *Put an advert for a mother's help in your local shop. An extra pair of hands for a few weeks could be well worth the cost, especially if you have other children.*

Getting over a Caesarean birth

Full recovery after a Caesarean birth takes anything between a month and two years, but the average is about six months. Your scar will be red, then pink; finally it will fade to white or silver, possibly remaining numb for several months. However, physical healing is only part of the process. Many women have no problems coming to terms with a Caesarean birth, but others say that the hurt in their body healed faster than the hurt in their heart.

An emergency Caesarean tests your reserves of courage far more than a normal birth. Most women are overwhelmed with fear. Fear does not always disappear once a crisis is over; the reaction can be delayed.

Initial acceptance of a Caesarean section can be a way of coping, like covering your ears while they adjust to a loud noise. You may feel so grateful that you deny sadness about not having a normal delivery until it surfaces later, perhaps when a close friend has a lovely birth. Sometimes it helps to talk about it, to your partner, your midwife or someone who has experienced it (contact the Caesarean Support Network – see Appendix).

Most women need to know the reason for their operation, to view it neither as their body's failure nor as unnecessary interference by the doctors. Try to find out before leaving hospital but if it's not possible make an appointment to see the consultant, however long ago the birth was.

In general it's wise to wait about a year before becoming pregnant again. Regardless of the reason for the previous operation, about two thirds of women go on to have a normal delivery. After an uncomplicated Caesarean with a bikini-line scar your care in labour would probably be little different from any other woman. You're likely to be emotionally vulnerable rather than physically at risk, and you may need extra support especially if your previous birth was traumatic. Contact the NCT (see Appendix) for information about VBAC (Vaginal Birth After Caesarean).

DISABILITY OR LOSS OF A BABY

It's a shock to learn that your baby has a disability. You'll need time to adjust, to find out the extent of the problem, the prognosis and the help available (see Appendix). Most parents want straightforward information even if a definite diagnosis is not available immediately. Many disabilities are not as bad as they seem at first.

If a baby dies you lose your hopes and dreams as well as your child. Such a tragedy can bring very negative emotions. You may feel angry and blame the staff or yourself for what happened, even when it was

Nobody knows why we lost our baby. It was just one of those things. He'd have been starting school now and I often wonder what he'd have been like. It was dreadful at the time but you come through and learn what really matters in life. You stop worrying about little things. We have two other children and John will always be a precious memory. TONI

This lovely baby has had a cleft lip and palate repaired. Although it's a shock to learn that your baby is not perfect, many problems such as this can be expertly treated. They're not the disaster they may seem at first!

nobody's fault. You may search endlessly for reasons, and feel guilty about anything from a missed antenatal appointment to simply being too happy.

Grieving is hard work and you'll feel exhausted and overwhelmed by the sadness at first. Later there will be short periods of respite when normal life takes over. These phases will become more frequent and longer, but for months or even years you may find something unexpected will trigger a flood of memories and your sadness will feel as raw as ever.

❛ *Joe is my first baby and it was a complete shock to be told that he only had one hand. I felt guilty, even though it probably happened before I knew I was pregnant. I wanted a reason and went through my diary looking for anything that could have caused it. One of the hardest things in the first few days was telling friends, when they were ready with their congratulations.*

I wish I could relive the time around the birth. We should have been so happy but we were upset as we didn't realize it would make no difference! Joe has an electronic hand now and he's quite a tomboy. There's nothing he can't do. ❜ JEAN

Some fathers find it hard to talk about the loss of a baby but this doesn't mean they don't care. There is no set way or time to grieve, but you often learn more from coping with sadness than you do from life's joys. If you feel the need to talk several weeks or even months later, when everyone else seems to have moved on, contact one of the organizations in the Appendix.

Life will never be quite the same. Just take one day at a time. Eventually you will come to accept what has happened and move forward again.

QUESTIONS AND ANSWERS

Q: I had a difficult first birth which ended in a Caesarean section, but for my second birth I've been offered a trial of scar. What does this mean?

A: Caesarean births are very safe but in most cases a normal delivery is even safer. Most Caesarean sections are performed for reasons that are not likely to happen a second time. For example, your previous birth may have been difficult because your baby was lying in an awkward position. If this baby is lying well curled up the birth will be much easier, so you'll labour normally but will be carefully monitored to ensure that you make good progress and that your baby copes well. Meanwhile everything will be ready so that there's no delay if another Caesarean section should become necessary, which you'll probably find reassuring.

A normal labour after a Caesarean is called 'trial of scar' because your previous scar could break down, although this is extremely rare if a bikini or vertical cut (see page 165) was made the first time. Occasionally it used to happen after a classical cut, which is seldom necessary these days.

If a woman has not had a Caesarean section but there is some doubt as to whether she will achieve a normal delivery she may be offered a 'trial of labour'. It's the same thing, and doctors often use this term when talking to women who have had a Caesarean.

Q: I have a spinal cord injury and use a wheelchair. Will I have a Caesarean section or a normal birth?

A: You have a good chance of a normal delivery unless there's an obstetric problem unrelated to your disability. If a Caesarean section is recommended make sure you understand the reason for it and feel happy with the decision. Women with disabilities often say that they were not sure why they needed an operation.

Q: My midwife thinks I could have a normal delivery for my breech baby. However, my consultant recommends a Caesarean section. Whose advice should I take?

A: A Caesarean birth is preferable to a difficult breech delivery, so it depends on your individual circumstances. Research suggests that it is not necessary to deliver all breech babies by Caesarean, so ask your consultant why he thinks it's needed in your case. If you feel unhappy about his answer you could ask to be referred for a second opinion to someone who delivers breech babies vaginally unless there's a particular reason not to.

Q: Can my husband stay if I need an emergency Caesarean section?

A: If there is plenty of time and you are having an epidural he could probably be there, but in a dire emergency there might not even be time to explain what is happening. You'd be suddenly surrounded by doctors, whisked dramatically down corridors into the bright lights of the theatre and given a general anaesthetic for speed. Neither you nor your husband would want any delay, but you'd probably be in the recovery room in less than an hour.

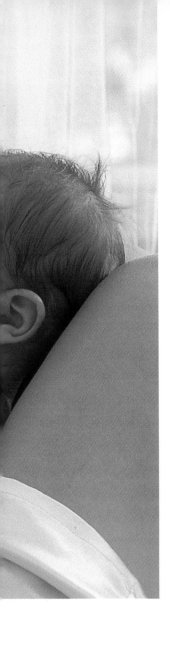

12

The Early Days

‘ *At first I floated about in a dream. Feeding, bathing and changing my baby took up all my attention. As the days passed, the tasks became familiar and comfortable. Within a month I couldn't remember life without a baby to love and care for.* ’

HOW YOU MAY FEEL

The days after a baby's birth are heady and exhausting. Excitement and elation may be mixed with bewilderment and frustration as your body undergoes rapid changes and your mind becomes preoccupied with your baby's needs. Take life slowly, give yourself space. Most women feel generally well, but emotional energy can mask physical tiredness. If visitors are overwhelming at the hospital ask them to visit when you get home.

You may feel afterpains for a day or two, a good sign that the uterus is returning to its non-pregnant size. They tend to be more pronounced with second and subsequent babies, and they are usually strongest during breast-feeding; if you prefer not to take paracetamol just relax, breathe gently and focus your attention elsewhere until they pass, as you did during labour.

You will have a discharge of blood and mucus (lochia), like a heavy period at first. It usually contains clots, but if these are larger than a walnut mention it to the midwife. Get out of bed slowly as you may have a sudden gush and feel faint. It is advisable to use sanitary pads rather than tampons to reduce the risk of infection. Breastfeeding helps reduce the flow as the uterus shrinks faster, sealing off the blood vessels. After the first week the lochia becomes pink, then brownish and intermittent for between two and six weeks. Sometimes it lasts longer, but if it's not bright red and does not smell offensive it usually tails off eventually with no problem. A heavier flow may occur if you have been doing too much. If you're worried contact your doctor.

It's important to empty your bladder to avoid problems such as infection, but it may be difficult for a day or two. If you can't manage it because of bruising or trauma you may be given a catheter until the problem rights itself.

Your first bowel movement may be uncomfortable, but try not to strain too much. It won't harm any stitches but can lead to haemorrhoids (piles). As your system returns to normal your motions will become softer and easier to pass. Drink plenty of fluids, eat roughage such as muesli, bran or wholemeal bread, move about to tone up your system – and wait. Don't feel under pressure to perform – a few days will make no difference and may be nature's way of giving your body time to heal. In the early days it's normal to have:

- Folds of loose skin and quite a 'bump' where your baby used to be. This will shrink and become firmer as the days pass.
- Tiny broken veins, bloodshot eyes, small bruises, piles or an aching pelvis, caused by the effort of pushing.
- Excess perspiration as your body gets rid of extra fluids.
- A feeling of unreality, whether it's your first baby or not.
- Mood swings, or general feelings of inadequacy or anxiety.
- A slightly raised temperature of up to 38°C (100°F) for a few hours around the third or fourth day when your milk comes in.
- Discomfort sitting or walking; soreness and exhaustion, especially if the delivery was difficult.

Coping with sore stitches

You are likely to feel bruised and sore after the birth simply because your tissues have been stretched. If your perineum is undamaged the soreness normally fades in a day or two. Megapulse treatment is offered in some hospitals: the physiotherapist uses a device that passes an electrical pulse over the area to reduce bruising.

A small episiotomy or tear may take up to 10 days to heal; a large episiotomy could take longer. The midwife will check your stitches daily to make sure they are healing normally. Good hygiene is important to avoid infection which would increase discomfort and delay healing. Wash your hands before and after changing sanitary pads and use medical wipes on toilet seats in hospital.

Here are some ways to help yourself:

- Tighten and release your pelvic floor muscles gently to help disperse the swelling.
- Let air circulate around your stitches.
- Stand up to pass urine, so that the flow avoids any sore places.
- Gently wash yourself afterwards to reduce stinging. If you don't have a bidet at home stand in the bath and use a jug or a shower spray (pointing downwards) with warm water. Dry yourself with soft tissues.
- Hold a clean sanitary pad over your stitches to support them when opening your bowels.
- Sit on a thick piece of foam rubber in the bath.
- Put ice cubes in a plastic bag, wrap it in a towel and hold the ice pack on your stitches.
- Stuff one leg of a pair of old tights with something soft and tie it into a ring to make a soft pad to sit on at home; or hire a 'valley cushion' from the NCT (see Appendix) to sit on.
- Ask the midwife to help you to breastfeed lying on your side.
- If your stitches do not feel considerably better after a week to ten days ask your midwife to check them again.

CHECKS FOR YOUR BABY

While you are in hospital a paediatrician will examine your baby thoroughly in your presence. For instance, he'll listen to her heart and make sure her hip joints are stable. He may check the reflexes that help her to adapt to independent life, such as breathing, sucking and swallowing, 'rooting' or searching for the nipple, grasping, 'stepping' when her feet touch a firm surface, and the 'Moro' reflex, where she throws out her arms if she is startled. On the fifth day after delivery a blood sample will be taken from your baby's heel to test for some rare disorders such as phenylketonuria.

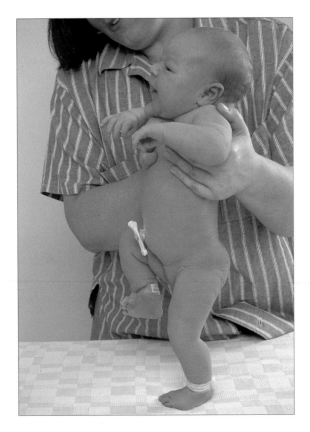

If you hold your newborn baby upright and let her feet come into contact with a firm surface such as a table top, she will lift each leg in turn and place it in front of the other as though she was going for a walk. This 'stepping' reflex is automatic and fades within a week or two of the birth.

Over half of all babies develop jaundice, which gives them a suntanned look caused by bilirubin, a yellowish substance in the blood. Jaundice is usually mild but babies are watched carefully as occasionally it proves more serious. It usually fades after a week, or it may take slightly longer for a premature baby; meanwhile the baby needs frequent feeding. High bilirubin levels can be lowered by phototherapy in hospital under a special light. Your baby's eyes will be covered for protection, but you can remove the blindfold during feeds.

A few babies suffer from low blood sugar (hypoglycaemia). It's more common with low birthweight or premature babies, and where the mother is diabetic or has had a difficult delivery. To avoid your baby becoming limp and apathetic, or alternatively jittery, the staff will want to be sure that she has a good feed within a few hours of birth. Sometimes a baby needs extra feeds, or even a drip.

If you have your baby at home the physical checks will be carried out by your GP, although your baby can be referred to a paediatrician if necessary. Your midwife will take routine blood samples and keep an eye open for things such as jaundice.

GOING HOME

Most mothers normally leave hospital within a day or two of the birth, although you may stay longer if there are any problems. Caring for your baby on your own can seem daunting, but your midwife will visit you for up to 10 days and longer if necessary. When she signs you off your health visitor will take over.

Make rest a high priority for at least 21 days after the birth. You'll want visitors, but the most welcome ones will admire your baby, tell you how clever you are, drop off a little present – and leave! Unless they are genuinely helpful, and you get on very well, having relatives to stay can be rather too much.

' When Freddie arrived the love I felt for him was indescribable. We are a close family and everyone kept asking me to bring him over and show him off. It was tempting to refuse because he had not been inoculated or he might have caught a cold from one of my nephews or nieces. I had to make myself believe that a cold would not be a disaster.

It would have been so easy to sit back and tell myself I didn't need my family, but I did; they gave me support and saw the funny side of life when I felt overwhelmed. My older sisters have children and they came up with suggestions I wouldn't have thought of, like not changing his nappy at night because it woke him up and he took another hour to settle again. Everyone threw in advice and I picked the bits I liked. ' LINDA

Although you may feel fine at first you'll soon run out of energy, so rest even if you feel energetic. If you have used up your reserves of emotional energy by trying to do too much something temporary, like your baby waking frequently at night or a minor feeding problem, can get blown up out of all proportion.

Here are some ways to help you avoid exhaustion. (See also page 168 on conserving energy after a Caesarean.)

WAYS TO CONSERVE ENERGY

◆ *Put a notice on the door asking people not to visit between certain times as you will be resting.*

◆ *Don't offer visitors refreshments unless you want them to stay around and chat.*

◆ *Take the phone off the hook when you want to rest or feed your baby. Record an answerphone message giving details of the baby.*

◆ *Make a list of jobs that need doing such as shopping, taking a toddler to the swings, or ironing. When somebody offers to help you'll have an answer ready.*

◆ *Forget the usual chores: grab an extra hour's rest in the morning and in the afternoon when your baby is asleep.*

◆ *Make sure everything (book, drink, remote control for TV) is within reach when your baby finally falls asleep in your arms.*

Most toddlers are naturally gentle with a new brother or sister, taking any unsettled feelings out on Mum or Dad. Try to respond positively when your toddler wants to show affection for the baby.

RELATIONSHIP WITH YOUR PARTNER

A birth of a wanted child touches tender feelings in most men. After such a highly emotional shared experience it may be hard for your partner to leave you in hospital, especially at night if he has to return to an empty house.

If the birth was difficult he will have found it as upsetting as you. He will be relieved that it is over but may feel angry, blaming the staff or the baby for what you went through. He may feel responsible for putting you in the situation and need reassurance to shake off the guilt.

Men are expected to be strong and supportive during and after a birth but many new fathers feel uncertain about their new role. As you adapt to the presence of a precious but demanding baby you'll need to find a new relationship that satisfies both of you. It takes time and can prove stressful.

The early days after a birth are unsettled. Enjoy the elation – it's a very special time in your lives – but be kind to each other, making allowances.

RELATIONSHIP WITH YOUR FAMILY

A new baby subtly changes the relationships within a family, creating aunts and uncles from sisters and brothers, grandmothers and grandfathers from mothers and fathers. It's unrealistic to expect everything to be back to normal after a fortnight!

A toddler needs to get to know his new brother or sister. Small children sometimes behave badly because they are too little to handle the excitement of having a brother or sister, which can be overwhelming. It helps to keep as far as possible to a normal routine. Show that you love and understand your toddler in the few weeks while he is coming to terms with the new arrival.

Babies can unite families very positively. Children from previous marriages are linked by a new baby who is a half-sister or brother to each of them. However, some family relationships may need tactful handling. Older relatives may have more experience of bringing up children but this is *your* child and it's your responsibility and privilege to make the decisions. It costs nothing to smile and thank them for their advice, while you decide whether or not to follow it. Instinct or experimentation will tell you whether something works for you.

CARING FOR YOUR NEW BABY

There is no single 'right' way to bring up a baby and nobody, however experienced, finds what works first time. Most parents use a mixture of guesswork and trial and error, trying different strategies without worrying. However, if you're new to parenthood you may feel more confident following simple guidelines. The first is to collect everything together before you start!

Nappy changes: You'll need a fresh nappy, something to clean your baby's bottom (baby lotion or warm water and cotton wool) and barrier cream.

- Lay your baby on a changing mat or towel.
- Take off the dirty nappy, clean her bottom with the cotton wool and baby lotion or water, dry it carefully and apply barrier cream to help prevent nappy rash.
- Holding her ankles, lift her bottom and slide the fresh nappy underneath.
- Bring it up between her legs and fasten the tabs. If you are using a terry nappy pin it in place and put on plastic pants.
- Put the dirty nappy in a bucket with sterilizing solution, or a polythene bag for disposal.
- Wash your hands thoroughly.
- Babies with very delicate skin sometimes get red, sore looking areas on their bottom. At the first sign of nappy rash, expose your baby to the air as much as possible. For example, lay her on her changing mat in a warm room, leaving her nappy unfastened.

Bathing: New babies don't need bathing every day. You can 'top and tail' your baby, washing just her face, hands and bottom, some days. To bath her you'll need fresh clothes; nappy changing requirements; boiled, cooled water and cotton wool; a soft towel; and soap or baby bath gel if you wish. Fill the bowl or bath with warm water and make sure the room is warm.

- Undress your baby except for her nappy. Wrap her in the towel.
- Wash her face with boiled, cooled water. Wipe each eye from her nose out, using separate cotton wool balls. Dry her face.
- Wash her head, rinse it using the bath water and dry it.
- Take off her nappy and clean her bottom.
- Lift her into the water by slipping your hands under her body and holding her arm and leg so that she is supported on your wrists. Keep an arm under her neck while you rest her legs on the base of the bath. Use the other hand to wash her.
- Slip the hand back under her bottom and hold her leg to lift her out. Dry her carefully. Put on a clean nappy and clothes.

Breastfeeding

Breastfeeding may be simple to establish, or it may be several weeks before you find it easy and rewarding. Babies are individuals: some are eager and can't wait to get at the food, while others fiddle around and seem not to know what's good for them. It helps to breastfeed soon after birth when your baby's

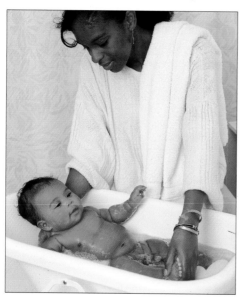

Hold your baby like this when you put her in the bath.

sucking reflex is strongest; but if there's a delay or the first feeds do not go smoothly, perseverance and good support usually lead to success.

Your midwife will help you with the early feeds. Take your time to find the right position for you. Good positioning helps to avoid sore nipples and allows your baby to take a good feed. It will depend on the shape of your breasts, how big your baby is and what feels comfortable. You should feel relaxed, not hunched up or distracted by discomfort.

Your baby's chest should face yours, with her head tipped back slightly so that her chin is close to your breast and her lips are near your nipple. Chest to chest and chin to breast is easy to remember. Use pillows for extra support if necessary.

HOW TO BREASTFEED

◆ *Support your baby's shoulders and neck with your forearm, cradling her head gently in your other hand. Use whichever hand and arm feels more comfortable.*
◆ *Brush her lips with your nipple until she opens her mouth.*
◆ *Wait until she opens her mouth really wide, like a baby bird. Be patient, this may take several minutes.*
◆ *When her mouth is wide open, bring her head towards your breast so that she takes a good mouthful of breast tissue as well as your nipple.*
◆ *If she is latched on properly her jawbone will move as she sucks. If not, slide a little finger into the corner of her mouth to break her suction. Relax and try again.*

You can help prevent sore nipples by making sure your baby is well supported and latched on properly. Wash your nipples once a day without using soap which removes natural oils and keep them dry. Cotton bras, and the old trick of putting tea-strainers (with the handles removed) over your nipples, can help air circulate. If they become sore expose them to the air as much as possible. Nipple creams may be soothing, although occasionally they also cause soreness. A change of feeding position to even out pressure on the nipple, or temporarily using a nipple shield may help.

Brief feeds as often as your baby will co-operate in the early days will give you both practice. You'll learn the positions that work for you and your baby will learn to latch on and feed well. This helps to minimize engorgement, where the rush of milk coming in on the third or fourth day leads to hard, swollen breasts. If you are engorged, expressing a bit of milk first may make it easier for your baby to latch on. You can encourage the milk to flow by applying warm compresses, or try cold compresses to reduce swelling. Sometimes alternate hot and cold compresses work, and some women swear by wearing a firm, supportive bra with cooling Savoy cabbage leaves inside for a few hours!

If you have any breastfeeding problem ask for support early on. Your midwife, health visitor or another mother who has breastfed successfully may be able to help, or contact one of the groups listed in the Appendix, who are happy to give advice and support.

' *I lived on excitement after Bianca was born. The birth was lovely and I felt fantastic. I lost weight and everyone said how well I looked, but I wasn't eating enough extra calories for breastfeeding. Bianca was always hungry and I never saw any milk, so she was on a bottle by the time she was six weeks old.*

I suppose I wanted to prove that parenthood was fun and that it didn't need to make any difference to your life. Breastfeeding failed because I did too much. I've learned to be more laid back! ' *NICKI*

Make sure you are sitting comfortably and that you hold your baby close to your body when you breastfeed.

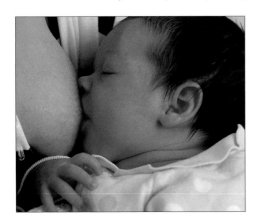

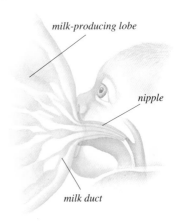

milk-producing lobe

nipple

milk duct

This baby is latched on well, taking a good mouthful of breast with her bottom lip curled back. In this position she has plenty of room to breathe.

When your baby is well positioned, with a good mouthful of breast tissue, your nipple will reach the back of her tongue and palate.

Bottlefeeding

If you are unable to breastfeed or choose to bottlefeed instead there is no reason to feel guilty. It can be a very satisfying experience. Cuddle your baby, and when it's practical open your shirt so that she can feel the warmth of your skin as she feeds.

Some babies like formula straight from the fridge. Others prefer the bottle warmed in a bottle warmer or jug of hot water. Keep the bottle tilted throughout the feed so that the teat stays full of liquid and your baby doesn't suck in air which could give her colic.

' I'd never thought about the intensity of caring for a baby before I had Kathryn. She knows nothing of the world and what I teach her will form the basis for her attitudes in life

I couldn't breastfeed because I had drugs for blood pressure problems, so at first she had bottles. When my milk came in she wouldn't latch on; sometimes she screamed solidly for a couple of hours. It would have been so easy to bottlefeed, but I really wanted her to be breastfed, and in time I succeeded. I was surprised at the warmth she brought from unexpected places. An old friend I'd not seen for years brought me a rose to plant in the garden in her honour. A friend of my mother's sent a little dress. ' ROSEMARY

Hygiene is especially important when you bottlefeed as your baby will not gain the immunities that breast-feeding offers. Germs multiply rapidly in stale milk, so be sure to clean all bottles and teats thoroughly before sterilizing them.

Instructions may vary slightly so read the label on the pack of formula, but in general make up feeds like this:

- Wash your hands and boil enough tap water for the number of bottles you intend to make.
- Cool the water and pour the correct amount into each bottle, using the measuring marks on the side.
- Measure the formula using the scoop provided. Don't pack it down as too much powder can be harmful. Level it off with the back of a knife.
- Add the powder to the bottle, screw on the cap and shake to dissolve it.
- Store bottles in the fridge, but throw away any unused formula after 24 hours.

Enjoy your baby

If you decide for good reasons to bottlefeed you may agonize that your baby will suffer and others may judge you – but other mothers will be busy agoniz-ing over their own supposed failings.

For many years you'll worry about making wrong decisions. Just as you gain confidence in your own sound judgement your children will reach their teens and tell you all over again that you're wrong! Life is for living, mistakes are inevitable – and a mother's place is in the wrong. It's best to accept this basic fact of life early and get on with enjoying your baby.

QUESTIONS AND ANSWERS

Q: My baby is five days old and I'm finding breastfeeding is agony, especially at the start of each feed. I don't want to give up but I've begun to dread it. What am I doing wrong?

A: Some women experience sharp pain at the beginning of a feed, when the milk lets down. It usually disappears after two or three weeks, as the ducts get accustomed to the sudden rush of milk. Anticipate it and deliberately relax your shoulders and take your mind elsewhere for a minute, until it passes.

If pain continues throughout the feed ask your community midwife to check that your baby is latched on well. Don't push your nipple between her lips so that she has to haul herself onto the breast; wait until she opens her mouth wide before you latch her on. She should take a good mouthful of breast with her bottom lip curled back.

Most babies come off the breast by themselves when they have finished feeding but some doze, wake up when they slide off the nipple and then jerk back on for another feed! This can make your nipple sore, so put your baby on your shoulder if you think she has finished. Cuddle her until she settles. Sore nipples usually heal within a day or two once the problem has been identified and solved.

Q: My baby is 10 days old and has had special care since birth. We are ready for discharge now but I'm afraid I won't be able to cope. There's always a midwife to help me here so I feel secure. Breastfeeding still isn't easy. Could I ask to stay longer?

A: It's easy to lose confidence in yourself when your baby needs the care of highly trained professionals, but the staff will reassure you that now she is better you can provide everything she needs to thrive. Breastfeeding is sometimes harder to establish when a baby is ill. With time and patience it will get easier, and when you go home your community midwife or your health visitor will continue to help. Your confidence will quickly return once you find out that you really can cope!

Q: I thought life would be wonderful once my baby arrived, but he's three weeks old and I still feel completely overwhelmed. All he does is howl and I feel trapped. I wanted him so much but now I long to get back to my old life. Do other mothers feel this way, or am I not suited to motherhood?

A: More mothers than you might imagine feel like this at first, but nobody likes to admit it. Try telling your health visitor, or a sympathetic older relative who will understand and support you.

You also need some practical help. It's not your fault that your baby cries so much! Ask a friend or relative to take him out for a walk so that you can have a bath or a rest without worrying about him. Plan an outing on your own leaving your partner to cope at home.

Anyone could feel trapped in your situation but getting out is wonderful for the morale, even if it is only for a couple of hours between feeds! This difficult phase will not last for ever. In time your baby will settle and become more contented and rewarding and you will adjust to your new life and get your energy back. Then you'll find that life with a baby can be fun.

Q: My baby's skin was beautiful when he was born but now I'm home his face is covered with spots. The health visitor didn't seem concerned but was it something I ate?

A: Your baby simply has especially fine, delicate skin, and the spots may come and go for a few weeks until his system matures. They are unlikely to be linked to anything you ate or did. Red spots appear sometimes if a baby becomes overheated and sweaty, but babies who are not too hot also get them. Tiny white spots (milia) are caused by temporary blockage of the glands that secrete sebum to lubricate the skin. They disappear after a few days and you should never squeeze them.

Just when you want your baby to look his best because everybody is coming to admire him, he comes out in spots! They look awful to you, but visitors are more likely to notice his tiny fingers, delicate ears and sweet expressions.

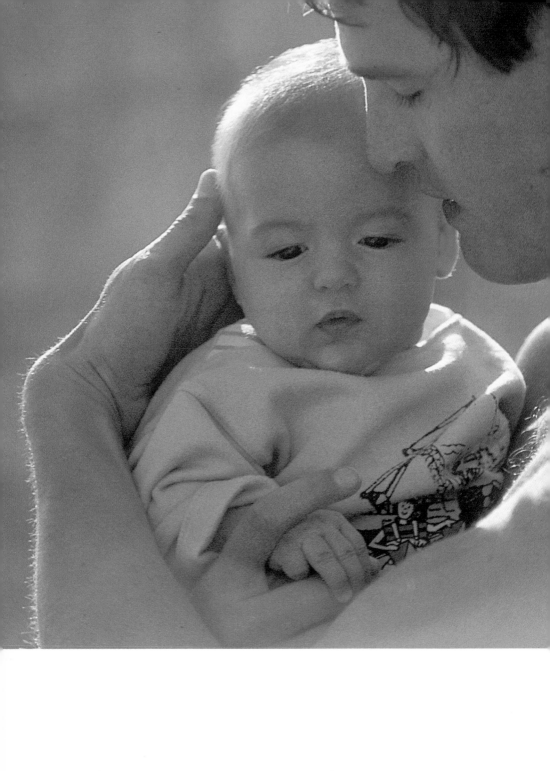

13

Getting Back to Normal

' *I never imagined that parenthood would make me feel so protective. Of course there are bad times when she won't stop screaming and I've really had enough. But then she smiles at me – and I forgive her everything!* '

ADJUSTING TO PARENTHOOD

Parenthood is nothing if not an intense experience. It involves a lot of giving in situations that arouse rather primitive emotions. At times your baby will fascinate and delight you; at other times you'll feel anxious, angry or inadequate. You may worry that his well-being lies largely in your hands and that you'll never be good enough for this responsibility. The ideal of a perfect mother is born of love and raised on other peoples' expectations, but a baby's ever-changing needs make perfection impossible!

Most mothers take several months to organize any sort of normal routine. Congratulate yourself if you manage to achieve one thing per day in addition to baby care. Breastfed babies often want to suckle happily all evening, every evening, and the cumulative lack of sleep sneaks up on you so you may find yourself operating in a daze. Most people believe they need eight hours' sleep every night, but your body will soon adjust to less. You won't feel on top form while this happens, but if you're really exhausted you will probably sleep anytime and anywhere!

For many months ahead you'll be a willing slave to a pint-sized boss. You may long for your baby to sleep to give you a little space of your own – but when he does you'll think about him constantly!

Babies sleep for as long as their body needs and are happy or miserable, according to their temperament. There is little you can do to influence this. If your baby cries despite your efforts to comfort him you may worry that he dislikes you or has failed to bond to you, but it will probably have more to do with his nature than your relationship or how you handle him. Follow his lead until a routine evolves naturally after a few months. When you have a baby your life takes on a slower rhythm. Somewhere within you you'll find the patience to respond to the day to day demands a baby makes, although you may also grieve for a 'lost' part of you – the independent woman who could do what she wanted when she wanted.

If you use a wheelchair or have another disability you may already live at a slower pace, so the change when a baby arrives is not so great. Physically able mothers often have to learn the hard way that rushing about is neither desirable nor comfortable. Slowing down can actually be a source of great vitality. It gives you time to enjoy your baby.

' *Before I had Lucien everybody warned me I'd get no sleep. I expected to look like a zombie with matchsticks propping up my eyes, but Lucien fed and went straight down. Everyone said that by the time he was six months old my time would not be my own, but he happily watched me pottering about, or the washing machine going round. I returned to work part time and went on holiday without him and he was fine!*

Now I'm pregnant again and the doom-and-gloom brigade are saying. "You won't have another one like Lucien, you know!" The awful things they warned me about never happened, and anyway he wasn't a baby for long. It's best to take each step as it comes and enjoy motherhood. **'** *YASMIN*

Who can help you?

There are many experts, supporters and other parents to help you make the most of parenting:

- Your health visitor can check your baby's growth and discuss immunization, feeding and baby care. She has access to national databases and may be able to help you contact other parents if you have a special situation.
- Relatives and friends can give advice, boost your confidence and look after your baby when you need a break.
- Childcare books can give you information and answer some questions.
- Magazines such as *Practical Parenting* publish informative articles on baby care written by experts. Keep copies for reference as your baby grows.
- The voluntary organizations listed in the Appendix provide a range of services. The Directory of British Organizations (ask at your local library) lists many more groups by subject.
- Your local Citizens' Advice Bureau (see telephone directory) has trained volunteers who give confidential advice on any topic including consumer rights, debt problems and welfare benefits.

CRYING BABIES

If your baby cries constantly it's neither your fault nor your sole responsibility. After two or three months he'll be more settled. Meanwhile, here are some things to try that might help:

- Check with your doctor that there's no physical reason for the crying, then stop worrying about this.
- Ask friends and relatives to help by taking your baby out for an hour or two to give you a regular break. This is essential to keep a sense of proportion.
- Take your baby out in the car, or walk around the block. You won't be the only parent to do this in pyjamas at 3am!
- Cranial osteopathy sometimes helps. The British School of Osteopathy (see Appendix) can give advice.
- Contact CRY-SIS (see Appendix) who can put you in touch with a telephone volunteer who has had a similar problem.
- If your baby has colic at roughly the same time every day, accept it and don't plan activities for this time.
- If you think you might harm your baby put her in a safe place such as her cot and go away for ten minutes to calm down; contact the NSPCC Helpline (see Appendix). They will offer practical support, not condemnation.

RELATIONSHIP CHANGES

A small baby changes life for both you and your partner. Here's what some fathers say about their new role:

'It's difficult to reconcile the demands of my job and the desire to be a good father. I'm not always there so I can't slot into Lucy's routine because I don't know what's going on.'

'I love being a father. It's much better for you than four pints of lager and a curry, a pleasure that has had to take a back seat recently! But I worry about my financial responsibility now that Carla isn't working.'

'Ben is growing and changing all the time. I really want to get back to see him each evening, but I feel a bit jealous of the time Abi spends with him. She seems closer to him than to me.'

If you look after your baby most of the time you'll go beyond following general advice (which only works up to a point) and start fine-tuning, adapting subtly to your baby's likes and dislikes. When your partner returns to work he may lose his confidence at baby care through lack of practice. Give him space to find his own ways to cope, without hovering over him or demonstrating your superior skills too readily!

Sadly, the most loving of mothers can be possessive over a baby, while even supportive partners often don't do as much as they think they do. There's a gap between the fantasy of domestic bliss where everyone has their needs met while chores are shared harmoniously, and the reality of family life with a demanding baby and adults who have feelings of power and vulnerability.

Potentially, parenthood means being on call for 24 hours a day with no holidays! Any division of labour is fine provided both partners are happy with the situation. If not, creeping resentment can easily sour your relationship. There can be no change if one partner keeps his or her feelings a secret.

❛ *Having a baby should change your life, and parenthood is rewarding, but my husband and I found the adjustment wasn't easy. If you want to work things out you really have to communicate. Our relationship has always been good as we had time to spend together.*

When Sophie arrived we couldn't keep up all our activities without getting frazzled, so for six months we decided to concentrate on looking after her and not expect much for ourselves. Every few weeks we made ourselves sit down and set some time aside for each of us. We organized a baby-sitter to spend time together. It sounds very planned but it certainly worked for us. ❜ JULIA

Start as you mean to go on: talk to each other and negotiate agreements that suit you both. Close relationships always involve ambivalence, so there will be conflicts. Resolving these through compromise will both challenge and strengthen your partnership.

Your baby should become a happy part of your lives, and not take over completely. After three or four months it's a good idea to sit down with your partner and review the situation. On the opposite page there are some ideas to help you balance everyone's needs.

BALANCING NEEDS

◆ *Time management: some jobs must be done every day; others, such as bathing your baby, could be done less frequently.*

◆ *Weekend lie-in: one partner looks after the baby while the other stays in bed for as long as they like on Saturday morning. On Sunday, reverse the roles.*

◆ *Forward planning: once a month you sit down and plan chores and time off for each partner.*

◆ *Talking time: every week you each spend five minutes listening without interruption while your partner talks and 20 minutes discussing any issues that come up.*

◆ *Regular night off together: you organize a baby-sitter and spend time doing something you both enjoy.*

◆ *Team work: you take turns with other couples or lone parents, looking after the children while the others have a break.*

Your sex life

Some women feel ready to make love again as soon as a week or two after giving birth but most take rather longer. If there has been a lull in your sex life, perhaps starting in late pregnancy and continuing after the birth, you may find that the spontaneity is lost and it is necessary for you and your partner to make a positive decision together to resume sexual relations. Sex may be painful or remind you of a negative birth experience. Full breasts may feel uncomfortable or messy when they leak milk, or you may need reassurance about your appearance. You may be exhausted because your baby does not sleep through the night, or distracted by his demands for attention. You may be so preoccupied with parenting that you forget about your adult relationship. It's not always easy to communicate if guilt or resentment are present, but talking with your partner may help you to find ways to set your sex life on course again.

Discomfort can often be improved by using a different position or a vaginal lubricant from the chemist. Having extra help at home could ensure that you are less tired or that you get a break from your responsibilities. Good humour and a willingness to communicate are essential. Your sex life will be different but it need not be less good; remember that penetrative sex is not the only form of lovemaking – there are many different ways of giving and receiving affection. Stroking, kissing and cuddling are all important ways of demonstrating your love. If you continue to show each other warmth and tenderness, and explore other means of providing each other with erotic pleasure, a full sexual relationship can follow in its own time when you both feel ready for it.

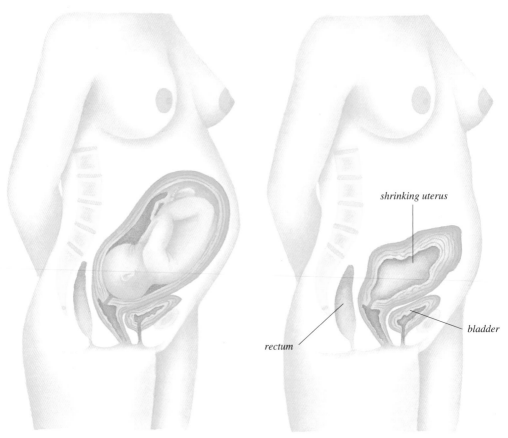

shrinking uterus

bladder

rectum

BEFORE THE BIRTH   AFTER THE BIRTH

YOUR POSTNATAL BODY

Your figure may look much the same as before pregnancy or you may notice some subtle changes. Your uterus will be slightly bigger than previously and your tummy may have a more rounded outline. It will feel flabby at first, becoming firmer after a few weeks. Your breasts may be larger if you are breastfeeding. If not, they'll be smaller and softer for several months while the fatty tissue that shapes them builds up, replacing the milk-producing tissue that developed in pregnancy.

Your pelvic floor is stretched during a normal birth and you may suffer stress incontinence when you cough or laugh. The muscle tone can be improved with pelvic floor exercises (see page 45), but it may be several months before you feel confident again.

The scar from a tear or episiotomy may feel strange and it can be reassuring to take a look using a hand mirror. Your periods might return in a few weeks, or not for a year or more if you are fully breastfeeding. You can conceive

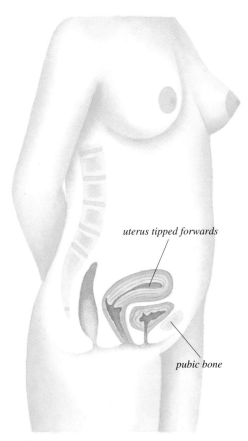

Far left: Your uterus takes up a lot of room a the end of pregnancy, stretching your abdomen and compressing your internal organs.
Centre: After your baby is born your uterus shrinks rapidly but you'll still look about five to six months pregnant. Your intestines have more room and they'll gradually resume their normal place.
Left: Six weeks after the birth your uterus will have contracted to the size of a small pear and returned to its normal position in your body.

uterus tipped forwards

pubic bone

SIX WEEKS LATER

before your first period. Becoming pregnant soon after giving birth could put a strain on your body, so use contraception unless you are sure that you really want another baby immediately.

Some women rapidly return to their pre-pregnancy weight, although this depends on body type. It's unwise to diet while breastfeeding, but after several months you'll naturally lose the extra fat stores laid down during pregnancy. If you bottlefeed and want to lose weight it may be necessary to watch what you eat and take more exercise.

When you're heavily pregnant you can't see over your bump and you may be dismayed to discover stretchmarks. These are red and unsightly at first. There's nothing you can do about them (they depend partly on skin type) but they fade to pink and eventually to a barely noticeable silvery cream.

Some women find their joints ache, especially after lifting or standing too long. Rest more and take care not to strain yourself – they'll stabilize as your hormones settle down.

Pelvic Tilting

*1. Lie on your back with knees bent
and hip-width apart and your feet
flat on the floor. Push your lower
back into the floor and tighten your
abdominal muscles.*

*2. Squeeze and lift your buttock
muscles, tilting your pelvis upwards
and draw in your pelvic floor. Hold
for a count of five then release back
down to the starting position.*

Postnatal exercises

In the early months, general exercise classes may be too strenuous as your
ligaments will still be soft and easily strained. Buy a video or find out about
special postnatal exercise classes.

If you cannot join a class near to home, here are some exercises you could
try. Warm up gently before you start and relax afterwards. Repeat each exercise six times to start with, working up to 10 or 12 repetitions. Ask your GP
or a physiotherapist for advice if you have any doubts – for example, if an
exercise feels too strenuous or you have a previous back or neck injury.

Don't push yourself; short, regular sessions are better than a marathon that
tires you out. However keen you are to get your figure back, respect your body
and put your baby's needs first.

Easy Curl-ups

1. Lie on your back with knees bent and hip-width apart and your lower back pushed into the floor. Place your hands on your thighs.

2. Lift your shoulders and slide your hands forward. Keep your head and neck up and your chin tucked in towards your chest. Slide your hands towards your knees. Hold for a count of four then slide down to the starting position.

Small Hip Rolls

1. Lie on your back with knees bent and feet together. Place your hands behind your head, elbows out.

2. Pull up your pelvic floor and tighten your abdominal muscles. Let your knees drop over halfway to the right. Hold them for a count of four then bring your legs back to the centre. Repeat to the left side.

Your straight abdominal muscles should be realigned before doing this exercise. If you are not sure ask your GP or physiotherapist to check.

1. Lay your baby on your chest. Press your lower back into the floor and bend your knees ensuring they are hip-width apart with your feet flat on the floor.

2. Support your baby under the armpits. Keeping your arms straight lift her towards the ceiling. Feel the push from your upper arms. Extend your arms to where it is comfortable but do not lock your elbows. Don't swing your baby in this position, or you may become unbalanced. Lower your baby back towards your lap.

Your postnatal checkup

About six weeks after the birth you'll be offered a check-up, usually with your GP. Your blood pressure and urine will be checked, and your breasts and tummy may be examined. You may be weighed, although many women will not have returned to their pre-pregnancy weight. You'll have an internal examination to make sure that everything is normal, including stitches and the muscle tone in your pelvic floor. A cervical smear may be taken and you'll be asked about your health in general.

Many women have minor discomforts after childbirth. You should discuss anything that is worrying you but on the opposite page there is a list of some common postnatal concerns that you might wish to talk over with your doctor.

When you begin this exercise, it is advisable to have your back supported.

Leg Lifts
1. Sit with your baby on your right thigh, facing towards you. Keep your back straight. Hold your baby under the armpits to support her.

2. Pull in your abdominal muscles, then lift your leg by straightening your thigh and turning your toes towards your nose. Hold this position for a count of four making sure that your weight is evenly distributed and not being thrown to one side. The leg will tone providing the thigh is tightened. Lower the leg. Repeat with your left leg.

- Any queries you have about what happened at the birth.
- How you really feel. Your GP cannot be of any help if you smile brightly and say you're feeling fine when you actually feel ill or depressed.
- Uncomfortable tear or episiotomy, sore nipples or any other pain.
- Stress incontinence. Your GP may suggest more pelvic floor exercises (up to 100 a day). If there's little improvement in another six weeks further treatment, such as small weighted cones that you hold in your vagina, may be offered.
- Any difficulties that you're experiencing with your sex life.
- Contraception. You may need a different size of cap or intra-uterine device, or a different pill if you are breastfeeding.

POSTNATAL DEPRESSION

Around 80 per cent of women experience 'baby blues' or some degree of temporary weepiness a few days after the birth. Some women go through a phase of feeling 'down' a few weeks later, when the novelty and excitement surrounding the birth have worn off, sleep deprivation has built up, and there is less practical help from family and friends.

About one woman in 10 suffers moderate postnatal depression, sometimes several months later. Severe depression requiring hospitalization or a long course of treatment affects fewer than one in 500.

Postnatal depression interferes with your enjoyment of life and should always be taken seriously. It's an illness, not a sign of inadequacy, and it's easier to treat if it's caught early. Don't struggle on, failing to recognize the symptoms or feeling too ashamed or lethargic to seek help.

It can be hard to admit to yourself that you feel depressed, especially if you have nothing to be depressed about. There's tremendous pressure to keep up the appearance of coping when everyone else seems to be doing so. If you don't fit the fantasy and nature has not come to your aid and turned you into a competent, contented mother you may feel many negative emotions. These are not signs of an unfeeling monster but of a mother who needs help.

Treatment might consist of individual or group psychotherapy, sessions with a counsellor to talk over your feelings, or a course of anti-depressants. These are not addictive but they usually have to be taken for some time to be effective. When suggesting treatment your GP will take into account your symptoms, your preferences and whether you are breastfeeding. The Association for Postnatal Illness and Meet A Mum Association (see Appendix) can also offer support.

POSTNATAL DEPRESSION SYMPTOMS

You may feel low for a few days without being clinically depressed, but it's worth seeking help if you're worried or if you experience any of these symptoms for two weeks:

◆ *An increasing loss of confidence so that you can't face meeting people, even friends, or you need to stick to a rigid routine because you cannot cope with the slightest change.*

◆ *Negative thoughts, feelings of worthlessness or hopelessness.*

◆ *A loss of interest in food, your baby and life in general.*

◆ *Butterflies in your tummy all the time, or a general feeling of panic every time your baby wakes up.*

◆ *An agitated feeling so that you have to keep busy all the time.*

◆ *A feeling of exhaustion but you're unable to sleep when you get the chance.*

Friendship is very important. You and your baby will enjoy sharing the company of other mothers and babies.

MEETING OTHER MOTHERS

The companionship and support of other mothers makes all the difference when you have children. Friends will discuss your baby's development over and over again. They'll understand the joys and difficulties of family life. They'll laugh with you, offer suggestions, reassure you that a phase will pass and find your toddler lovable at times when you secretly find him impossible.

In these early stages it is important to meet and make some new friends. Invite some women from your antenatal class round for coffee – someone has to start the ball rolling. Try looking on your clinic notice board for details of a local parent and toddler group (babies are included). Think about joining a class at your local college, sports or leisure centre – there may well even be a crèche for your baby. Spend time watching the toddlers playing at the local park and chat to the other parents. Ask your health visitor to introduce you to some other mothers. Contact Meet A Mum Association or the NCT (see Appendix). They run postnatal groups nationwide.

It's very easy to stay at home and tell yourself that you don't need anything else in your life; to use the possibility that your baby might catch a cold as an excuse for not meeting people. But sooner or later you'll feel lonely, and wish that you and your baby had some friends.

' I thought I'd work freelance from home, but I hadn't realized just how much time a baby takes up. I hated the thought of someone else looking after Ben and found my career was less important to me than I'd thought! Now I live at a child's pace, not by the clock. I make decisions according to events at the time and ignore the five-year plan that used to rule my life. We can't afford holidays, but now our quality of life is good. ' KATE

RETURNING TO WORK

Returning to work has both positive and negative aspects; just accept this without feeling guilt or any regrets! The popular image of an organized woman with her family life under control so that it never interferes with her work is a myth. The best you can hope for is that your arrangements hold up most of the time. You'll juggle work and motherhood and may feel that you are doing neither job well, but your baby will probably be perfectly happy!

Even if your employer has never considered it before it's worth trying to negotiate a work schedule that suits you. Decide what you want, work out how it could benefit your company, and present your plan to the personnel manager. New Ways to Work (see Appendix) give advice about flexible working practices. You have nothing to lose by taking the initiative.

Parents at Work (see Appendix) have publications on balancing work and home commitments, and choosing childcare. Local social services (see telephone book) keep lists of nurseries and registered childminders. Make arrangements for your return to work in plenty of time and plan a phased handover as peace of mind is very important. Many women carry on breast-feeding night and morning, but allow a week to drop each feed before you start work so that your body can adjust. If your baby won't take a bottle, talk to his carer. He may accept one from her, or he may start to use a beaker.

QUESTIONS AND ANSWERS

Q: I worry about my baby all the time. I even wake him up to make sure he's breathing. I fret over every decision in case it turns out to be wrong. Why am I so twitchy?

A: You worry because you care so much and because your baby still feels part of you. Call it love – or just motherhood!

These feelings can be overwhelming, especially the first time round when each stage your baby goes through is new. You'll gradually learn to relax about day-to-day events as they become familiar, but you may go through phases of intense, stomach-churning anxiety as each new stage arrives.

Babies respond individually so it's rarely possible to be sure that you've made the right decision except with hindsight. This applies whether it's your first baby or your fourth. Experienced mums watch what happens and have no hesitation in changing their mind if a decision proves wrong. If you do your best you'll get it right most of the time.

Q: My hair has been coming out in handfuls since my baby was born. When I brush it more falls out and my pillow is covered with it every morning. What can I do?

A: Hair has growing and resting phases. Pregnancy hormones encourage growth, but when they stop circulating some women's hair stays in the resting phase until the normal growth pattern reasserts itself. Hair loss may start around three to four months after the birth but it usually stops by about six months when the hormone levels stabilize.

Make sure that you get plenty of rest and your diet includes leafy green vegetables. Some people recommend eating seaweeds (from health food shops) to aid normal hair growth.

A small number of women have a continuing problem, so if the loss continues after six months see your GP, who might suggest a private prescription for Regaine, a lotion that is applied to the hair to help regrowth.

Q: My nine-week-old baby has colic. The doctor says she's fine and not to worry, but I'm exhausted breastfeeding her as she's so demanding. Would she settle better on the bottle?

A: A change to bottlefeeding rarely solves the problem, although it may seem to work for a few days. Breast milk consists of foremilk (more dilute and sweet), and hindmilk (richer in fat and more sustaining). Try to space breastfeeds at least two or three hours apart, so that your baby has room in her tummy for both. Between feeds comfort her by cuddling or rocking her. Give her a dummy or your little finger to suck (up to the second joint, fleshy side up). Frequent snacks of foremilk may produce gas so she cries and you give her more foremilk, a vicious circle!

Your doctor may be able to prescribe medication that helps, but for most parents the answer is patience. She's not crying because you're doing something wrong; accept this and walk her about. Most babies are more settled when they're three to four months old.

Q: As a single parent, I'm not coping very well with motherhood. I love my daughter but I have no energy and I miss my workmates. How can I start enjoying my life again?

A: Most mothers feel that they are not coping from time to time! Ask your health visitor if she knows a group or another mother whom you could meet. If you do not have any transport other mums may be willing to help out.

Contact Gingerbread and the National Council for One Parent Families (see Appendix) or ask your library for the address of a pen friend group. Borrow a book of action rhymes to enjoy with your daughter, or a pattern book to make something for her.

Even if you don't feel like it at first, making the effort to think beyond chores and to get out and meet people will raise your morale and give you the energy to enjoy life again. Babies are hard work but they are also enormous fun to be with.

APPENDIX

These organizations offer support and information when you are pregnant or have a baby. The Directory of British Organizations (ask at your local library) lists many more groups by subject. Voluntary organizations want their services to be used so don't hesitate to contact them. Many operate nationwide and can put you in touch with your nearest branch, but some are small initiatives run by individuals who give what help they can. Often their services have to be fitted in around family demands, so please offer to phone back at a convenient time and enclose a stamped addressed envelope if requesting information.

UMBRELLA ORGANIZATIONS

Good sources of general information and services, or can put you in touch with the right organization for your needs.

Association for Improvements in the Maternity Services (AIMS), 21 Iver Lane, Iver, Buckinghamshire SL0 9LH (01753 652781). Website: www.aims.org.uk. Support and information about maternity rights and options; list of home birth support groups and independent midwives; local groups.

Maternity Alliance, 45 Beech Street, London EC2P 2LX (Helpline: 020 7588 8582). Over 70 organizations that campaign for parents and babies. Information on health issues, disability and rights at work.

National Childbirth Trust (NCT), Alexandra House, Oldham Terrace, London W3 6NH (020 8992 8637, weekdays 9.30am-4.30pm). Website: www.nct-online.org.uk. Antenatal classes, postnatal support, breastfeeding counselling, information, study days, leaflets and merchandise. Branches nationwide.

Regional Health Information Services: Freephone 0800 665544. Can put you in touch with your local health information service for information on health matters; help to find or change any health professional, make a complaint or contact a self-help group; details of the Maternity Services Patient's Charter.

CONCEPTION

Family Planning Association, 2-12 Pentonville Road, London N1 9FP (020 7837 4044). Website: www.fpa.org.uk. Information on fertility, contraception, sexual health, licensed sperm clinics, techniques of sperm separation and achieving a successful pregnancy; addresses of family planning clinics nationwide.

The Miscarriage Association, c/o Clayton Hospital, Northgate, Wakefield, W Yorks WF1 3JS (0192 420 0799). Website: www.miscarriageassociation.org.uk. Information, support and volunteer contact; local groups.

PREGNANCY

Action on Pre-Eclampsia (APEC), 2nd Floor, 31-33 College Road, Harrow, Middlesex HA1 1EJ. Helpline: 020 8427 4217 (weekdays 10am-1pm). Website: www.apec.org.uk. Information, support and advice about pre-eclampsia.

Alcohol Concern, Waterbridge House, 32-36 Loman Street, London SE1 0EE (020 7928 7377). Website: www.alcoholconcern.org.uk. Advice for women concerned about their drinking during pregnancy.

Antenatal Results and Choices (ARC), 73-75 Charlotte Street, London W1T 4PN. (Helpline: 020 7631 0285, weekdays 9am-6pm). Support for parents making decisions about testing, or who discover that their unborn baby is abnormal.

Birth Defects Foundation, 1 Martindale, Cannock, Staffordshire WS11 2XN (08700 707020). Website: www.birthdefects.co.uk. E-mail: help@birthdefects.co.uk. Information and support where a defect, with or without a specific name, is diagnosed.

British School of Osteopathy, 275 Borough High Street, London SE1 1JE (020 7407 0222). Website: www.bso.ac.uk. E-mail: admin@bso.ac.uk. List of registered osteopaths; expectant mothers clinic for back/postural problems and massage for labour.

National AIDS Helpline: Freephone 0800 567123. A confidential helpline for anyone concerned about HIV or AIDS. Lines available in various languages; Minicom service for people with hearing/speech difficulties.

QUIT, Victory House, 170 Tottenham Court Road, London W1P 0HA. Pregnancy Quitline (0800 002211) offers counselling; free Quitpacks; referral to local stop smoking groups.

Vegan Society, 7 Battle Road, St Leonards on Sea, East Sussex TN37 7AA (0142 442 7393). Website: www.vegansociety.com E-mail: info@vegansociety.com. Advice about vegan diet during pregnancy.

The Vegetarian Society, Parkdale, Dunham Road, Altrincham, Cheshire WA14 4QG (0161 928 0793). Website: www.vegsoc.org.uk. Advice about vegetarian diet during pregnancy.

WellBeing, 27 Sussex Place, Regent's Park, London NW1 4SP (020 7723 9296). Eating in Pregnancy Helpline: 0114 242 4084. E-mail: wellbeing@rcog.org.uk. Nutrition in pregnancy, prematurity, early miscarriage and early diagnosis of fetal abnormalities.

Women's Health, 52 Featherstone Street, London EC1Y 8RT (Helpline: 020 7251 6580, weekdays 9.30am-1.30pm). Information to help you make informed decisions about your health.

BIRTH

Active Birth Centre, 25 Bickerton Road, London N19 5JT (020 7482 5554). Website: www.activebirthcentre.com. Information, literature and teachers (nationwide) to help you have a natural birth.

Caesarean Support Network, 55 Cooil Drive, Douglas, Isle of Man IM2 2HF (01624 661269, weekdays 6-9pm). Support for women before or after a Caesarean birth.

AFTER THE BIRTH

Association for Postnatal Illness (API), 25 Jerdan Place, Fulham, London SW6 1BE (020 7386 0868). Website: www.apni.org.uk. E-mail: info@apni.org.uk. Nationwide telephone support for mothers throughout illness by volunteers who have themselves suffered from postnatal illness.

Association of Breastfeeding Mothers (ABM), PO Box 207, Bridgwater, Somerset TA6 7YT (020 7813 1481). Recorded list of breastfeeding counsellors throughout the UK.

Breastfeeding Network, PO Box 11126, Paisley PA2 8YB (0141 884 2472; Supporter line: 0870 900 8787). Website: www.breastfeeding.co.uk. Breastfeeding counsellors nationwide.

CRY-SIS, London WC1N 3XX (Helpline: 020 7404 5011, 8am-11pm). Parents with a sleepless or excessively crying baby can be put in touch with a telephone volunteer who has experienced a similar problem.

La Leche League (Great Britain) BM 3424, London WC1N 3XX (020 7242 1278, 24 hours). Breastfeeding information and support through local groups and telephone counselling.

Meet a Mum Association (MAMA), 26 Avenue Road, South Norwood, London SE25 4DX (020 8239 1152). Website: www.mama.org.uk. Postnatal support groups and mother to mother support if you have postnatal depression.

New Ways to Work, 22-25 Northumberland Avenue, London WC2N 5AT (Helpline: 020 7930 3355). Website: www.new-ways.co.uk. Information and advice about job sharing and flexible working patterns for individuals and employers.

NSPCC Helpline: (0800 800 500, 24 hrs). Practical support for parents who feel they may harm their child.

Parentline Plus, 520 Highgate Studios, 53-79 Highgate Road, Kentish Town, London NW5 1TL (0808 800 2222). Website: www.parentlineplus.org.uk. Advice on issues affecting step families.

Parents at Work, 45 Beech Street, London EC2Y 8AD (Helpline: 020 7628 3578, Tues, Thurs, Fri 9am-1pm, 2-4pm). Website: www.flametree.co.uk. Email: info@parentsatwork.org.uk. Practical advice on work-related issues, including childcare; booklets, workshops, local support groups.

LONE PARENTS

Gingerbread, 1st Floor, 7 Sovereign Close, Sovereign Court, London E1W 3HW (Helpline: 0800 018 4218). Website: www.gingerbread.org.uk. Support for lone parents via a network of self-help groups; advice on holidays, legal and welfare rights.

National Council for One Parent Families, 255 Kentish Town Road, London NW5 2LX (Helpline: 0800 018 5026). Website: www.oneparentfamilies.org.uk. Information on issues affecting lone parents; advice for single pregnant women; training courses to help lone parents become financially independent.

BEREAVEMENT

Child Death Helpline: (020 7829 8685, Mon, Thurs, 7-10pm, Weds 10am-1pm). For all those affected by the death of a child.

Foundation for the Study of Infant Deaths (FSID), Artillery House, 11-19 Artillery Row, London, SW1P 1RT (020 7222 8001). Helpline (020 7233 2090, 24 hours). Website: www.sids.org.uk/fsid. E-mail: fsid@sids.org.uk. Information, advice, support and individual befriending for parents coping with a sudden infant death.

Stillbirth and Neonatal Death Society (SANDS), 28 Portland Place, London W1N 4DE (020 7436 5881, Mon, Tues, Wed 10am-3pm). Self help groups and befriending after pregnancy loss, stillbirth or neonatal death; booklet: 'Saying Goodbye to Your Baby'.

SPECIAL SITUATIONS

BLISS The National Charity for the New Born, 2nd Floor, Camelford House, 87-89 Albert Embankment, London SE1 7TP (020 7820 9471, Helpline: 0500 618140). Website: www.bliss.org.uk. E-mail: information@bliss.org.uk. Support for parents of babies who are premature or need special or intensive care.

Contact a Family, 170 Tottenham Court Road, London W1P 0HA (020 7383 3555). Website: www.cafamily.org.uk. E-mail: info@cafamily.org.uk. Directory of rare conditions and their support networks. Factsheets, parents' guides and telephone helpline.

Council for Disabled Children, 8 Wakley Street, London EC1V 7QE (020 7843 6000). Website: www.ncb.org.uk. E-mail: jkahn@ncb.org.uk. Central co-ordinators of information on all types of help available for disabled children.

Disabled Parents Network, PO Box 5876, Towcester, NN12 7ZN (0870 241 0450). Website: www.DisabledParentsNetwork.com. Support for disabled parents and prospective parents.

Disability, Pregnancy & Parenthood international (DPPi), 5th Floor, 45 Beech St, London EC2P 2LX (0800 018 4730). Website: http://freespace.virgin.net/disabled.parents. Information service for disabled parents, prospective parents and professionals.

Twins and Multiple Births Association (TAMBA), 309 Chester Road, Little Sutton, Ellesmere Port CH66 1QQ. (Twinline: 0173 286 8000, weekdays 7-11pm; weekends 10am-11pm). Website: www.tamba.org.uk. Local clubs and specialist support for families with twins, triplets or more.

INDEX

ACKNOWLEDGEMENTS

Special Photography: **Daniel Pangbourne**
Stylist: **Sheila Birkenshaw**
Hair and Makeup: **Leslie Sayles**
Illustrations: **Melanie Northover**

PICTURE CREDITS

ANGELA HAMPTON - FAMILY LIFE PICTURES; 60 top, 136 centre, 137 top, 167 bottom, 167 top, 199

BUBBLES; 94, 134 top and bottom, 135 top and bottom, F. Rombout 2, 34, 64, 82, Ian West 158

CLEFT LIP AND PALATE ASSOCIATION; 170

COLLECTIONS; Anthea Sieveking 92, Sandra Lousada 154

SALLY AND RICHARD GREENHILL; 89, Sally Greenhill 88

ROBERT HARDING PICTURE LIBRARY; S. Villeger 186

HEA BUSINESS UNIT PICTURE LIBRARY; 12

IMAGE BANK; Anthony A. Boccaccio 84

SANDRA LOUSADA; 6

LUPE CUNHA PHOTOGRAPHY; 144, 180

NATIONAL MEDICAL SLIDE BANK; 24, 60 centre

PETIT FORMAT; Taeke Henstra 172

PETER PUGH-COOK; 194-197

RASCALS; Joanna Mungo 178

REFLECTIONS PHOTO LIBRARY; Jennie Woodcock 48, 126, 139 bottom, 139 top, 176, 182 bottom left, Martin Dohrn 163

SCIENCE PHOTO LIBRARY; David Scharf 22 centre, Petit Format/Nestle 20 , 36 top left, 66 top left, Professors P. M. Motta & J. Van Blerkom 23 top right

TONY STONE IMAGES; Andre Perlstein 8

ZEFA PICTURES LTD; 108

*The publishers would like to thank the parents and babies
who kindly modelled for this book.*

KU-235-249

Gill Langley

MA PhD

The Vegan Society
St Leonards-on-Sea

Published December 1988 by
The Vegan Society Ltd
7 Battle Road
St Leonards-on-Sea
East Sussex
TN37 7AA

First reprint July 1990
Second reprint May 1991

© Gill Langley

All rights reserved. No part of this
book may be reproduced or transmitted
in any way or by any means without the
prior permission of the publisher

ISBN 0–907337–15–5

Produced by *Up Design*, Kingston-upon-Thames

Printed and bound in Great Britain by
KSC Printers Ltd., Tunbridge Wells, Kent

Text printed on 100%-recycled paper

Vegan Nutrition is dedicated to the memory of the late Roy McIntyre Smith (1913–86) and to those other ethical pioneers without whose vision and steadfastness veganism's potential contribution to the well-being of humans, animals and the environment would not enjoy the recognition it does today.

CONTENTS

FOREWORD

There is considerable public interest in ways of eating a more healthy diet. Many people have been shifting toward a low-fat, high-fibre diet, often achieved by the substitution of vegetable and cereal foods for meat products. The end-point of such a change is a vegan diet — which is free of all animal products, including milk and eggs. There are, however, relatively few people at present who are strictly vegan. One of the reasons for this may be concern that vegan diets do not provide adequate levels of essential nutrients. This belief, often incorrectly perpetuated by health professionals, is generally not based on research results from studies of vegan populations. Occasional case reports of vitamin deficiencies among children avoiding animal products have been misinterpreted to mean that vegan diets are unsafe. Closer examination of these case reports almost always shows that the diets of such children are not those recommended by responsible vegan nutritionists. All diets need to contain nutrients from a wide variety of food sources, and this applies equally to vegan and any other dietary pattern. This book will enable people to make these choices more easily.

Concern over these rare cases of deficiency in infants fed inappropriate plant-based diets has sometimes overshadowed the considerable potential long-term benefits of balanced vegan diets on rates of major chronic diseases. Vegans and vegetarians have been shown to have lower rates of heart disease. They have also been shown to have lower rates of diseases which particularly affect the quality of life, such as gallstones and diverticulitis. These differences may be explained in part by the avoidance of high-fat animal products on the one hand, and by the greater consumption of wholegrain cereals, fruit and vegetable products on the other.

This book brings together in a concise and carefully-researched manner all that is currently known about vegan nutrition. It fills a real gap in the literature and will be a valuable contribution in two ways. Firstly, it will provide health professionals with a clear summary of research in this area, which will enable them to give better-informed counsel. Secondly, it will provide those people who want to become vegans, or who are already practising vegans, with information that will enable them to follow a vegan diet with assurance about the short-term safety and long-term benefits of such a diet.

Dr. Barrie M. Margetts PhD

Medical Research Council Environmental Epidemiology Unit, University of Southampton

i

INTRODUCTION

The results of a 1987 survey indicated that 3% of the British population are now vegetarian — almost half as many again as in 1984[1]. Some of these 1.5 million-plus people go further than omitting meat, poultry and fish from their diets, and eliminate *all* animal produce. These complete vegetarians — vegans — derive their nourishment exclusively from the plant kingdom.

The reasons for becoming vegan are numerous, and include ethical concern for the rights and welfare of animals, and of people in the Third World — much of whose cereal harvest is exported to feed farm animals in Western countries. Anxiety about the degradation of the environment can be another prompt to adopting a vegan diet, as people see the planet's ecological balance being disturbed increasingly by the cereal monoculture necessary to feed farm animals; pollution from nitrogen fertilizers and farm slurry which contaminate our waterways; and clearance of rainforests and other woodlands to create short-term grazing, which can lead to erosion and desertification. Some turn to veganism in the interests of maintaining or restoring good health (*See Section 8 — **Vegan Diets as Therapy***), and yet others for religious, aesthetic or philosophical reasons.

The vegan population is scattered geographically and, despite popular preconceptions, is by no means homogeneous. Many of the early pioneers of veganism in the late 1930s and 1940s are now over 70 years old; there are also senior citizens who are recent 'converts'; there are infants, teenagers and adults who have been vegan from birth; there are animal rightists of every political persuasion (and none); there are orthodox Rastafarians for whom animal products are not 'I-tal' or 'whole' food; there are university professors, business executives, medical doctors, clergymen, professional athletes and others from a wide, and ever-widening, variety of backgrounds and occupations; and while many vegans are well-informed on nutritional matters and eat a varied, wholefood diet, there are some who subsist mainly on convenience or junk foods. Thus it is difficult to talk of 'typical' vegans or of a 'typical' vegan diet.

Recent years have witnessed considerable growth in the acceptance and popularity of veganism, but a clear understanding of the concept and practice still eludes many people, perhaps most notably the media, whose treatment of the subject is often as ill-informed as it is dismissive. Vegetarians and others who may be attracted to veganism in principle can be concerned, understandably in the face of the propaganda from the meat and dairy lobbies, about the ability of a plant-based diet to sustain good health. And vegan parents, like their omnivore and vegetarian peers, also require informed advice on the dietary requirements of their children.

Experience shows, however, that health professionals such as nutritionists, dietitians, health visitors, community health workers and general practitioners are often ill-equipped to advise on various aspects of vegan nutrition. Much information available in standard reference works is out of date, while more recent publications tend to repeat earlier dogma without re-examining original research.

A survey of members of the California Dietetic Association conducted a few years ago revealed that their knowledge of vegetarianism in general was surprisingly low. They recognized that there are economic and health benefits in being vegetarian, but in simulated counselling sessions they often did not support people's dietary choice and tried to persuade children and pregnant and lactating women to eat meat. Nutrition professionals can sometimes be more influenced by text-book theories of nutrition than by the evidence of their own eyes and the documented health and well-being of vegans of all ages.

A report in a 1988 issue of the *Journal of the Royal Society of Medicine*[2] emphasized the lack of co-ordinated teaching about nutrition in medical curricula. The results of a questionnaire revealed that only half the house physicians at medical schools had been taught about nutritional matters such as dietary fibre, salt, sugar, and obesity, and several doctors commented on their lack of nutritional knowledge and expressed a wish to learn more. While we cannot, of course, expect every GP to be an expert on veganism, we can at least hope that they will have ready access to a reliable and up-to-date reference work on the subject. *Vegan Nutrition* aims to meet precisely this need. In addition, it is hoped that it will be of assistance to hospital dietitians with the responsibility of providing balanced and tasty meals for vegans in their care.

Vegan Nutrition is an attempt to make available sound and well-referenced information for all the above groups. I have taken considerable pains to avoid repeating myths, by consulting original research papers, some of them historical and some very recent indeed. All these are fully referenced at the end of the sections. Each section begins with brief nutritional notes as background for lay readers, and then reviews studies of vegans and the results, which shed light on various aspects of vegan nutrition.

Officially recommended daily amounts (RDAs) of nutrients are provided where available, but it is important to realize that nutrition is still an inexact science and that RDAs are only estimates. They have wide in-built safety margins but are calculated for a generalized population, so that they may be over- or under-estimates of the needs of many individuals. That RDAs are educated guesses is shown by some very large variations in values for the same nutrient recommended by different countries. British RDAs tend to be lower, for example, than those of the USA, although in the latter recommended intakes for several nutrients have recently been reduced.

Another point needs to be stated clearly: the fact that daily intake of a nutrient may fall below recommended levels is not on its own indicative of a deficiency. Deficiency refers to a state characterized by adverse symptoms; a lower than recommended consumption, or even a lower than average blood level of a nutrient, does not necessarily mean deficiency if a person remains in good health and has no adverse symptoms. This is especially true while estimates of daily needs remain uncertain; and in many instances the human body is able to adapt to lower levels of nutrient intake by increasing absorption efficiency and reducing excretion.

Sections 1–6 of the book end with a brief summary, and throughout the text major points are highlighted so that readers can scan quickly through and identify areas of particular interest. A number of tables, including some showing the nutrient content of various vegan foods, are also provided.

As suggested by its title, this book is concerned with veganism. It does not review the extensive literature on vegetarianism, except where strictly relevant or where data on veganism are not available. Similarly, as a general rule research and reports on other food philosophies, such as macrobiotics or fruitarianism, are not dealt with here except where they have a direct bearing on vegan nutrition.

Vegan Nutrition shows that a vegan diet can provide all the essential nutrients for health and fitness at any age, without the need to take supplements, as long as a few elementary rules are observed. This proviso is particularly relevant to infants and young children, who are vulnerable to poor nutrition, whether omnivore, vegetarian or vegan. Since its foundation in 1944, and ahead of current nutritional thinking, the Vegan Society has recommended the use of a wide variety of wholefoods, along with fortified products where there is justifiable concern about the availability of a particular nutrient. (See **Guidelines on Vegan Diets** below.)

Any dietary philosophy can encompass regimes which are healthy and nutritious to greater or lesser extents. The informed consensus is that the average British omnivore's diet is largely responsible for a range of degenerative diseases — from obesity to cancer, and from haemorrhoids to heart disease. We all need to look more closely at our own diets and those of our children and old people. For vegans, and those aspiring to veganism, and for those whose task is to advise on dietary matters, it is hoped that *Vegan Nutrition* will prove a useful reference volume.

GILL LANGLEY

Hitchin, Hertfordshire. December 1988.

References

1. *The 1987 Realeat Survey of Meat Eating and Vegetarianism*, conducted by Social Surveys (Gallup Poll) Ltd.
2. JUDD, P.A. (1988) 'Teaching Nutrition to Medical Students', *Journal of the Royal Society of Medicine*, 81, 176–178.

GUIDELINES ON VEGAN DIETS

In the interests of sound, ethically-based nutrition the Vegan Society recommends choosing a wide variety of foods from the following groups:

- Fresh and dried fruits
- Vegetables, including green leafy vegetables
- Whole grains and grain products — e.g. barley, rice, sweetcorn, wheat; wholemeal bread, pasta, rice cakes
- Nuts
- Pulses (peas, beans and lentils)
- Seeds — e.g. sunflower, sesame, pumpkin

Don't overcook vegetables, and where possible conserve the cooking water for stocks and soups. Include salads and some raw vegetables. Some people find fortified soya products useful. A dietary supply of vitamin B_{12} can be ensured by the use of foods naturally containing the vitamin, such as edible seaweeds and tempeh, or of fortified foods — e.g. most yeast extracts; some soya milks, cereals and margarines; textured vegetable protein (TVP). Vitamin D is most easily derived from the action of sunlight on the skin.

Parents of vegan infants should use energy-dense foods — e.g. suitably-prepared grains, cereals and nuts — after weaning, as well as some fresh fruit and vegetables. Low-Calorie fibrous foods, such as leafy vegetables and fresh fruit, can fill small stomachs easily and shouldn't be overused at first. Low-salt yeast extracts and fortified soya milks provide vitamin B_{12}, and daylight is a source of vitamin D. Mashed beans, dried fruit spreads, tofu and tahini are good sources of calcium for small children. See also *Table 5 — Diet guidelines for vegan children*.

SYMBOLS & ABBREVIATIONS

μg	microgram(s)
<	*(in tables)* Less than...
approx.	Approximate(ly)
Calorie(s)	Kilocalorie. This has been used in preference to the newer kilojoules (kJ) or megajoules (MJ) to assist the lay reader. 1MJ = 239 Calories.
COMA	Committee on Medical Aspects of Food Policy (UK)
DHSS	Department of Health and Social Security (UK)
EEC	European Economic Community
equiv.	equivalent(s)
FAO	Food and Agriculture Organization
HDL(s)	High-density lipoprotein(s)
g	gram(s)
kg	kilogram(s)
LDL(s)	Low-density lipoprotein(s)
MAFF	Ministry of Agriculture, Fisheries and Foods (UK)
mg	milligram(s)
ml	millilitre(s)
MMA	Methylmalonic acid
mmole	millimole(s)
n.a.	*(in tables)* Values not available
NACNE	National Advisory Committee on Nutrition Education (UK)
NCHS	National Center for Health Statistics (USA)
ng	nanogram(s)
oz	ounce(s)
pg	picogram(s)
P/S ratio	The ratio of PUFAs *(see below)* to saturated fatty acids
PUFA(s)	Polyunsaturated fatty acid(s)
RDA(s)	Recommended Daily Amount(s) *(of a nutrient)*. Equivalent to the US Recommended Daily Intake or Allowance
tbsp	tablespoonful(s)
tsp	teaspoonful(s)
TVP	Textured vegetable protein
UK	United Kingdom
unspec.	Unspecified
UNU	United Nations University
US(A)	United States of America
VLDL(s)	Very low-density lipoprotein(s)
WHO	World Health Organization

TABLES

Proteins are large molecules made from smaller units called amino acids, and when eaten are digested in the stomach and small intestine into their component amino acids which are then absorbed into the bloodstream. The body synthesizes the proteins it needs for maintaining tissues and for sustaining growth from the amino acids made available by digestion; amino acids are also vital precursors of hormones and other physiologically active substances.

There are twenty amino acids commonly found in both plant and animal proteins. Plants can synthesize all the amino acids they need from simple inorganic substances such as carbon, nitrogen, sulphur and water. Humans, like other animals, cannot, and we have only a limited ability to convert one amino acid into another. So there are eight essential amino acids which must be present in the food we eat, and these are isoleucine, leucine, lysine, methionine, phenylalanine, threonine, tryptophan and valine. Histidine (and possibly taurine) is an essential amino acid during infancy only. If one of these essential amino acids is not available in adequate amounts the ability of the body to use those which *are* present can be limited. If the proportions of amino acids in our food are not ideal, then a higher protein level may be necessary to ensure that our requirements for the essential amino acids are met.

Protein Requirements

Experts are still not entirely sure how much protein we need, and estimates have been revised often in recent years. The national and international organizations which advise on nutrient requirements suggest standards which are calculated to meet or exceed the requirements of practically everyone, explicitly taking into account individual variation, and so these levels have a wide in-built safety margin. In 1985 the World Health Organization (WHO) published revised figures as follows[1]:

The WHO protein figures translate into 56g of protein a day for an 11.5-stone (75kg) man, and 48g for a 10-stone (64kg) woman. The recommendations of the UK Department of Health and Social Security (DHSS) are slightly higher, at about 68g a day for sedentary or moderately active men, and 54g a day for women[2]. Both these **official recommendations suggest that eating 10% of our daily energy as protein will provide an adequate amount.** The NACNE report[3] proposed a protein intake of 11%. National and international recommendations for protein intake are based on animal sources of protein such as meat, cow's milk and eggs. Plant proteins may be less digestible because of intrinsic differences in the nature of the protein and the presence of other factors such

Table 1. Protein requirements estimated by FAO/WHO/UNU

Age group	Protein per kg body weight per day
Infants	
0 – 12 months	1.85 – 1.5g
12 – 24 months	1.5 – 1.2g
Children	
2 – 10 years	1.2 – 1.0g
10 – 18 years	1.0 – 0.85g
Young adults	0.75g
Older adults and the elderly	0.75g

(The recommendations for pregnant or lactating women are slightly higher.)

as fibre, which may reduce protein digestibility by as much as 10%. Nevertheless, dietary studies show the adequacy of plant foods as sole sources of protein (*See* **Combining Proteins** *below*), as does the experience of many thousands of healthy vegans of all ages.

The main protein foods in a vegan diet are the pulses (peas, beans and lentils), nuts, seeds and grains, all of which are relatively energy-dense. As the average protein level in pulses is 27% of Calories; in nuts and seeds 13%; and in grains 12%, it is easy to see that **plant foods can supply the recommended amount of protein as long as energy requirements are met.**

People are not Rats

Tradition has it that plant proteins are of a poorer quality than animal proteins, because the essential amino acids are present in proportions which may not be ideal for human requirements. In the early years of research into protein quality this belief derived from experiments with laboratory rats, when it became clear that amino acid supplementation of a plant source of protein improved its biological value to the point where it would support the growth of weanling rats. The parameters of

Table 2. Portions of some vegan foods that provide 10g of protein

Food group	Food	Weight (g)	Weight (oz)
Nuts (shelled)	Pistachios	50	1.8
	Cashews	58	2.0
	Almonds	59	2.1
	Brazils	83	2.9
	Hazels	131	4.6
Pulses	Soya flour	25	0.9
	Soya beans, raw	29	1.0
	Red lentils, raw	42	1.5
	Haricot beans, raw	47	1.7
	Chickpeas, raw	50	1.8
	Tofu, steamed	135	4.8
	Haricot beans, boiled	151	5.3
	Peas, boiled	200	7.0
Grains	Wholemeal wheat flour	76	2.7
	Whole barley, raw	95	3.4
	Wholemeal wheat bread	114	4.0
	Wholemeal rye flour	122	4.3
	Brown rice, raw	149	5.3
Seeds (husked)	Sesame	38	1.3
	Pumpkin	40	1.4
	Sunflower	44	1.6
Other	Spinach, boiled	200	7.0
	Dried apricots, raw	208	7.3
	Potatoes, baked (excl. skin)	384	13.5

1 oz = 28.4 g. Values taken from Paul and Southgate, 1978[38], Tan et al, 1985[39] and US Department of Agriculture, 1979[40].

WHO estimate for an adult's daily protein requirements: 48–56 grams.

British DHSS recommended daily protein intake: 54–68 grams.

these experiments were set in such a way that differences in the quality of plant and animal proteins were maximized; the second major problem with the experiments is that rats and humans have different nutritional requirements[4].

The weanling rat grows, relatively, at a much faster rate than the human infant and therefore requires a more concentrated source of nutrients, including protein. A comparison with human milk makes the difference quite clear: protein comprises only 7% of the Calorie content of breast milk, while rat milk contains 20% protein. If weanling rats were fed solely human milk, they would not thrive. Using the same logic as was applied in the early experiments, it could be argued from this that breast milk is also inadequate for human infants!

Some early studies further demonstrated the differences in nutritional requirements between rats and humans. In 1955[5] an experiment with three male volunteers showed that the amino acid cystine is able to substitute for 80–89% of the body's requirement for another essential amino acid, methionine, whereas in rats the substitution value is only 17%.

Combining Proteins

Although the terms 'first-class' and 'second-class' proteins are no longer used, in some circles the belief persists that a vegan diet, containing only plant proteins, may be inadequate. This is because cereals, nuts and seeds contain less of the amino acid lysine, while being high in methionine; and pulses are rich in lysine but contain less methionine. This has given rise to concern that the amino acid present in lower amounts in each food will limit the availability to the body of the others, and the suggestion has been made[6], and adopted quite widely — even among vegans — that complementary protein foods, such as beans and grains, should be eaten at each meal in order to enhance amino acid availability. Vegetarians are also sometimes advised to ensure that they complement vegetable proteins with dairy foods. Are these precautions necessary?

Protein combining may reduce the amount of protein required to keep the body in positive protein balance[7], but several human studies have indicated that this is certainly not always the case. For example, over a 60-day period seven human subjects were fed diets in which the protein was derived solely either from beans, corn and refined wheat; beans, rice and refined wheat; or a combination of the plant foods with the addition of cow's milk[8]. All subjects remained in positive nitrogen balance (a measure of the adequacy of dietary protein), and there were no significant differences in nitrogen balance between the subjects eating only plant foods and those whose diet was supplemented with milk.

Another study looked at the nutritive value of a plant-based diet in which wheat provided 76% of the protein[9]. The aim was to determine whether this regime could be improved by adding other sources of plant protein — such as pinto beans, rice and peanut butter. The diets were entirely vegan, contained only 46g of protein, and were fed to 12 young men over a 60-day period, during which they continued with their normal daily activities. **The researchers found that all subjects remained in positive nitrogen balance, and that replacement of 20% of the wheat protein with beans, rice or peanut butter did not result in significant changes in the levels of essential amino acids in the bloodstream.**

Even more startling perhaps were the findings of a 59-day investigation with six male subjects who consumed diets in which virtually the sole source of protein was rice[10]. At two protein levels (36g and 48g per day) the diets comprised rice as the sole source of protein, or regimes where 15% and 30% of the rice protein was replaced with chicken. The partial replacement of rice with chicken protein did not significantly affect the nitrogen balance of the volunteers (in contrast to earlier experiments with rats which showed that a rice diet did not sustain normal growth). **In this *human* study, even on the low-protein diet, rice as the sole source provided between 2 and 4.5 times the WHO-recommended amounts of all essential amino acids, except lysine — of which it supplied 1.5 times the suggested level.** On the higher protein diet, rice alone provided between two and six times the essential amino acid levels suggested by the WHO, and all subjects were in positive nitrogen balance.

When cornmeal was fed as virtually the sole source of protein to ten male volunteers during a 100-day study it was found that at an intake of 6g of nitrogen per day (approx. 36g protein) not all the subjects were in positive nitrogen balance[11]. Yet all the essential amino acids were eaten in amounts which met or exceeded standard requirements, with the exception of tryptophan — of which 91% was provided. **These results suggest that on a corn-protein diet, non-specific nitrogen is the first limiting factor, not lack of essential amino acids.**

The 1988 position paper of the American Dietetic Association[12] emphasized that, because amino acids obtained from food can combine with amino acids made in the body, it is not necessary to combine protein foods at each meal. Adequate amounts of amino acids will be obtained if a varied vegan diet — containing unrefined grains, legumes, seeds, nuts and vegetables — is eaten on a daily basis.

These and other similar experiments show clearly that diets based solely on plant sources of protein can be quite adequate and supply the recommended amounts of all essential amino acids for adults, even when a single plant food, such as rice, is virtually the only source of protein. The American Dietetic Association emphasizes that protein combining at each meal is unnecessary, as long as a range of protein-rich foods is eaten during the day.

Studies of Vegans

Of course, a vegan diet does not comprise a single plant source of protein, but rather a well-balanced mixture of foods, so vegans need not force themselves to consume 450g rice each day! What levels of protein intake have been measured in studies of vegans, and how do these compare with those found in vegetarians and omnivores? There have now been several such surveys, extending back to 1954. In 1967 Ellis and Mumford[13] reviewed several early studies and found that vegans took 10–11% of their daily energy intake in the form of protein, compared with 11–12% in the case of vegetarians. In 1966 Hardinge *et al*[4] calculated that vegan men and women achieved their recommended daily allowances of all essential amino acids and that the pattern of their amino acid intake quite closely resembled that of the protein in human milk, while that of vegetarians and omnivores (with a generous intake of animal proteins) was more similar to the amino acid pattern of cow's milk.

In 1981, Abdulla and co-workers[15] used the duplicate portion sampling technique to measure, among other nutrients, protein intakes in six healthy Swedish middle-aged vegans whose diet was deliberately somewhat restricted. Protein intake was 10% of total energy, compared with 12% for Swedish omnivores of similar age. **Although energy consumption in this vegan community was low, their intake of all essential amino acids was, at the minimum, almost *double* the recommendations of the US National Academy of Sciences, and *more than double* the WHO recommendations. This was despite the fact that these subjects deliberately suppressed their protein intake in the belief that too much protein is deleterious to health.**

The protein intake of 22 British vegans was compared with age- and sex-matched omnivores and mean values found to be slightly lower[16]. Lockie and colleagues[17] found from their study of male and female vegans, vegetarians and omnivores that the mean protein intake of the ten vegans was somewhat lower than that of omnivores and vegetarians, and the same was true of a survey published in 1987[18] comparing 11 vegans

Table 3. Mean daily protein intake of vegans, vegetarians and omnivores as % of total energy

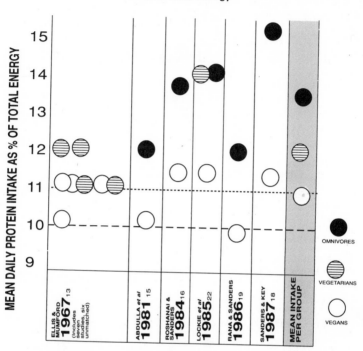

· — — — WHO and DHSS recommendations: Protein intake 10% of energy
··········· NACNE recommendations: Protein intake 11% of energy consumed

with 11 omnivores. A dietary analysis reported in 1986[19] similarly showed that a sample of 18 vegans had protein intakes lower than those of omnivores. Interestingly, this study also suggested that adults are able to synthesize the amino acid taurine from other amino acids in the diet, since the level of taurine in the plasma and breast milk of vegan subjects was adequate — even though taurine is not present in plant foods.

A high-protein diet can adversely affect calcium balance in the body, so that the less excessive intake in a vegan diet facilitates the absorption of calcium — a significant factor in preventing osteoporosis, which may be less prevalent in vegans and vegetarians. This is discussed in some detail in Section 5 — **Minerals**.

Studies show that the protein intake of vegans, expressed as a percentage of energy consumed each day, is close to the levels suggested by WHO and NACNE and although it is similar to that of vegetarians and omnivores, the latter two groups eat more protein than guidelines recommend.

Energy Intake in Vegans

The DHSS recommends[2] an average energy intake for men and women of 2,395 Calories. Ministry of Agriculture figures[20] suggest that the average energy consumption of people in the UK, including alcohol, was higher than this at 2,800 Calories in 1982. However the intake of vegans, vegetarians and omnivores, as measured in the recent studies summarized in *Table 4*, was below this national average (possibly reflecting an above-average interest in health and nutrition among the volunteers). Comparisons of energy intake are difficult because of variations between individuals in age, physical activity and basal metabolic rate, and differences in methods of measuring or estimating energy intake. The individuals studied in these investigations, of whatever dietary persuasion, ate fewer Calories than the population at large.

Table 4. Mean daily energy intake of vegans, vegetarians and omnivores

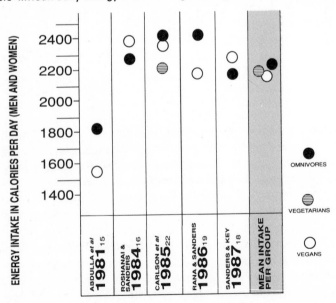

DHSS recommendations: 2,395 Calories.
MAFF figures for UK population: 2,800 Calories.

Most vegans and vegetarians are lighter in weight than omnivores and have a lower proportion of body fat[22] — characteristics which are likely to protect against obesity-related diseases such as diabetes mellitus, some cancers and heart disease.

Protein and Energy Requirements of Infants and Children

Vaghefi et al[4], while writing of protein requirements, concluded that the over-riding need of the body is for energy. Unless energy intake is adequate an individual will be in negative nitrogen balance regardless of the amount of protein in the diet, and evidence for this has been provided by research into the type of diet best able to remedy oedema caused by kwashiorkor in Jamaican children[23]. It was found that of six different diets given to 103 children, six of them with a very low protein intake (2.5% of total energy) lost oedema as fast as children given five times as much protein. The authors suggest that protein deficiency does not cause the oedema of kwashiorkor, but that energy deficiency is the major, although not only, factor involved.

In short-term studies with male infants who had been malnourished but rehabilitated nitrogen balance was similar whether the protein source was cow's milk, cottonseed and rice, soya beans, rice, soya beans and peanuts, soya beans and rice, cottonseed and peanuts, or cottonseed alone[24]. With these mixtures no effort was made to supply the 'limiting' amino acid in one plant protein by an excess in another. Only peanut protein on its own was less well retained. In crossover studies, lasting 2–3 months on each diet, babies fed rice and cottonseed or rice and peanuts as protein sources grew as well as infants fed wheat supplemented with lysine. All gained weight satisfactorily and at equivalent rates, although two infants fed rice alone did not grow as well as those fed cow's milk.

As long as an infant's energy needs are being met it will thrive on a diet where protein is available from a mixture of plant foods.

Surveys of Vegan Infants and Children — Protein and Energy

There have been surprisingly few thorough studies of the health of vegan infants and children. Infancy and childhood are times of rapid growth and development when a good supply of nutrients is particularly important. There is growing concern about the food eaten by children generally in the UK, as it is often high in saturated fat and sugar and low in fibre — features identified as contributing to ill-health in adulthood. On

11

the other hand, many nutritionists are concerned that a vegan diet may prove an inadequate source of protein and energy. What do investigations show?

An American study published in 1980[25] reported on 48 pre-school children from The Farm, a large (800-member) vegan community in Tennessee which was virtually self-sufficient in food. The community's diet was based on beans and peas, a variety of grains and vegetables, soya milk and other soya products, some fruit, margarine, and yeast. Parents completed a three-day diet diary for their children, whose ages were 2–5 years, and each child was measured and weighed.

The authors reported that energy intake for all age groups and both sexes exceeded RDAs, with the exception of the 4-year-old girls whose mean energy intake of 1,621 Calories was slightly below the US recommendation of 1,800 Calories for this group. The equivalent British RDA of 1,500 Calories was, however, exceeded and the authors pointed out that all the 4-year-old girls consumed more than two-thirds of the suggested energy allowances in the USA.

Protein consumption in all groups exceeded US-recommended intakes; in the case of 2-, 3- and 5-year olds by more than double. Intake of protein also exceeded the UK RDA for each age group. **Although there were individual variations, mean intakes by the American vegan children of amino acids — cystine, histidine, isoleucine, leucine, lysine, methionine, phenylalanine, threonine, tryptophan and valine — were all higher than those of children reported by the US National Academy of Sciences.**

Average values for height and weight were below the national average in the 3- to 5-year-olds, although not the 2-year-olds, and all groups met or exceeded reference values for triceps skinfold thickness, except 4- and 5-year-old girls; the latter may be due to the slightly lower average age of the 5-year-olds in the sample compared with the reference 5-year-old population. Most, but not all, age groups exceeded the reference data for arm and arm muscle circumference. In interpreting the anthropometric data it should be borne in mind that hereditary factors were not taken into account in this study.

In 1981 a study of 23 British vegan pre-school children was published[26]. The children, born of vegan mothers, were 1 to 4.5 years old and were located with the help of the Vegan Society, which also part-funded the study. Parents completed a 7-day diet diary for their children — one of the most accurate methods of measuring food intake. Energy consumption of all but two children was less than the UK recommendations, but the mean (85% of the RDAs) fell inside the normal range. Where energy intakes were low, the bulky nature of the diets was the probable cause — a problem easily overcome by reducing the consumption of fruit and vegetables and increasing that of grains, pulses and nuts. (See earlier **Guidelines on Vegan Diets** and **Table 5** below). By way of comparison, a report published in 1986[27] showed that the energy intake of more than 3,000 *omnivore* schoolchildren in Britain averaged 90% of the DHSS RDAs; and two-thirds of omnivore pre-school children had energy intakes below DHSS values according to a 1975 report[28].

The mean protein intake of the vegan children was 109% of DHSS recommendations, and only five children's protein consumption fell below these values. All children had protein intakes greater than those recommended by WHO[1]. Wholegrain cereals and pulses each provided about one-third of the children's protein intake, with nuts contributing 18%.

Anthropometric measurements showed a tendency for the vegan children in this study to be lighter in weight than standard values, but all were within the normal range for weight and height, with the exception of two children whose parents were of short stature. The Dugdale Index (an expression of weight for height) was a mean of 97 in the children, compared with a nominal value of 98–100, and head and mid-arm circumferences were normal. All the children had been breast-fed for the first six months of life, and most well into their second year.

A 1986 UK report[29] showed that, while growing faster at first than the standard reference curves predict, infants of omnivore parents who were exclusively breast-fed for more than four months fell into the 10th centile of the Tanner reference curves[30] for triceps and subscapular skinfold thickness after three months of age. The breast-fed children also fell below the American NCHS reference curves[31]. British vegan women tend to breast-feed their children for much longer than the average omnivore, and the same may well be true in the USA and elsewhere. Reports that vegan infants grow more slowly than omnivore children should be interpreted in the light of this fact. A US study measured the mental age of vegan and vegetarian children and found it well above their chronological ages (See Section 7 — **The General Health of Vegans**).

Infants and children reared on a varied vegan diet obtain adequate protein and energy, are healthy and grow normally, and although they tend to be of lighter build than omnivore children they are within the normal ranges for height and weight.

Protein and Energy Problems in Infancy

Reports in the medical press of vegan infants suffering from protein and energy deficiencies are extremely rare, and case studies must be interpreted with caution, as they are often not typical of vegans as a whole. When such cases are scrutinized it becomes clear that usually the infants have not been weaned onto a varied and balanced vegan diet, as recommended by the Vegan Society, but onto a more restricted fruitarian or macrobiotic regime. In other cases, parents have not adopted a vegan diet for themselves and their children, but rather have eliminated certain foods from their infants' diets on a piecemeal basis and without seeking advice on this course of action. In those very few cases where nutritional deficiencies have occurred in vegan infants of vegan parents the cause has been either over-dilution of foods and/or a lack of energy-dense foods (e.g. suitably-prepared nuts, seeds, grains and pulses).

Four cases were reported in 1979 of malnutrition in infants raised on fruitarian and macrobiotic diets[32]. The first concerned a 13-month-old boy who had been weaned onto a strict *fruitarian* diet, receiving no legumes or grains, but only breast milk and uncooked vegetables and fruit. Investigations confirmed kwashiorkor and **his diet was assessed as being deficient in protein and Calories (as well as iron and vitamin B$_{12}$). After acute hospital treatment he was brought back to health on a *vegan* diet and at the age of two years was well, his weight and height being within normal limits.** The other cases in this study were infants reared on *macrobiotic* diets leading to Calorie deficit and emaciation.

In all of these cases the parents were not providing a varied and balanced vegan diet, but following more restrictive fruitarian or macrobiotic principles. Without care these diets can be deficient in nutrients, especially in the case of infants. The authors of the report failed to distinguish between these regimes and a balanced vegan diet, consequently damning all as "obviously inadequate for growing children", despite the fact that one infant was nursed back to full health on a vegan diet.

Unfortunately, the authors also described all three diets as "cults" and "fads" and, apparently because one mother was suffering from puerperal psychosis, speculated that the followers of "extreme faddist" diets may be mentally ill. Such generalized and inaccurate value judgments are out of place in a medical report; moreover, **when parents follow a particular dietary philosophy — which, when sensibly implemented, is perfectly adequate and has been shown to offer distinct health benefits to children and adults alike — efforts to force the inclusion of ethically-**

offensive foods, such as meat and fish, are misplaced and can cause unnecessary anguish.

Two cases of kwashiorkor in infants in Cleveland, Ohio, were reported in 1975[33]. Although these children's diets, as described, contained no animal products, the parents were not vegans or vegetarians, but had restricted their children's diets because they believed that foods such as cow's milk were causing problems in their particular cases. Both children were receiving a little cereal, fruit juices, baby fruit and in one case rice, and both were suffering from protein and energy deficiency.

Two reports of kwashiorkor and other nutritional deficiencies in infants raised on a vegan diet illustrate the need for energy-dense foods to be included in the diets of very young children. In one case[34] a child in Chicago, Illinois, was being fed a restricted diet of honey water and small amounts of cereal, bananas, fruit juices, soya formula and wheat germ oil; he was not receiving enough Calories and protein. The first reaction of medical staff was to try to introduce dairy or meat protein, but when this was resisted by the parents, the child was managed successfully on a vegan diet. As the authors pointed out, such a diet is "nutritionally feasible" and doctors should develop more open-mindedness about various feeding regimes and dietary beliefs.

The second instance of protein-Calorie malnutrition in vegan infants concerned a community of black Hebrew Americans living in Israel[35]. The diet of the community's children was uniform and regulated by the group's leaders. It comprised fruits, vegetables, oats, yeast and home-made almond or soya milk — the latter forming the single most important dietary item for infants aged 3–12 months.

Twenty five infants, mainly in this age group, showed evidence of protein and Calorie deficiency. All but one of these children had been weaned or partly weaned, and the main problem seems to have been that the plant milks made by the community were over-diluted and the remaining foods were insufficiently energy-dense. Forty seven infants under the age of three years from the community were well, although those aged 4–18 months were small for their age. Catch-up growth meant that children older than 18 months were within the normal range for height and weight. Although, as superficially described, the diet given to infants in this community may appear balanced, the inclusion of more concentrated preparations of pulses, nuts and seeds — such as in spread or puréed form — would have ensured adequate energy and protein intakes.

There have been only two recent reports of protein and Calorie malnutrition in infants reared by vegan mothers on a vegan diet, and these were due to over-dilution of weaning foods or insufficient en-

Table 5. Diet guidelines for vegan children

Food group	Approx. serving size	Daily servings per age group		
		6 mo–<1 yr	1–<4 yrs	4–<6 yrs
Bread	1 slice	1	3	4
Grains[a]	1–5 tbsp	0.5 (finely ground, cooked)	1	2
Fats	1 tsp	0	3	4
Fruit				
citrus	0.25–0.5 cup	0	2 (juice or chopped)	2
other[b]	2–6 tbsp	3 (puréed)	2 (chopped)	3
Protein foods[c]	1–6 tbsp	2 (cooked and sieved)	3 (chopped)	3
Vegetables	0.25–0.3 cup			
green leafy/ yellow[d]		0.25 (cooked and puréed)	0.5 (chopped)	1
other[e]		0.5 (cooked and puréed)	1 (chopped)	1
Soya milk (fortified)[f]	1 cup	3	3	3
Miscellaneous				
molasses	1 tbsp	0	1	1
wheat germ	1 tbsp	0	optional	optional
yeast extract (fortified with B_{12})	1 tsp	0	1	1

[a] e.g. dry bulghur wheat, wheat flakes, rice, millet, macaroni, wheat grains, oats.

[b] e.g. apples, peaches, avocados, bananas, pears, berries, apricots and grapes. Dried fruit spreads include those made with dried peaches, apricots, raisins and figs.

[c] e.g. nuts (almonds, cashews, walnuts, pistachios), nut 'butters', legumes (soya beans, peanuts, black-eyed beans, pinto beans, peas, split peas, lentils), miso (fermented soya paste), seeds (pumpkin, sesame and sunflower), seed 'butters' and tofu. *Nuts, seeds and legumes should be ground or cooked and sieved for infants and small children.*

[d] e.g. carrots, broccoli, spinach, kale, spring greens.

[e] e.g. potatoes, tomatoes, lettuce, cabbage, corn, celery, onions, cucumbers, cauliflower and bean sprouts (mung, soya and alfalfa).

[f] e.g. *Plamil* (a range of liquid soya milks) and *Soyagen* (a dried soya milk powder).

This table is based on one in Truesdell and Acosta *(1985), ref. 37.*

ergy-dense foods. Other published cases of protein and energy deficiency in infants referred to restrictive macrobiotic or fruitarian regimes or to dietary limitations imposed by non-vegan parents for 'health' reasons.

Summary

A varied wholefood vegan diet contains adequate levels of energy and protein to sustain good health in all age groups, as evidenced by studies of vegans across the world. National and international recommendations for protein intake can be easily met on a vegan diet. The main protein-rich foods — pulses, nuts, grains and seeds — are energy-dense, and their use ensures that appropriate levels of nitrogen and essential amino acids are available. Potatoes and other vegetables also provide useful amounts of protein. From a wider health perspective it is significant that, as the COMA Report on Diet and Heart Disease[36] pointed out, animal protein is often associated with saturated fat, while plant protein is usually associated with fibre. The NACNE Report[3] also stated that the "healthful" diet will contain larger amounts of cereal and vegetable protein, and less protein from animal foods.

Although protein complementing *may* increase the availability of amino acids, experimental studies with human volunteers have shown that adequate protein is present in an all-plant diet even when only one protein food, such as rice, is eaten. There is no need to worry about combining proteins in each meal. A varied vegan menu, with foods from two or more plant protein groups each day, will ensure adequate protein is obtained.

Care should be taken that infants, when weaned, have an adequate intake of dietary energy and this can be ensured by the use of suitably prepared pulses, grains, nuts and seeds. These foods should be used as staples, with smaller amounts of bulky, less energy-dense fruits and vegetables, so that the latter do not fill the small stomachs of infants and preclude the consumption of adequate energy and protein. These guidelines are easy to follow, once understood, and allow children to be reared in good health on a vegan diet, as evidenced by the studies cited.

References

1. FOOD AND AGRICULTURE ORGANIZATION/WORLD HEALTH ORGANIZATION/ UNITED NATIONS UNIVERSITY (1985). 'Energy and protein requirements', WHO *Technical Report Series 724*. Geneva, WHO.

2. DEPARTMENT OF HEALTH AND SOCIAL SECURITY (1979). *Recommended*

Daily Amounts of Food Energy and Nutrients for Groups of People in the United Kingdom. London, HMSO.

3. NATIONAL ADVISORY COMMITTEE ON NUTRITION EDUCATION (1983). *Proposals for Nutritional Guidelines for Health Education in Britain.* London, Health Education Council.

4. VAGHEFI, S.B., MAKDANI, D.D. and MICKELSEN, O. (1974). 'Lysine supplementation of wheat proteins, a review', *Am. J. Clin. Nutr.*, 27, 1231–1246.

5. ROSE, W.C. and WIXOM, R. L. (1955). 'The amino acid requirements of man. XIII The sparing effect of cystine on methionine requirement', *J. Biol. Chem.*, 216, 763–773.

6. LAPPÉ, F.M. (1976). *Diet for a Small Planet.* New York, Ballantine Books.

7. KOFRÁNYI, E., JEKAT, F. and MÜLLER-WECKER, H. (1970). 'The minimum protein requirements of humans, tested with mixtures of whole egg plus potatoes and maize plus beans', *Z. Physiol. Chem.*, 351, 1485–1493.

8. CLARK, H.E., MALZER, J.L., ONDERKA, H.M., HOWE, J.M. and MOON, W. (1973). 'Nitrogen balances of adult human subjects fed combinations of wheat, beans, corn, milk, and rice', *Am. J. Clin. Nutr.*, 26, 702–706.

9. EDWARDS, C.H., BOOKER, L.K., RUMPH, C.H., WRIGHT, W.G. and GANAPATHY, S.N. (1971). 'Utilization of wheat by adult man: nitrogen metabolism, plasma amino acids and lipids', *Am. J. Clin. Nutr.*, 24, 181–193.

10. LEE, C., HOWE, J.M., CARLSON, K. and CLARK, H.E. (1971). 'Nitrogen retention of young men fed rice with or without supplementary chicken', *Am. J. Clin. Nutr.*, 24, 318–323.

11. KIES, C., WILLIAMS, E. and FOX, H.M. (1965). 'Determination of first limiting nitrogenous factor in corn protein for nitrogen retention in human adults', *J. Nutr.*, 86, 350–356.

12. HAVALA, S. and DWYER, J. (1988). 'Position of the American Dietetic Association: vegetarian diets — technical support paper', *J. Am. Diet. Assn.*, 88, 352–355.

13. ELLIS, F.R. and MUMFORD, P. (1967). 'The nutritional status of vegans and vegetarians', *Proc. Nutr. Soc.*, 26, 205–212.

14. HARDINGE, M.G., CROOKS, H. and STARE, F.J. (1966). 'Nutritional studies of vegetarians. V. Proteins and essential amino acids', *J. Am. Diet. Ass.*, 48, 25–28.

15. ABDULLA, M., ANDERSSON, I., ASP, N-G., BERTHELSEN, K., BIRKHED, D., DENCKER, I., JOHANSSON, C-G., JÄGERSTAD, M., KOLAR, K., NAIR, B.M.,

NILSSON-EHLE, P., NORDÉN, Å., RASSNER, S., ÅKESSON, B. and ÖCKERMAN, P-A. (1981). 'Nutrient intake and health status of vegans. Chemical analyses of diets using the duplicate portion sampling technique', Am. J. Clin. Nutr., 34, 2464–2477.

16. ROSHANAI, F. and SANDERS, T.A.B. (1984). 'Assessment of fatty acid intakes in vegans and omnivores', Hum. Nutr.: Appl. Nutr., 38A, 345–354.

17. LOCKIE, A.H., CARLSON, E., KIPPS, M., and THOMSON, J. (1985). 'Comparison of four types of diet using clinical, laboratory and psychological studies, J. Roy. Coll. Gen. Pract., 35, 333–336.

18. SANDERS, T.A.B. and KEY, T.J.A. (1987). 'Blood pressure, plasma renin activity and aldosterone concentrations in vegans and omnivore controls', Hum. Nutr.: Appl. Nutr., 41A, 204–211.

19. RANA, S.K. and SANDERS, T.A.B. (1986). 'Taurine concentrations in the diet, plasma, urine and breast milk of vegans compared with omnivores', Br. J. Nutr., 56, 17–27.

20. MINISTRY OF AGRICULTURE, FISHERIES AND FOODS. NATIONAL FOOD SURVEY COMMITTEE. 'Household food consumption and expenditure', Annual Reports of the National Food Survey Committee. London, HMSO.

21. SANDERS, T.A.B. (1983). 'Vegetarianism: Dietetic and medical aspects', J. Plant Foods, 5, 3–14.

22. CARLSON, E., KIPPS, M., LOCKIE, A. and THOMSON, J. (1985). 'A comparative evaluation of vegan, vegetarian and omnivore diets', J. Plant Foods, 6, 89–100.

23. GOLDEN, M. (1982). 'Protein deficiency, energy deficiency, and the oedema of malnutrition', Lancet i, 1261–1265.

24. KNAPP, J., BARNESS, L.A., HILL, L.L., KAYE, R., BLATTNER, R.J. and SLOAN, J.M. (1973). 'Growth and nitrogen balance in infants fed cereal proteins', Am. J. Clin. Nutr., 26, 586–590.

25. FULTON, J.R., HUTTON, C.W. and STITT, K.R. (1980). 'Preschool vegetarian children', J. Am. Diet. Assn., 76, 360–365.

26. SANDERS, T.A.B. and PURVES, R. (1981). 'An anthropometric and dietary assessment of the nutritional status of vegan pre-school children', J. Hum. Nutr., 35, 349–357.

27. WENLOCK, R.W., DISSELSUFF, M.M. and SKINNER, R.K. (1986). 'The diets of British schoolchildren. Preliminary report of a nutritional analysis of a nationwide dietary survey of British schoolchildren'. Middlesex, DHSS Leaflets Unit.

28. COMMITTEE ON MEDICAL ASPECTS OF FOOD POLICY (1975). 'A nutrition survey of preschool children, 1967–68', *DHSS Report on Health and Social Subjects 10*. London, HMSO.

29. WHITEHEAD, R.G., PAUL, A.A. and AHMED, E.A. (1986). 'Weaning practices in the United Kingdom and variations in anthropometric development', *Acta. Paed. Scand. Suppl.*, 323, 14–23.

30. TANNER, J.M., WHITEHOUSE, R.M. and TAKAISHI, M. (1966). 'Standards from birth to maturity for height, weight, height velocity and weight velocity: British children 1965', *Arch. Dis. Child.*, 41, 613–635.

31. HAMILL, P.V.V. (1977). 'NCHS growth curves for children, birth to 18 years', National Center for Health Statistics, US Dept. of Health, Education & Welfare publ. no. (PHS) 78–1650.

32. ROBERTS, I.F., WEST, R.J., OGILVIE, D. and DILLON, M.J. (1979). 'Malnutrition in infants receiving cult diets: a form of child abuse', *Br. Med. J.*, 1, 296–298.

33. LOZOFF, B. and FANAROFF, A.A. (1975). 'Kwashiorkor in Cleveland', *Am. J. Dis. Child.*, 129, 710–711.

34. BERKELHAMER, J.E., THORP, F.K. and COBBS, S. (1975). 'Kwashiorkor in Chicago', *Am. J. Dis. Child.*, 129, 1240.

35. SHINWELL, E.D. and GORODISCHER, R. (1982). 'Totally vegetarian diets and infant nutrition', *Pediatr.*, 70, 582–586.

36. COMMITTEE ON MEDICAL ASPECTS OF FOOD POLICY (1984). 'Diet and cardiovascular disease', *DHSS Report on Health and Social Subjects 28*. London, HMSO.

37. TRUESDELL, D.D. and ACOSTA, P.B. (1985). 'Feeding the vegan infant and child', *J. Am. Diet. Ass.*, 85, 837–840.

38. PAUL, A.A. and SOUTHGATE, D.A.T. (1978). *McCance & Widdowson's The Composition of Foods (4th edition)*. London, HMSO.

39. TAN, S.P., WENLOCK, R.W. and BUSS, D.H. (1985). *Immigrant Foods. 2nd Supplement to McCance & Widdowson's The Composition of Foods*. London, HMSO.

40. US DEPARTMENT OF AGRICULTURE (1979). *Agriculture Handbook No.8–11 and 8–12*. Washington, US Department of Agriculture.

Simple Carbohydrates — the Sugars

Sugar, Dental Decay and Obesity

Sugar and Other Diseases

Sugar and Vegan Diets

Complex Carbohydrates — the Starches

Complex Carbohydrates — Official
Recommendations and Vegan Diets

Complex Carbohydrates — Fibre

Recommended Fibre Intakes and Vegan Diets

Fibre and Disease

Summary

References

Carbohydrates are the main source of energy in most human diets worldwide, in Britain providing 45% of total energy intake. Plants synthesize carbohydrates from carbon dioxide and water in the presence of sunlight. The structural components of plant cells — known in dietary terms as fibre or roughage — derive from carbohydrates, which also provide energy for growth, as well as being stored as sugars and starches. In plants stored carbohydrates are found in the fruits and seeds, where they provide nutrients for growth of the seedling; and in roots and tubers, where they are an energy reserve for the plant throughout winter and for accelerated growth in the spring. Generally, fruits contain simple carbohydrates in the form of sugars, while seeds, roots and tubers contain complex carbohydrates in the form of starches. Sugars and starches have similar energy levels of 4 Calories per gram.

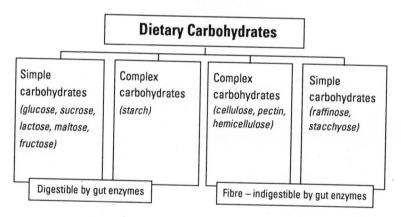

Simple Carbohydrates — the Sugars

Sugars are small, simple carbohydrate molecules and the common sugars in food, in descending order of sweetness, are: fructose (natural fruit sugar), sucrose (refined table sugar), glucose (grape sugar or dextrose), maltose (malt sugar) and lactose (milk sugar). Glucose is the basic unit from which many other sugars are built up, and to which most sugars and starches are broken down during digestion. Each type of sugar is absorbed from the intestine at a different rate, and causes a different rise in blood sugar levels. Sucrose, derived from sugar beet or sugar cane, is highly refined and contains no other nutrients; even raw sugar from cane or beet contains only low levels of iron and the B vitamins. Black molasses is, however, a good source of iron.

Sugar, Dental Decay and Obesity

Excess sugar in the diet has been linked with many conditions, the most obvious being tooth decay (caries) and obesity. The frequency with which sugars are eaten and their physical form are thought to be the two main factors affecting the amount of caries caused, although quantity of sugar also plays a part. Quantities of sucrose eaten, and its frequent combination with fat in foods, are major factors influencing obesity.

Although sucrose intake in Britain has dropped during the last ten years, the calculated intake per person being 20% lower than in 1974, it is still a massive 30kg per year, which translates into about 82g (about 3oz) of sucrose — that is, *added* sugar — a day. These figures exclude the consumption of natural sugars, as found in unprocessed foods. The NACNE Report[1] recommended that sucrose intake, in particular from confectionery and soft drinks, should be reduced to 20kg per person each year over the next fifteen years, and the COMA Report[2] recommended that sugar intake should not increase.

In its natural form, sugar is combined with plant fibre and is diluted with water, as well as coming 'packaged' with important nutrients such as vitamins and minerals. But extracted, refined, concentrated and added to foods such as cakes, biscuits, sweets and soft drinks, sugar has become the main cause of tooth decay — a problem which has been exported to some third world countries such as Nigeria, where caries increased by 65% each year between 1982 and 1987.

A study[3] at a children's home in Australia showed that children who ate a vegetarian diet high in complex carbohydrates — based mainly on wholemeal bread, beans, oats, rice, potatoes and fruit, with some treacle and molasses — developed fewer and smaller tooth cavities than other children of their age. Those who ate more sugar on leaving the home developed more decay. Some scientists believe that all types of sugar are equally damaging to the teeth and that starchy (complex carbohydrate) foods, which are common in a vegan diet, also contribute. However, investigations have shown that at a constant sugar intake, eating more starch does *not* cause more decay. Moreover, a meal high in complex carbohydrates induces a feeling of fullness (satiety) sooner, which may help prevent excessive consumption of foods containing added sugar, thus reducing the likelihood of caries and overeating.

Sugar and Other Diseases

The connections between sugar and diseases such as diabetes, heart disease, some cancers, Crohn's disease (inflammation of the gut) and gallstones are less clear-cut. Some population studies in a number of countries have suggested a link between a high sugar intake and the onset of **diabetes**, while others have failed to show this connection. It seems likely that it is a *combination* of high sugar and high fat intakes which predispose towards diabetes. Epidemiological surveys in 41 countries have shown a strong association between sugar and fat intakes; sugar makes fat more palatable and is frequently combined with it in cakes, biscuits, confectionery and many processed foods. The two ingredients together provide a concentrated source of Calories, which contributes to obesity, and many scientists now believe that obesity is a key factor in the aetiology of adult-onset diabetes.

In diabetes the body is unable to control the level of sugar in the blood, and after a meal blood sugar rises and may stay elevated, while in a normal person it is regulated by the pancreatic hormones insulin and glucagon. An experiment with healthy human volunteers showed that a meal of chocolate and tea, or crisps and a cola drink, caused much greater swings in blood sugar than the same number of Calories taken as raisins, peanuts and tea, or as bananas, peanuts and tea. The two types of meal had similar proportions of fat and sugar in them, so it seems likely that fibre can modify rapid changes in blood sugar which otherwise stress the pancreas. This knowledge is now reflected in the advice given to diabetics to eat a wholefood diet.

Some human studies have indicated a link between sugar and **heart disease**, but the evidence is not conclusive. The most likely connection may be through contributing to overweight and obesity, which are risk factors for heart disease. The COMA Report[2] on diet and heart disease acknowledged this and recommended that intake of simple sugars should not be allowed to increase but that fibre-rich complex carbohydrates should be eaten in greater amounts; and that obesity should be avoided by appropriate food intake and regular exercise.

A recent investigation showed that populations with a high sugar consumption have higher rates of **breast cancer**, but again it has not been possible to separate the influences of sugar and fat in the diet. These two nutrients are also associated with the development of **large bowel cancer**, this disease being more common in people whose diet is high in fat, sugar and Calories, but low in fibre, and who become overweight[4]. While it is quite possible to consume large amounts of sugar and fat on a vegan diet, it seems that most vegans do not.

Sugar and Vegan Diets

A plant-based diet, containing ample amounts of fruit and vegetables, is likely to be well supplied with natural sugars, and such surveys as have been made have shown this to be the case. A Swedish study[5] of six middle-aged vegans analyzed sugar intake and found that sucrose was eaten in slightly smaller amounts than in an omnivorous diet. This was not unexpected since this particular group of vegans used no added sugar, and indeed a greater difference might have been predicted. The men consumed twice as much sucrose as the women in the sample.

Glucose and fructose figured more prominently than in the omnivorous diet. Although the total intake of sugars of all sorts by these vegans was higher than that of a comparable omnivorous group, because they were taken in natural form, in association with fibre and water, overeating and stress on the pancreas would be less likely to occur.

A British study of ten vegans[6] also analyzed sugar intake separately from total carbohydrate consumption, revealing again that the intake of all sugars by the vegans was higher, at 20.6% total energy, than either vegetarians (15.2%) or omnivores (17.7%). The relatively high all-sugars consumption by the vegans was due in part to natural sugars in fruit and vegetables, although another report of the same study[7] showed that the vegans in this group also ate more added sugar than the vegetarians and omnivores. As a proportion of total carbohydrate intake sugar intake was relatively less in the vegans than in the other dietary groups analyzed.

Since these two surveys report on only 16 individuals in total, information is clearly too scanty to allow conclusions to be drawn about sugar intake by vegans in general. **It seems likely, however, that there is wide variation in sugar consumption by vegans, as there is among omnivores, but that natural sugars in plant foods may well figure more prominently in the former group.**

Complex Carbohydrates — the Starches

Starches are complex carbohydrates, consisting of long chains of glucose molecules joined together. When eaten, these are broken down by enzymes in the mouth and small intestine mainly to glucose, which is then absorbed into the bloodstream for distribution to all tissues in the body. Some carbohydrates are stored in the liver and muscles in the form of glycogen which, when required, is converted back to glucose for use as a fuel. This process is under the dual control of the hormones insulin and glucagon, and allows endurance athletes to continue competing long after blood glucose has been exhausted as a source of fuel for the muscles. 'Glycogen loading' with complex, unrefined carbohydrate foods — such as wholemeal bread, potatoes and pasta — for two or three days immediately before an event is now commonly practised by competitive long-distance runners and cyclists — a far cry from the 'wisdom' of only a few years ago that plenty of red meat was required for stamina!

The sugars released from complex carbohydrates by digestion are generally absorbed into the bloodstream more slowly than when simple sugars are eaten, especially if unprocessed plant foods, containing fibre, are the source. The presence of fibre also modulates extreme changes in blood glucose (*See above and* **Complex Carbohydrates — Fibre** *below*). However, different kinds of complex carbohydrates produce different blood glucose responses — apples, lentils and fructose (fruit sugar), for example, give rise to only a quarter to a third of the elevation of blood glucose caused by glucose, parsnips and carrots[8].

Complex Carbohydrates — Official Recommendations and Vegan Diets

In 1983 the report of the National Advisory Committee on Nutrition Education (NACNE)[1], looking at the health of the British nation in general, recommended that **carbohydrate intake should increase from the present average of 45% to a minimum of 50% total energy consumed.** It stated that "a key feature of nutrition education should deal with counteracting the results of decades of teaching aimed at reducing carbohydrate intakes", and that fat and sugar intakes should be reduced by partially substituting brown and wholemeal bread, fruit, potatoes and other vegetables. The COMA report on diet and heart disease[2] suggested compensating for a reduced fat intake with more "fibre-rich carbohydrates (e.g. bread, cereals, fruit, vegetables)".

Investigations between 1954 and 1967 found total carbohydrate intake in vegans varying between 54% and 82% of energy consumed[9]. A later, 1985 comparison of total carbohydrate intake among vegans, vegetarians and omnivores in Britain[7] showed that only the vegans, at 55% of energy, met the NACNE recommendations. The same was true in another survey of a group of vegan subjects whose intake was 52% compared with 41% in omnivores[10]. Two other studies[11,12] have recorded higher carbohydrate intakes in vegans compared with age- and sex-matched omnivores.

The carbohydrate intake recommended by the National Advisory Committee on Nutrition Education is higher than that presently consumed by omnivores in the UK and, according to surveys, is achieved only by vegans as a dietary group.

Complex Carbohydrates — Fibre

Dietary fibre is found *only* in plant foods and consists of lignin and fibrous or viscous polysaccharides, such as cellulose, hemicellulose, pectins and other substances which give plant cells their stable structure. They are not digested enzymically in the human body, but are fermented to a variable extent by bacteria in the colon and are therefore unavailable as nutrients; for this reason, nutritionists believed for many years that fibre was not a valuable constituent of the diet. Fibre occurs naturally in grains, pulses, nuts, seeds, fruit and vegetables which have not been refined or processed, but refining, processing and cooking may remove or break down the fibrous content of these foods.

Recommended Fibre Intakes and Vegan Diets

During the last century average fibre consumption in Britain has fallen by about two-thirds to its present level of 20g a day, compared with the 50-120g eaten by rural Africans, who rarely suffer from bowel and other complaints associated with low-fibre intakes. The COMA Report[2] on dietary changes for reducing cardiovascular disease suggested that the daily intake of fibre should be *in excess* of 30g a day, and the NACNE Report[1], concerned with health in general, made similar proposals, further suggesting that **extra fibre should be eaten in foods such as whole grains, fruit and vegetables, rather than added as bran**.

Recent surveys[6, 10-13] of amounts of fibre eaten by vegans have shown that their average intake is 45g a day, compared with 22g for omnivores and 38g for vegetarians in the same studies.

Vegans and vegetarians, but not omnivores in general, equal or exceed the fibre intake recommended by nutrition advisory committees.

Fibre and Disease

The most obvious role of fibre in the diet is to provide bulk for intestinal muscles to work on, thus helping food pass though the gut more quickly and without straining. This effect is emphasized by fibre's ability to hold water, increasing its bulk further. Adequate fibre in the diet induces satiety and hence reduces the likelihood of **obesity**. **Irritable bowel syndrome** and **constipation** account for between one-third and two-thirds of new consultations at gastroenterology clinics in Britain, yet adequate dietary fibre prevents constipation, and consequently the likelihood of **varicose veins** and **haemorrhoids** is decreased. **A 1986 study[13] con-**

Table 6. Portions of some vegan foods that provide 5g of fibre

Food group	Food	Weight (g)	(oz)
Nuts (shelled)	Brazils	56	2.0
	Almonds	59	2.1
	Hazels	82	2.9
Pulses	Haricot beans, raw	20	0.7
	Chickpeas, raw	33	1.2
	Soya flour	42	1.5
	Red lentils, raw	43	1.5
	Haricot beans, boiled	68	2.4
	Peas (fresh), boiled	96	3.4
	Butter beans, boiled	98	3.5
	Broad beans, boiled	119	4.2
Grains	Wholemeal wheat flour	52	1.8
	Wholemeal bread	59	2.1
	Oatmeal, raw	71	2.5
	Sweetcorn, canned	88	3.1
	Brown rice, raw	119	4.2
Dried fruits	Dried apricots, raw	21	0.7
	Dried figs, raw	27	0.9
	Dried currants, raw	77	2.7
Other	Spinach, boiled	79	2.8
	Mushrooms, raw	200	7.0
	Potatoes, baked (excl. skin)	200	7.1

1oz = 28.4g. Values taken from Paul and Southgate, 1978[25] and Tan *et al*, 1985[26]. Fibre intake recommended by COMA Report (1984): more than 30g fibre a day.

firmed that mean transit time (passage of food through the digestive system) in vegans is shorter than in omnivores, and that the former passed softer faeces, more frequently.

Diverticular disease is characterized by pouching and inflammation of the wall of the bowel, and several studies have suggested that a high-fibre diet can help prevent it. In 1979 a group of researchers in Oxford showed that **across the age range diverticular disease was consistently more common in omnivores than in vegetarians**[14]. Moreover there was a major correlation between fibre intakes and occurrence of diverticular disease in the two groups, cereal fibre seeming to be the most important protective factor. Diets providing 30g of fibre or more each day are beneficial in treating diverticular disease.

Many factors are involved in the aetiology of **bowel cancer**, including the amount and type of fat in the diet, as well as fibre intake. Populations whose diets are high in fibre have a low prevalence of bowel cancer[15], and here fibre may contribute both by diluting the presence of mutagens (substances which cause mutations, and may therefore pose a cancer risk) in the faeces, and by hastening their transit through the gut. **A comparison of the levels of mutagens in the faeces of 12 omnivores, 6 vegetarians and 11 vegans**[16] **showed significantly lower levels in the vegans and vegetarians.** A 1987 laboratory study of 12 male volunteers[17] who were housed in a metabolic ward while following 20-day experimental diets, showed that while on a vegan diet the level of bile acids in their faeces fell lower than when they were on an omnivore or a vegetarian diet. A high concentration of bile acids is associated with risk of colorectal cancer, as is the concentration of cholesterol in the faeces, which was also lowest while volunteers were on a vegan diet. **The authors note that a higher mortality from colorectal cancer has been reported for omnivores than for vegetarians and vegans.**

There is also reason to believe that adequate dietary fibre can help prevent the recurrence, and so possibly the development, of **duodenal ulcers**. In one study[18] 73 patients with recently-healed duodenal ulcers were randomly allocated to a low- or high-fibre diet for six months, the fibre being provided mainly by wholemeal bread, unleavened bread, whole grains and vegetables. 80% of the low-fibre group suffered a recurrence of their ulcers, while only 45% of the high-fibre group did so.

Several factors are associated with the development of **gallstones**, but only obesity, gender and age have been confirmed as risk factors. A study designed to examine the role of these risk factors and to compare the prevalence of gallstones in vegetarian and omnivorous women was reported in 1985[19]. Whereas a quarter of the omnivores had gallstones, only one in eight of the vegetarians did. Taking into account differences in age and body weight between the two groups, it was found that **omnivores were twice as likely to have gallstones as vegetarians.** The main dietary factors implicated are fat, sugar, cholesterol, energy and fibre, and the vegetarians ate less saturated fat and more fibre than the omnivores.

Numerous studies have shown that a high-fibre diet, or added fibre, reduces the surge in blood glucose which follows a meal and can allow type 2 (maturity-onset) **diabetics** to stop taking insulin, and can improve some aspects of blood glucose control in type 1 (juvenile-onset) diabetics[20-22]. Such a diet can also reduce pancreatic stress in non-diabetics.

In studies of human populations, high intakes of dietary fibre or complex carbohydrates are the strongest or only dietary factors related to a lower incidence of **coronary heart disease**[2]. When given in high doses, viscous types of fibre such as pectin and guar cause major reductions in blood cholesterol, a known risk factor for heart disease, and a recent study[23] has confirmed that vegans have lower levels of low-density lipoprotein and total cholesterol in their bloodstream than vegetarians and omnivores. **The authors predicted that lifelong vegans might show a 57% reduction in coronary heart disease compared to meat-eaters.** While some investigations have shown that fibre contributes to the lower blood pressure generally observed in vegans and vegetarians, it is not the only factor in a non-meat diet — as shown by a recently-published randomized controlled trial[24], in which omnivores put on a low- (20g per day) or high- (58g) fibre diet for six weeks at a time did not show a drop in blood pressure, in contradiction to other similar studies.

Concern has been expressed that, especially in infants, a very high dietary fibre intake may interfere with the availability of various nutrients. Studies with adult human volunteers have shown increasing faecal loss of nitrogen, carbohydrate, fat and energy as fibre intake rises to high levels, and it has been speculated that for this and other reasons, a vegan diet may not be suitable for infants and small children[25]. In fact it is easy to ensure that infants eat enough suitably-prepared high-energy foods such as beans, grains and nuts. The adequacy of a vegan diet for these age groups, especially with respect to protein and energy, is discussed more fully in Section 1 — **Protein and Energy**. The significance of fibre intake to mineral status is discussed in Section 5 — **Minerals**.

Summary

Internationally, advisory bodies on nutrition have recommended an increase in the consumption of complex carbohydrates from legumes, whole grains, fruits and vegetables. Vegans, as a dietary group, are most likely to achieve the levels of intake recommended. It is also recognized that intake of dietary fibre by the general population should increase by at least one-third. Animal foods — such as meat, milk or eggs — are devoid of fibre and, in contrast to that of the average omnivore, vegans' and vegetarians' consumption of fibre meets or exceeds recommended intakes. Vegans and vegetarians also suffer less often from the 'diseases of civilization' associated with low-fibre diets. A high consumption of sugar (and fat) is linked with several diseases, but too few studies have been conducted to allow us to determine with any certainty the average intake of sugar by vegans.

References

1. NATIONAL ADVISORY COMMITTEE ON NUTRITION EDUCATION (1983). *Proposals for Nutritional Guidelines for Health Education in Britain*. London, Health Education Council.

2. COMMITTEE ON MEDICAL ASPECTS OF FOOD POLICY (1984). 'Diet and cardiovascular disease', *DHSS Report on Health and Social Subjects 28*. London, HMSO.

3. HARRIS, R. (1963). 'Biology of the children of Hopewood House, Bowral, Australia, 4. Observations on dental caries experience extending over 5 years (1957–61)', *J. Dent. Res.*, 42, 1387–1399.

4. BRISTOL, J.B., EMMETT, P.M., HEATON, K.W. and WILLIAMSON, R.C.N. (1985). 'Sugar, fat and the risk of colorectal cancer', *Br. Med. J.*, 291, 1467–1470.

5. ABDULLA, M., ANDERSSON, I., ASP, N-G., BERTHELSEN, K., BIRKHED, D., DENCKER, I., JOHANSSON, C-G., JÄGERSTAD, M., KOLAR, K., NAIR, B.M., NILSSON-EHLE, P., NORDÉN, Å., RASSNER, S., ÅKESSON, B. and ÖCKERMAN, P-A. (1981). 'Nutrient intake and health status of vegans. Chemical analyses of diets using the duplicate portion sampling technique', *Am. J. Clin. Nutr.*, 34, 2464–2477.

6. CARLSON, E., KIPPS, M., LOCKIE, A. and THOMSON, J. (1985). 'A comparative evaluation of vegan, vegetarian and omnivore diets', *J. Plant Foods*, 6, 89–100.

7. LOCKIE, A.H., CARLSON, E., KIPPS, M. and THOMSON, J. (1985). 'Comparison of four types of diet using clinical, laboratory and psychological

studies', *J. Roy. Coll. Gen. Pract.*, 35, 333–336.

8. JENKINS, D.J.A., TAYLOR, R.H. and WOLEVER, T.M.S. (1982). 'The diabetic diet, dietary carbohydrate and differences in digestibility', *Diabetologica*, 23, 477–484.

9. ELLIS, F.R. and MUMFORD, P. (1967). 'The nutritional status of vegans and vegetarians', *Proc. Nutr. Soc.*, 26, 205–212.

10. ROSHANAI, F. and SANDERS, T.A.B. (1984). 'Assessment of fatty acid intakes in vegans and omnivores', *Hum. Nutr.: Appl. Nutr.*, 38A, 345–354.

11. RANA, S.K. and SANDERS, T.A.B. (1986). 'Taurine concentrations in the diet, plasma, urine and breast milk of vegans compared with omnivores', *Br. J. Nutr.*, 56, 17–27.

12. SANDERS, T.A.B. and KEY, T.J.A. (1987). 'Blood pressure, plasma renin activity and aldosterone concentrations in vegans and omnivore controls', *Hum. Nutr.: Appl. Nutr.*, 41A, 204–211.

13. DAVIES, G.J., CROWDER, M., REID, B. and DICKERSON, J.W.T. (1986). 'Bowel function measurements of individuals with different eating patterns', *Gut*, 27, 164–169.

14. GEAR, J.S.S., FURSDON, P., NOLAN, D.J., WARE, A., MANN, J.I., BRODRIBB, A.J.M. and VESSEY, M.P. (1979). 'Symptomless diverticular disease and intake of dietary fibre', *Lancet* i, 511–514.

15. DOLL, R. (1979). 'Nutrition and Cancer: A review', *Nutr. & Cancer*, 1(3), 35–45.

16. KUHNLEIN, U., BERGSTROM, D. and KUHNLEIN, H. (1981). 'Mutagens in feces from vegetarians and non-vegetarians', *Mutation Res.*, 85, 1–12.

17. VAN FAASSEN, A., BOL, J., VAN DOKKUM, W., PIKAAR, N.A., OCKHUIZEN, T. and HERMUS, R.J.J. (1987). 'Bile acids, neutral steroids, and bacteria in feces as affected by a mixed, a lacto-vegetarian, and a vegan diet', *Am. J. Clin. Nutr.*, 46, 962–967.

18. RYDNING, A., AADLAND, E., BERSTAD, A. and ØDEGAARD, B. (1982). 'Prophylactic effect of dietary fibre in duodenal ulcer disease', *Lancet* ii, 736–739.

19. PIXLEY, F., WILSON, D., MCPHERSON, K. and MANN, J.I. (1985). 'Effect of vegetarianism on development of gallstones in women', *Br. Med. J.*, 291, 11–12.

20. ANON. (1981). 'High-fibre diets and diabetes', *Lancet* i, 423–424.

21. SIMPSON, H.C.R., LOUSLEY, S., GEEKIE, M., SIMPSON, R.W., CARTER,

R.D., HOCKADAY, T.D.R. and MANN, J.I. (1981). 'A high-carbohydrate leguminous fibre diet improves all aspects of diabetic control', *Lancet* i, 1–5.

22. ANON. (1983). 'High carbohydrate, high fibre diets for diabetes mellitus', *Lancet* i, 741–742.

23. THOROGOOD, M., CARTER, R., BENFIELD, L., McPHERSON, K. and MANN, J.I. (1987). 'Plasma lipids and lipoproteins in groups with different dietary practices within Britain', *Br. Med. J.*, 295, 351–353.

24. MARGETTS, B.M., BEILIN, L.J., VANDONGEN, R. and ARMSTRONG, B.K. (1987). 'A randomized controlled trial of the effect of dietary fibre on blood pressure', *Clin. Sci.*, 72, 343–350.

25. ACOSTA, P.H. (1988). 'Availability of essential amino acids and nitrogen in vegan diets', *Am. J. Clin. Nutr.* In press.

26. PAUL, A.A. and SOUTHGATE, D.A.T. (1978). *McCance & Widdowson's The Composition of Foods (4th edition)*. London, HMSO.

27. TAN, S.P., WENLOCK, R.W. and BUSS, D.H. (1985). *Immigrant Foods. 2nd Supplement to McCance & Widdowson's The Composition of Foods*. London, HMSO.

Recommended Fat Intake

Fat and Vegan Diets

Fats and Disease

Summary

References

The main constituents of all fats are the fatty acids, which may be saturated, monounsaturated or polyunsaturated, depending on the number of double or triple bonds between the carbon atoms in the molecule. The more of these bonds in a fatty acid, the less it is saturated with hydrogen. Fats containing a high proportion of saturated fatty acids are solid at room temperature, and these are mainly animal fats such as lard, suet and butter — although coconut and palm fat are also highly saturated. Most plant fats are high either in polyunsaturated fatty acids — such as safflower seed, sunflower seed, corn and soya oils — or in monounsaturated fatty acids, such as olive oil.

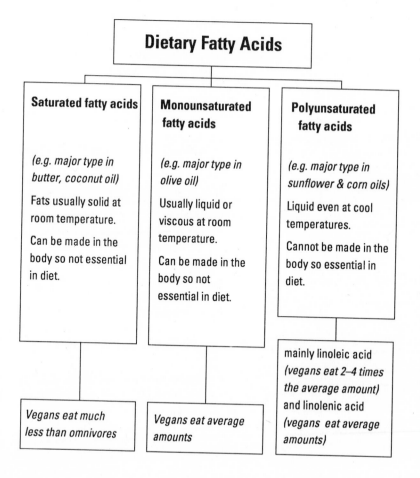

Dietary Fatty Acids

Saturated fatty acids

(e.g. major type in butter, coconut oil)

Fats usually solid at room temperature.

Can be made in the body so not essential in diet.

Vegans eat much less than omnivores

Monounsaturated fatty acids

(e.g. major type in olive oil)

Usually liquid or viscous at room temperature.

Can be made in the body so not essential in diet.

Vegans eat average amounts

Polyunsaturated fatty acids

(e.g. major type in sunflower & corn oils)

Liquid even at cool temperatures.

Cannot be made in the body so essential in diet.

mainly linoleic acid *(vegans eat 2–4 times the average amount)* and linolenic acid *(vegans eat average amounts)*

Saturated and monounsaturated fatty acids can be made in the human body, and so are not essential components of the diet; over-consumption of saturated fats is linked to a number of diseases. Trans fatty acids are isomers of the natural (cis) form of fatty acids and are formed mainly by the hydrogenation of fats in processes such as the manufacture of margarine; trans fats are solid at room temperature. There is some evidence that they may increase cholesterol levels in the blood and may be associated epidemiologically with cancer, although the link is not clear. Polyunsaturated fatty acids (PUFAs) cannot be made in the body, and so are essential in the diet. The two main dietary polyunsaturated fatty acids are linoleic and linolenic, and both can be converted in the body to longer-chain fatty acids, which are vital components of the cell membranes — especially in the brain.

In the body, PUFAs are precursors of the prostaglandins which regulate a great many body processes, and also affect platelet function. Another requirement for fat in the diet is to enable the absorption of fat-soluble vitamins. Fat is a source of energy, and in adipose tissue it acts as insulation and provides support and protection for organs such as the heart and kidneys. Cholesterol is a constituent of nerves and some hormones and is used for the synthesis of bile, but is not necessary in the diet as the body can make enough for its own requirements.

Fat is a major source of dietary energy and contains 9 Calories per gram compared to the 4 Calories of protein and carbohydrate. In the small intestine fats are emulsified by bile and then digested by lipase enzymes (from the pancreas) into their constituent fatty acids and glycerol (triglycerides). Mainly via the lymph system and then the bloodstream, triglycerides are carried to peripheral tissues (especially adipose tissue and skeletal muscle), where they are hydrolyzed to release free fatty acids for oxidation (as fuel) or incorporation into tissue glyceride.

In the circulation are a number of lipoproteins which carry cholesterol: high-density lipoproteins (HDLs), very low-density lipoproteins (VLDLs) and low-density lipoproteins (LDLs). Lipoproteins generally have the structure of a sphere with triglyceride or cholesteryl ester in the core, with a coat of cholesterol or phospholipid outside. VLDL transports triglycerides in the bloodstream, and LDL and HDL carry cholesterol as well. Triglycerides (fatty acids plus glycerol) and cholesterol are found in animal foods but probably not in plant foods, although other sterols are. Levels of cholesterol in the bloodstream are determined more by the amount of saturated fat in the diet than dietary intake of cholesterol itself, although the latter has some effect on plasma cholesterol levels.

Recommended Fat Intake

The need for dietary fat varies with age. The infant requires a relatively high fat intake for rapid growth, and human breast milk contains about 55% of its energy as fat. Numerous nutritional committees have made recommendations for fat intake (*See below*), but these usually apply to adults and children over the age of five.

Eating too much or the wrong kind of fat is linked to a number of serious diseases, most notably cardiovascular disease. In 1982, the average consumption of all fats in the UK was 90–105g a day. This represents 38% of energy intake when alcohol is included in calculations, and 40–41% when alcohol is excluded. The ratio of PUFAs to saturated fatty acids (known as the P/S ratio) in the diet has altered in the last 25 years, with consumption of saturated fats decreasing and that of PUFAs increasing, so that the P/S ratio in 1982 was 0.27 — compared to 0.17 in 1959. Nevertheless, about half the fat eaten by the general population is saturated fat, derived mainly from dairy products and meat.

It is recognized by British and other nutrition advisory bodies that consumption by Westernized countries of total fat and of saturated fatty acids should be decreased, in particular because of the link with high blood levels of cholesterol. **The COMA Report**[1] **on diet and heart disease recommended a lowering by one-sixth of total fat consumption to 35% energy intake, with saturated fats accounting for only 15%** (one-quarter down on present levels). This would mean a total fat consumption of 77–87g a day, and relatively higher intakes of PUFAs, altering the P/S ratio to 0.45.

The NACNE Report[2] **suggested a long-term reduction in fat consumption to a level of 30% of energy intake, with saturated fatty acids contributing only about 10% of total energy consumption.** It recognized that achieving this will require the partial substitution of saturated fats in foods and in cooking with polyunsaturated fats and oils. Similar recommendations have been made by American committees on nutrition and health, and the World Health Organization has proposed that 30% of food energy should be derived from fat[4].

The major sources of saturated fatty acids in the British diet are butter, margarines and cheese (about one-third), meat and meat products (about one-quarter), milk and cream (about one-fifth), and cooking fats and oils (about one-tenth). Milk and cheese are now more widely available in low-fat forms, and the COMA Report pointed out that nearly half of the recommended decreases in fat and saturated fatty acids could be achieved by avoiding cream and switching to fat-reduced milk and cheese. Vegetable margarines with high levels of polyunsaturated and monounsaturated fats are also available.

Scientific opinion is divided regarding the effect of dietary cholesterol on health. Neither of these two expert committees made specific recommendations about reducing intake, except for people at risk of coronary heart disease, in whose case it was proposed that cholesterol consumption should be limited to less than 100g per 1000 Calories of food energy a day. A report by the Royal College of Physicians[3] in 1976 advised that egg consumption should be reduced — one standard egg contains 280mg cholesterol — and the WHO Expert Committee on heart disease in 1982 recommended limiting dietary cholesterol to less than 300mg a day[4]. In the UK average consumption by adults is 350–450mg a day, and this is likely to fall if suggested decreases in saturated fat intake are implemented, since cholesterol is associated with foods also containing these — such as meat, milk and animal fats.

Fat and Vegan Diets

In a vegan diet containing grains, pulses and nuts, the 'hidden' fat intake will comprise a high proportion of polyunsaturated rather than saturated fatty acids. In addition, as animal fats (including butter) are not used, vegan alternatives — such as vegetable oils for cooking and vegetable margarines or spreads made from nuts, or seeds for use with bread — mean that the P/S ratio of a vegan diet is high. At the same time, total fat intake is lower than for the general population, although this is not of necessity a feature of a plant-based diet.

Recent dietary calculations and analyses[5–10] measured the mean total fat consumption of Swedish, British and American vegans as 34% of energy intake, the comparable figure for vegetarian subjects being 38%[7] and for omnivore subjects 39%[6–10]. All these levels of fat intake are considerably lower than those measured in the general British population, so the control non-vegetarian subjects studied were not representative of the population as a whole.

Of these groups, only in the case of vegans is the total fat intake likely to be within the limit proposed by the COMA Report, and even so it may be higher than the goal of 30% of energy consumption set by the NACNE Report.

The fatty acid composition of the vegan diet does, as expected, differ markedly from that of an omnivorous diet. Using the duplicate portion technique, the composition of the diets of six Swedish middle-aged vegans was analyzed in detail[5]. The daily intake of linoleic acid was 30g, which represented 50–60% of the total fatty acid consumption, and the P/S ratio was very high at 3.7, compared to 0.18 in Swedish omnivores. Total sterol intake was 381mg, of which only 28mg appeared to be cholesterol. Cholesterol may be found in small quantities in vegetable oils, although analysis may be unable to distinguish between unidentified plant sterols and cholesterol. An American investigation[10] of 23 vegans calculated a P/S ratio of 1.9 and a cholesterol intake of less than 10mg.

A British study[7] of 10 vegans also showed a low apparent cholesterol intake of 29mg, compared to 296mg in vegetarians and 357mg in omnivores, and another[9] measured a P/S ratio for fatty acids of 1.1 in vegans and 0.4 in omnivore subjects. A very detailed analysis of fat consumption by 22 British vegans was published in 1984, and confirms these figures[6]. There was little difference in total fat intake between the vegan subjects and age- and sex-matched omnivores, but the vegans ate only 18g of saturated fatty acids a day, compared to 31g for the omnivores. Intake of monounsaturated fatty acids was similar in both groups (33g a day), as was consumption of linolenic acid, but the vegans ate 26g linoleic acid a day compared with only 10g eaten by the omnivores.

In a vegan diet polyunsaturated fatty acids (PUFAs), which have a beneficial effect on blood cholesterol levels, are more abundant than saturated fatty acids. Cholesterol is virtually non-existent in a vegan diet.

Fats and Disease

A high fat consumption is associated with a number of serious and common diseases, as shown mainly by population studies. The relationship between fats and **coronary heart disease** has been reviewed by the Royal College of Physicians[3], the World Health Organization[4] and the Committee on Medical Aspects of Food Policy[1]. Death rates for coronary heart disease in the UK remain among the highest in the world, accounting for nearly one in three deaths in men. Diet is a major factor in the development of heart disease whose basis is atherosclerosis, the narrowing of arteries by cholesterol-containing deposits (plaque), which starts in childhood. Thrombosis superimposed on atherosclerotic plaque is the usual trigger for a heart attack, and both these processes are affected by fat in the diet.

More than 20 studies in 14 different countries have shown that, along with high blood pressure (hypertension), cigarette smoking and social class, plasma levels of cholesterol and LDL-cholesterol are key factors associated with heart disease[11]. The main dietary influence on plasma total and LDL-cholesterol is the amount and type of fat eaten, saturated and trans fats tending to raise levels, and PUFAs lowering them (to a lesser degree). Monounsaturated fats have little effect either way.

There is also evidence from comparisons of different countries that as dietary intake of linoleic acid increases (and hence blood and adipose tissue levels of linoleic acid), deaths from coronary heart disease decrease. Recent evidence also suggests that PUFAs known as long-chain omega-3 fatty acids, such as eicosapentaenoic (EPA) and docosahexaenoic acids (the main source in the omnivore diet being fish oils), have beneficial effects on triglycerides and inhibit thrombosis, as does linoleic acid (from plant foods) to a lesser extent. There is apparently no EPA or docosahexaenoic acid in a plant-based diet[6], and vegans have lower levels of docosahexaenoic acid in their plasma and red blood cell lipids[12]. However, another omega-3 fatty acid, called linolenic acid, is present in plants, especially in walnuts, wheat germ oil, rapeseed oil, soya beans and tofu, seaweeds and purslane. Linolenic acid can be converted in the body to eicosapentaenoic acid.

As noted above, vegans have a lower than average intake of fat and a high proportion of that consumption is in the form of PUFAs, so it would be expected that levels of total and LDL-cholesterol in their bloodstream would be low, while HDL-cholesterol would be about the same as in omnivores. Investigations have shown this to be the case, and also that vegans (and vegetarians) are at less risk of heart disease than meat-eaters.

A British report[12] in 1978 analysed the composition of substances in the blood and other tissues, and found that total plasma cholesterol in vegan subjects was 4.1mmole/l, compared with 6.1mmole/l for omnivore subjects. The proportion of linoleic acid in all tissues studied was higher in the vegans, implying a higher intake in the diet, while the proportion of linolenic acid in tissues of vegans was lower than in omnivores. A comparison of plasma cholesterol levels in vegans and other dietary groups revealed[7] an average level of 3.9mmole/l in vegans, compared with 4.3mmole/l in vegetarians and 5.3mmole/l in omnivores. The difference was significant between the vegans/vegetarians and the omnivores. A very detailed analysis of the fatty acid composition of substances in the bloodstream of vegetarians, vegans and omnivores published in 1987 showed that linoleic and linolenic acids were predominant in the first two groups compared with the third.

A 1987 British study[14] compared the levels of total, LDL- and HDL-cholesterol in the plasma of vegans, vegetarians, fish-eaters and meat-eaters. After adjustments made for differences in age and sex of the sub-jects, it was found that total and LDL-cholesterol were highest in meat-eaters and lowest in vegans compared with other groups. HDL-choles-terol was higher in fish-eaters than in other groups. Vegans had the lowest LDL/HDL ratio. The authors speculated that dietary causes of these characteristics in vegans, apart from lower intakes of saturated fats, might be plant protein, fibre, total carbohydrate or high P/S ratio for fatty acids. They suggested that, because of their low plasma cholesterol, life vegans and vegetarians in Britain might show a 57% and 24% reduction in coronary heart disease compared with meat-eaters. This study will be following the morbidity and mortality of individuals in these dietary groups over a period of ten years.

An earlier American investigation[10] also found that plasma levels of VLDL- and LDL-cholesterol in vegan men and women were lower than in omnivore men and women of similar age and that they had a lower LDL/HDL ratio, which suggests a low risk of atherosclerosis. A later study in the USA[15] looked at the effects of fat from dairy products on the plasma lipoprotein levels of strict macrobiotics (virtually vegans) and vegetarians. Dairy products were the main source of dietary saturated fat and cholesterol for the vegetarians, whose LDL-cholesterol was 24% higher than in the macrobiotics. HDL-cholesterol did not seem to be related to any dietary component, but analysis within and among the vegetarians suggested that fatty dairy products raise plasma LDL-choles-terol on a percentage basis about three times more than they raise the beneficial HDL-cholesterol.

Fatty meals and high intakes of saturated fats are risk factors for coronary heart disease, causing damaging changes in levels of choles-terols in the blood. Vegans eat the least total and saturated fat of all dietary groups, and have the lowest levels of LDL-cholesterol as well as the lowest LDL/HDL-cholesterol ratio in their bloodstream. Their risk of coronary heart disease is thus likely to be much smaller than that of meat-eaters or even vegetarians.

It has been estimated by experts that a third of all **cancer** deaths could be attributed to dietary causes (although the development of any cancer is affected by a number of interacting factors). While all the connections between diet and cancer are not yet understood, there is evidence from population studies that cancers of the breast, womb, pancreas, prostate and colon are linked to a high fat intake and that breast[16] and colon cancer[17] are correlated with the consumption of meat and animal fat and protein. In a 1987 laboratory study[18] twelve male **volunteers followed** three experimental diets for 20-day periods while housed in a metabolic ward. While on a vegan diet the concentrations of bile acids and cholesterol in their faeces — factors both known to be positively associated with colorectal cancer — were lowest; while on a meat diet, with its high levels of fat and low amounts of fibre, these potential risk factors were highest.

Obesity is linked with certain cancers, including cancers of the womb, breast and gallbladder[16], and about one-third of adult men and women in Britain are overweight. Fatty foods, because of their high Calorie content, contribute particularly to problems of overweight. Vegans are generally lighter in weight with less body fat than the general population[9,19].

A high-fat diet is also linked to the development of maturity-onset diabetes (*See Sugar and Other Diseases in Section 2 — Carbohydrates.*)

Summary

Numerous expert committees on nutrition have recommended the adoption of a diet lower in total fat. Only vegan diets have been found to comply consistently with guidelines that fat should not comprise more than 30–35% of our total energy intake. Saturated fats contribute to high levels of cholesterol in the blood — a risk factor for atherosclerosis and heart disease, while polyunsaturated fats (PUFAs) have the opposite effect. A vegan diet, containing no meat and dairy fats, is low in saturated fatty acids and high in beneficial PUFAs. The blood of vegans has lower total and LDL-cholesterol levels than any other dietary group and as a result they are likely to be less susceptible to coronary heart disease. Infants require a higher fat intake than adults, and the polyunsaturated vegetable oils are a useful source of energy on weaning. Nutritional guidelines proposing a fat consumption not exceeding 35% of total energy consumption apply to adults and children older than five years.

References

1. COMMITTEE ON MEDICAL ASPECTS OF FOOD POLICY (1984). 'Diet and cardiovascular disease', *DHSS Report on Health and Social Subjects 28.* London, HMSO.

2. NATIONAL ADVISORY COMMITTEE ON NUTRITION EDUCATION (1983). *Proposals for Nutritional Guidelines for Health Education in Britain.* London, Health Education Council.

3. ROYAL COLLEGE OF PHYSICIANS AND BRITISH CARDIAC SOCIETY (1976).

'Prevention of coronary heart disease', *J. Roy. Coll. Phys.*, 10, 213–275.

4. WHO EXPERT COMMITTEE (1982). 'Prevention of coronary heart disease', *WHO Technical Report Series 678*. Geneva, WHO.

5. ABDULLA, M., ANDERSSON, I., ASP, N-G., BERTHELSEN, K., BIRKHED, D., DENCKER, I., JOHANSSON, C-G., JÄGERSTAD, M., KOLAR, K., NAIR, B.M., NILSSON-EHLE, P., NORDÉN, Å., RASSNER, S., ÅKESSON, B. and ÖCKERMAN, P-A. (1981). 'Nutrient intake and health status of vegans. Chemical analyses of diets using the duplicate portion sampling technique', *Am. J. Clin. Nutr.*, 34, 2464–2477.

6. ROSHANAI, F. and SANDERS, T.A.B. (1984). 'Assessment of fatty acid intakes in vegans and omnivores', *Hum. Nutr.: Appl. Nutr.*, 38A, 345–354.

7. CARLSON, E., KIPPS, M., LOCKIE, A. and THOMSON, J. (1985). 'A comparative evaluation of vegan, vegetarian and omnivore diets', *J. Plant Foods*, 6, 89–100.

8. RANA, S.K. and SANDERS, T.A.B. (1986). 'Taurine concentrations in the diet, plasma, urine and breast milk of vegans compared with omnivores', *Br. J. Nutr.*, 56, 17–27.

9. SANDERS, T.A.B. and KEY, T.J.A. (1987). 'Blood pressure, plasma renin activity and aldosterone concentrations in vegans and omnivore controls', *Hum. Nutr.: Appl. Nutr.*, 41A, 204–211.

10. BURSLEM, J., SCHONFELD, G., HOWALD, M.A., WEIDMAN, S.W. and MILLER, J.P. (1978). 'Plasma apoprotein and lipoprotein lipid levels in vegetarians', *Metabolism*, 27, 711–719.

11. BRITISH MEDICAL ASSOCIATION BOARD OF SCIENCE AND EDUCATION (1986). *Diet, Nutrition and Health*. London, BMA.

12. SANDERS, T.A.B., ELLIS, F.R. and DICKERSON, J.W.T. (1978). 'Studies of vegans: the fatty acid composition of plasma choline phosphoglycerides, erythrocytes, adipose tissue, and breast milk, and some indicators of susceptibility to ischemic heart disease in vegans and omnivore controls', *Am. J. Clin. Nutr.*, 31, 805–813.

13. MELCHERT, H.-U., LIMSATHAYOURAT, N., MIHAJLOVIC, H. and EICHBERG, J. (1987). 'Fatty acid patterns in triglycerides, diglycerides, free fatty acids, cholesteryl esters and phosphatidyl choline in serum from vegetarians and non-vegetarians', *Atherosclerosis*, 65, 159–166.

14. THOROGOOD, M., CARTER, R., BENFIELD, L., MCPHERSON, K. and MANN, J.I. (1987). 'Plasma lipids and lipoproteins in groups with different dietary practices within Britain', *Br. Med. J.*, 295, 351–353.

15. SACKS, F.M., ORNISH, D., ROSNER, B., McLANAHAN, S., CASTELLI, W.P. and KASS, E.H. (1985). 'Plasma lipoprotein levels in vegetarians: the effect of ingestion of fats from dairy products', *JAMA*, 254, 1337–1341.

16. DE WAARD, F. (1986). 'Dietary fat and mammary cancer', *Nutr. and Cancer*, 8(1), 5–8.

17. DOLL, R. (1979). 'Nutrition and Cancer: A review', *Nutr. and Cancer*, 1(3), 35–45.

18. VAN FAASSEN, A., BOL, J., VAN DOKKUM, W., PIKAAR, N.A., OCKHUIZEN, T. and HERMUS, R.J.J. (1987). 'Bile acids, neutral steroids, and bacteria in feces as affected by a mixed, a lacto-vegetarian, and a vegan diet', *Am. J. Clin. Nutr.*, 46, 962–967.

19. SANDERS, T.A.B. (1983). 'Vegetarianism: Dietetic and Medical Aspects', *J. Plant Foods*, 5, 3–14.

Vitamin A (Retinol)

The B Group Vitamins
Vitamin B_1 (Thiamin)
Vitamin B_2 (Riboflavin)
Niacin (Nicotinic Acid and Nicotinamide)
Vitamin B_6 (Pyridoxine)
Folic acid (Folate)
Pantothenic Acid and Biotin
Vitamin B_{12} (Cobalamins)

Daily Requirement of B_{12} — a Controversy
Vegan Sources of B_{12}
Vitamin B_{12} — the Vegan Experience
Occasional B_{12} Deficiency
Vitamin C (Ascorbic acid)
Vitamin D (Ergocalciferol D_2, Cholecalciferol D_3)
Vitamin D Deficiency
Vitamin E (Tocopherols)
Vitamin K
Summary
References

Vitamins are essential nutrients required in relatively small amounts in the diet. They cannot be made in the body, with the exception of vitamin D which is synthesized in the skin in response to daylight, and vitamins B_{12} and K which are synthesized by gut bacteria. There are two main types: the fat-soluble vitamins A, D, E and K — which are found mainly in fatty foods; and those soluble in water — the B group vitamins and vitamin C.

Vitamin A (Retinol and ß-carotene)

Vitamin A or retinol is a fat-soluble vitamin found only in animal foods such as liver, kidney, dairy produce and eggs (foods which also contain high levels of saturated fat). However carotenes, of which the most important is ß-carotene, are common in deep yellow and orange-coloured plant foods, and in the body are converted to retinol. ß-carotene in plant foods is the only type of vitamin A available to vegans, but is also one of the prime sources for omnivores. **Plant foods rich in ß-carotene include carrots, dark green leafy vegetables — such as spinach, parsley and watercress; sweet potatoes, dried apricots and mangoes.** By law in Britain vitamin A (as retinol or ß-carotene) is added to **margarine**, which is a major source for the general population and is also acceptable to vegans when the margarine contains no animal products.

Vitamin A is essential for vision (especially in dim light), and is also necessary for healthy skin and surface tissues, especially those which secrete mucus. At least 21 human studies have suggested a relationship between low dietary ß-carotene and cancer[1]. The DHSS[2] recommends a daily intake of 450µg for infants, increasing to 750µg retinol equivalents from the age of 17 years onwards, and more for lactating women. The comparable recommendations of the US National Academy of Sciences[3] are 420µg retinol equivalents for infants, rising to 1,000µg for men and 800µg for women. 1µg retinol equivalent is equal to 1µg retinol or 6µg of ß-carotene. A very high intake of vitamin A can be harmful.

There have been few analyses of the vitamin A and ß-carotene contents of vegan diets. Early reports show vitamin A intake in vegans to be equal to or in excess of the recommended amounts[4-6]. One comparison of vegan and omnivorous diets[7] found that the former contained significantly fewer retinol equivalents than the omnivorous diet, while a similar study the following year[8] found average levels to be about the same in vegans and omnivores. There is a large individual variation in intake, but another British study[9] found that vegans consumed 165% of the RDA for vitamin A, compared to 208% for vegetarians (who obtain additional

Table 7. Vitamin A content of some vegan foods

Food	Retinol equivalents µg/100g	Retinol equivalents per average portion
Cabbage	50	57 (4oz)
Spinach	1,000	1133 (4oz)
Watercress	500	283 (2oz)
Carrots, old	2,000	2266 (4oz)
Tomatoes	100	113 (4oz)
Apricots, dried	600	510 (3oz)
Mango	200	170 (3oz)
Margarine *(animal-free)*	800	243 (1oz)
Pumpkin, cooked	108	123 (4oz)

100g = 3.5oz. Values taken from Ministry of Agriculture, Fisheries and Food[10]. British DHSS-recommended daily intake of retinol equivalents: 750µg for adults.

amounts from dairy produce and eggs), 255% for wholefood omnivores, but only 110% for average (non-wholefood) omnivores. **There have been no reports of vitamin A deficiency in vegans**, and it seems highly likely that they obtain plenty of ß-carotene from plant foods.

The B Group Vitamins

The chemical structure of each B vitamin is different, but because they have several features in common vitamins B_1, B_2, niacin, B_6, B_{12}, folic acid, pantothenic acid and biotin are usually considered as a group. Vitamin B_{12} is of particular significance in vegan diets, and so will be considered separately in a following section. The B vitamins are water-soluble (and therefore some can be lost if cooking water is thrown away), tend to be found in the same foods and act as co-factors in various enzyme systems in the body.

Vitamin B_1 (Thiamin)

Thiamin is widely available in both animal and plant foods. Rich sources — such as offal, pork, milk and eggs and, for vegans, **vegetables, fruit, yeast extracts, and whole grains** — contain more than 0.04 mg per 100 Calories. In whole grains, thiamin is found in the outer bran layer of the grain, thus much is lost when wheat is refined and for this reason white flour must by law be fortified with thiamin. Cooking can also partly destroy the vitamin. Thiamin is needed so that the body can release energy from carbohydrates, and when it is in short supply glucose is not properly utilized. The more carbohydrate consumed, the more thiamin is required, and this can lead to deficiency if high levels of mainly refined carbohydrates are eaten. A wholefood vegan diet in particular contains adequate thiamin because it includes whole grains. Deficiency of thiamin causes palpitations and muscular weakness, and in severe cases beri-beri.

The Department of Health (DHSS)[2] suggests a daily thiamin intake of about 1mg for adults, less for children, and the US recommended amounts[3] are slightly higher at 1–1.5mg. Recent analyses[7,8] indicate that **the thiamin content of vegan diets is significantly higher than that of omnivorous diets,** and exceeds both US and UK requirements. Similarly, a comparison of thiamin intake in vegans, vegetarians and omnivores showed that the former consumed 176% of DHSS RDAs, compared to 160% for vegetarians and an average of 120% for omnivores[9]. Since the main sources of thiamin even in an omnivorous diet is, in descending order, bread and cereal products, potatoes, milk and meat, this is hardly surprising.

Vitamin B$_2$ (Riboflavin)

Riboflavin is widely available in animal foods such as liver, kidney, dairy products and eggs, and in plant foods such as **whole grains, wheatgerm, pulses, dark green leafy vegetables, yeast and yeast extracts.** Cooking can destroy 30–40% of the riboflavin in vegetables.

Riboflavin is needed in the body for the utilization of energy from food and the daily intake recommended by the British[2] and US[3] authorities is 1.3–1.7mg for adults, and less for children. Two recent dietary analyses[7,8] indicated that vegan and omnivore subjects were consuming the same amounts of riboflavin — between 1.7 and 1.9mg, daily. Another study has shown that the intake of vegan volunteers, in contrast with that of vegetarians and omnivores, was below the recommended amount — although there were no signs of clinical deficiency[9]. A report of levels of riboflavin in the diet and in breast milk[11] indicated that vegans had a mean daily intake of 1.33 mg riboflavin, compared to 2.45mg in omnivores — both levels satisfying official recommendations. The mean concentration of riboflavin in breast milk was lower in the vegan subjects, but similar to values reported for pooled milk samples from five different areas in the UK. An assessment of 23 British vegan pre-school children published in 1981 found that the children's mean intake of riboflavin was 130% of the recommended daily amount[12]. **A deficiency of riboflavin in vegans is unlikely.**

Niacin (Nicotinic acid and Nicotinamide)

Nicotinic acid and nicotinamide are known collectively as niacin. The nicotinic acid in grains is mainly a bound form which is largely unavailable for use by the body. However the amino acid tryptophan can be converted to nicotinic acid in the body, and so again (as with vitamin A) equivalents of niacin are used as follows: 1mg of niacin equivalent is equal to 1mg of *available* niacin or 60mg of tryptophan. Rich food sources of niacin include meat, fish, cheese and eggs; and, of foods acceptable to vegans, also **yeast and yeast extracts, wheatgerm, whole grains, some pulses and some fruits and vegetables** (*See Table 9 below*). Cooking destroys 30–40% of the niacin in vegetables.

Niacin, like thiamin and riboflavin, is required by the body for the release of energy from food, and deficiency causes pellagra, characterized by muscular weakness, dermatitis, and mental and digestive disorders. The British RDAs[2] are 15–19mg niacin equivalents for adults and about half this for children, and the US RDAs[3] are similar.

Dietary analyses[7,8] indicate that **niacin intake by vegans is not significantly different from that of omnivores**, while a comparative study[9] showed that subjects in four dietary groups all met recommended amounts, with vegans, vegetarians and 'average' (i.e. non-wholefood) omnivores eating nearly double official requirements, and wholefood omnivores consuming smaller, but still adequate amounts.

Vitamin B$_6$ (Pyridoxine)

Pyridoxine is found widely in the same sorts of foods as the other B complex vitamins: meat, fish and eggs, as well as in plant foods such as **whole grains, wheatgerm, and fruits and vegetables. Potatoes and other vegetables** are the main source of pyridoxine in the diet of the general population, even though cooking destroys up to 40% of B$_6$ in vegetables. The DHSS has not set a recommended intake because deficiency of this vitamin is very rare, while the US RDA[3] is 2–2.2mg a day for adults. Very high amounts are harmful. Pyridoxine is essential in the body for the metabolism of amino acids, and requirements are thus related to protein intake. The vitamin is also needed for the formation of haemoglobin. Little research into the content of this vitamin in the vegan diet has been done; one dietary analysis indicated that vegan subjects had a daily pyridoxine intake of 1.9mg compared to 1.5mg for omnivores[7]. The higher protein intake of omnivores compared with vegans probably means that vegans have a lesser requirement for pyridoxine.

Table 8. Thiamin and riboflavin content of some vegan foods

Food	mg thiamin/ 100g	average portion	mg riboflavin/ 100g	average portion
Wholemeal bread	0.34	0.19 (2oz)	0.09	0.05 (2oz)
White bread (fortified with thiamin)	0.21	0.12 (2oz)	0.06	0.03 (2oz)
Brown rice, raw	0.59	0.33 (2oz)	0.07	0.04 (2oz)
Oats	0.90	0.51 (2oz)	0.09	0.05 (2oz)
Muesli	0.33	0.28 (3oz)	0.27	0.23 (3oz)
Peas, frozen	0.31	0.35 (4oz)	0.09	0.10 (4oz)
Potatoes	0.20	0.34 (6oz)	0.02	0.03 (6oz)
Mushrooms	0.10	0.09 (3oz)	0.40	0.34 (3oz)
Watercress	0.10	0.06 (2oz)	0.10	0.06 (2oz)
Soya beans, boiled	0.26	0.22 (3oz)	0.16	0.14 (3oz)
Almonds, shelled	0.24	0.07 (1oz)	0.92	0.26 (1oz)
Peanuts, shelled and roasted	0.23	0.07 (1oz)	0.10	0.03 (1oz)
Dried figs	0.10	0.06 (2oz)	0.08	0.05 (2oz)
Yeast extract, e.g. *Marmite*	3.10	0.16 (0.18oz)	11.0	0.57 (0.18oz)

100g = 3.5oz. Values taken from Ministry of Agriculture, Fisheries and Foods[10] and Tan *et al*[53].
Recommended amounts: 1mg/day thiamin (UK); 1.3–1.7mg/day riboflavin (UK).

Table 9. Niacin and pyridoxine content of some vegan foods

Foods	mg niacin equiv/ 100g	average portion	mg pyridoxine/ 100g	average portion
Wholemeal bread	1.8	1.0 (2oz)	0.12	0.07 (2oz)
White bread	2.3	1.3 (2oz)	0.07	0.04 (2oz)
Wholemeal flour	8.3	2.4 (2oz)	0.50	0.29 (2oz)
Wheatgerm	5.3	0.76 (0.5oz)	0.95	0.14 (0.5oz)
Brown rice, raw	5.8	3.3 (2oz)	n.a.	n.a.
Oats	3.3	1.9 (2oz)	0.12	0.07 (2oz)
Peas, frozen	1.6	1.8 (4oz)	0.10	0.11 (4oz)
Mushrooms, raw	4.6	3.9 (3oz)	0.10	0.08 (3oz)
Potatoes	1.5	2.6 (6oz)	0.25	0.43 (6oz)
Soya beans, boiled	3.4	2.9 (3oz)	n.a.	n.a.
Almonds, shelled	4.7	1.3 (1oz)	0.10	0.03 (1oz)
Peanuts, shelled and roasted	21.3	6.1 (1oz)	0.40	0.11 (1oz)
Dried apricots	3.8	3.3 (3oz)	0.17	0.15 (3oz)
Yeast extract, e.g. *Marmite*	67.0	3.4 (0.18oz)	n.a.	n.a.

100g = 3.5oz. Values taken from Paul and Southgate[13]. n.a. = values not available.
Recommended amounts: 15–19mg niacin equiv/day (UK); 2–2.2mg pyridoxine/day (USA).

Folic acid (Folate)

Folic acid (known as folacin in the USA) occurs in small amounts in many foods, but the richest sources are liver and, for vegans, **yeast and yeast extracts, as well as raw green leafy vegetables. Nuts and whole grains also contain useful amounts.** Most fruits, meat and dairy produce contain little, and heating food destroys 20–50% of its folate content. Folate is required for the metabolism of certain amino acids, and in conjunction with vitamin B_{12} for rapidly dividing cells; deficiency leads to megaloblastic anaemia. The British Medical Association[1] recommends a diet rich in vegetables, especially for women of child-bearing age and others at possible risk of defiency, to boost liver stores of folate. The DHSS[2] recommends a daily intake of 300µg folic acid for adults, while the US official recommendation is for 400µg[3], although there is a growing school of thought that this amount is unnecessarily high.

This vitamin is generally abundant in a vegan diet and apparently present in higher amounts than in an omnivorous diet. Dietary analyses[7,8] have shown the mean intake of vegan volunteers to be about 300µg, compared with nearer 200µg for omnivores. In another British study[9] vegans and vegetarians were the only dietary groups which came close to the DHSS-recommended intake, with omnivores consuming only about 65% of this level. A Swedish report found even higher levels of total folate (mean 545µg) in the vegan diet[14], and a study of British vegan pre-school children showed their intake of folic acid to be 160% of the RDA[11].

Pantothenic Acid and Biotin

Pantothenic acid is found in animal products, **whole grains and pulses** and is used in the body to release energy from fat and carbohydrate. Dietary deficiency of this vitamin is unlikely because it is widespread in food, and there is no recommended daily intake. **Biotin is found in** offal and egg yolk and, for vegans, in **whole grains, fruits and vegetables. It is also made by certain bacteria in the intestine** and sufficient may be available from this source. Biotin is required only in very small amounts for the metabolism of fat, and there is no official recommended level. One study[7] found slightly less biotin in the diet of vegan subjects than in that of omnivores (19µg, compared to 24µg) but both groups had an adequate intake.

Vitamin B_{12} (Cobalamins)

Vitamin B_{12} is of special relevance to vegans because it is commonly, but inaccurately, believed that this vitamin is found solely in animal

foods. B_{12} is unique among vitamins in being made only by micro-organisms such as bacteria, yeasts, moulds and some algae; and also in requiring the presence of intrinsic factor to enable absorption from the intestine to take place. Meat (especially offal) and dairy products contain high concentrations, which derive from micro-organisms widely distributed throughout the environment. Cooking, including the boiling of milk, reduces B_{12} content.

The vitamin is needed, with folic acid, by rapidly dividing cells such as those in the bone marrow which form the blood. Deficiency, which is rare, leads to a characteristic (megaloblastic) anaemia and degeneration of the nervous system. Symptoms include sore tongue, weakness, tingling and numbness of fingers and toes, and gastro-intestinal problems. Folic acid, which is plentiful in the vegan diet, can protect against the anaemia of B_{12} deficiency but not against the neurological degeneration. Most cases of B_{12} deficiency in the general population are due to a lack of the intrinsic factor, normally produced in the stomach, which allows the vitamin to be absorbed actively in the small intestine. Other **possible factors in B_{12} deficiency include small bowel disorders, the effects of drugs, smoking and alcohol, and some parasitic infections.**

Daily Requirement of B_{12} — a Controversy

There is no British RDA for vitamin B_{12}, but the general consensus[15] among nutritionists is that 2µg fulfils the body's requirements, and this is the level recommended for adults by the World Health Organization[16]. The US RDA is 3µg[2], although a leading American expert (advised by the US Recommended Daily Amount Committee) suggested[17] in 1987 that this should be reduced to 2µg, which has been shown to maintain health and a substantial body reserve of the vitamin with a wide margin of safety. He also stated that 1µg of vitamin B_{12} a day will sustain the average person[18]. The debate is complicated by the very tiny amounts involved which are not easy to measure accurately; by the susceptibility of the vitamin to degradation on cooking and storage; and by the fact that assay techniques do not always distinguish between biologically-active B_{12} and its various analogues, which are not used by the body.

Vitamin B_{12} is stored in the liver, which normally contains sufficient (2–5mg) to sustain the body for a period of 3–6 years, and for this reason it is not necessary to have a supply of the vitamin every day. Furthermore, since the main route of excretion of B_{12} is via the bile, the body is able to recycle the vitamin by reabsorbing it from the bile as it passes through the small intestine. At lower intakes of the vitamin there is a higher absorption rate into the bloodstream[17]. These mechanisms provide considerable leeway when dietary sources of B_{12} are scarce and may account for the fact that even vegans of 20 years standing, some with no obvious sources of dietary B_{12}, usually show no signs of deficiency.

Baker[19] studied the minimum requirements of five Southern Indian volunteers with B_{12}-deficiency anaemia by measuring blood responses to different doses of the vitamin. He found that 0.07–0.25µg of dietary B_{12} a day was inadequate, but that 0.3–0.65µg was sufficient, and possibly more than sufficient, to return the subjects to normal health. He concluded that the minimum daily requirement for Southern Indian adults is about 0.5µg B_{12}, and that an intake of 1µg would satisfy the needs of the vast majority of people and allow a wide safety margin. This conclusion was foreshadowed by an earlier report of an experiment where radio-labelled B_{12} was given to volunteers to estimate the daily rate of loss of the vitamin from the body[20]. It was found that less B_{12} was lost from the body in healthy subjects when stores in the liver were low, so that a steady state was maintained; and that 0.6–1.2µg was adequate for blood cell formation and to maintain health.

Vegan Sources of B_{12}

Grains, nuts, pulses, vegetables and other unprocessed plant foods generally contain none of the vitamin unless they are contaminated with B_{12}-producing micro-organisms. Vegans using lightly-washed home-grown produce may well obtain small amounts of the vitamin in this way. **Some drinking water** may contain B_{12}. Variable, but in some cases (e.g. *nori*, *wakame*) very high, levels of B_{12} are found in a number of **edible sea-weeds**[21,22]. Spirulina, an alga which is available as a supplement in health-food shops, was thought to be a rich source, but a study[23] using a radioimmunoassay technique to measure B_{12} has indicated that much of this is in the form of analogues which are not absorbed by the body. Two tablespoons of **nutritional yeast** (occasionally available in health-food shops in this country, but more common in the USA) contain about 4µg of B_{12}; the yeast is grown on B_{12}-enriched molasses medium. Fermented soya foods such as **tempeh, miso and shoyu (soya sauce), and barley malt syrup, sourdough bread and parsley** may contain variable (but generally low) amounts of the vitamin[21], and some of these foods are used fairly widely by vegans. Small amounts of B_{12} are found in **beer and cider**, and trace levels in **wine, yeast and tofu** (soya bean curd). Cooking destroys some of the B_{12} content in foods.

Other sources of the vitamin in a vegan diet are **fortified foods**. There is now a wide range of processed foods suitable for vegans and fortified with commercially-produced B_{12}. These include numerous **yeast extracts, soya-based textured vegetable proteins** (which, when sold as meat substitutes, must be fortified by law in the UK) and products made from them, as well as **certain brands of soya milk and margarine** which are acceptable to vegans. There are **vitamin tablets** containing B_{12} which are suitable for vegans, but again these may contain varying proportions of clinically-active B_{12}, as they have also been shown to contain some analogues of the vitamin[23].

In addition to these dietary sources of B_{12}, there is considerable evidence that the vitamin may be available from bacterial activity in the small intestine. In a study published in 1980, samples of bacteria were taken from the jejunum and ileum (small intestine) of healthy Southern Indian subjects, cultured in the laboratory and analysed for B_{12} production using two microbiological assays, as well as chromatography[24]. Five groups of micro-organisms produced considerable amounts of B_{12}-like material (as measured by the *Euglena gracilis* assay), and these were further tested with the *Ochromonas malhamensis* technique. Two groups of bacteria, *Pseudomonas* and *Klebsiella*, synthesized biologically-active vitamin B_{12}. It has been shown that free intrinsic factor (necessary for the absorption of the vitamin) is often present in the small intestine, so if these bacteria also produce B_{12} inside the body they could contribute significant amounts of the vitamin. Similar studies with Western vegans would be interesting.

Vitamin B_{12} — the Vegan Experience

Because of a generally high level of awareness among vegans of the importance of vitamin B_{12}, many individuals ensure that they receive an adequate supply by the use of fortified foods or supplements (usually tablets); others, however, make no special effort to incorporate these sources in their diets. Generalizations about the B_{12} content of a vegan diet are therefore hard to make.

A few investigations[25–27] have documented the use of B_{12} supplements among British vegans. Tablets were used by 8%[26] and 18%[27] of vegans in groups studied in 1970 and 1978 respectively, but a 1986 survey[28] recorded tablet use by 41% of vegan runners. Between 1967[25] and 1978[26,27] an average of 57% of vegans studied used foods fortified with B_{12}, while in the group of vegan runners surveyed all individuals used fortified foods (yeast extracts, soya milk, TVP) or foods naturally containing B_{12} (seaweeds, fermented soya products)[28]. This variation may be due to an increasing awareness of the B_{12} issue in recent years, or to the fact that the latter survey assessed practising athletes — who are, perhaps, particularly strongly motivated to ensure optimal nutrition.

Dietary intakes of the vitamin by vegans have been measured in several studies. The more recent (1985–1987) indicate an average B_{12} intake (including fortified foods) of 1.2–1.8µg[7-9], at which levels about half the vitamin is absorbed from the gut. In a Swedish study in which subjects did not use fortified foods[14] an average intake of 0.35µg was recorded, and analysis of various foods used, including fermented vegetables, showed contents of 10–70ng B_{12} per 100g wet weight, which may have been due to the activity of micro-organisms. British vegan pre-school children had a mean intake of 280% of the British RDA, although five of the 23 consumed less than the recommended intake[12]. Similarly, at a vegan community called The Farm, in Tennessee, USA — where B_{12} was obtained from supplemented soya milk and from the yeast *Saccharomyces cerevisae* (used as a flavouring) — the mean intake of 48 two- to five-year-old children was 15µg — about 660% of the US RDA[29]. None of the vegans in these groups showed any clinical signs of deficiency and all were healthy.

One measure of the adequacy of B_{12} intake is the level of the vitamin found in the blood. Accepted normal serum levels fall within a wide range — from 100–900pg/ml. Values below 80pg/ml suggest a possible deficiency of B_{12} while between 80 and 140pg/ml there may or may not be symptoms of deficiency. **Lower than normal serum levels of the vitamin are not, of themselves, indicative of a deficiency.** As already mentioned, vegans of up to 20 years standing with no obvious source of the vitamin in their diets only very rarely have clinical symptoms of deficiency. Although their serum level of B_{12} does fall over a number of years it often stabilizes at about 100pg/ml. Vegans who take supplements or fortified foods generally have higher serum levels of the vitamin, while **vegan macrobiotics or smokers may be predisposed to B_{12} deficiency.**

Consequently, surveys of vegans document a wide variation of serum levels of B_{12}. One report[25] mentions values between 30 and 650pg/ml with a mean value (of 20 subjects) of 236pg/ml, compared with a range of 120–740pg/ml and a mean serum value of 441pg/ml in matched omnivore control subjects. There was **no clinical evidence of B_{12} deficiency even in those vegans with the lowest serum levels,** although one 80-year-old subject who had been a vegan for only two years had pernicious anaemia. Three vegans who had been on the diet for 17 years without taking supplements were healthy, with serum B_{12} levels of 150, 375 and 450pg/ml, and normal amounts of haemoglobin in the blood.

Haematological measurements[27] of 34 vegans who had been on the diet for between one and 30 years revealed a range of serum B_{12} levels from 94–675pg/ml — all *above* the value of 80pg/ml at which deficiency symptoms can be expected. The majority of subjects took B_{12} tablets or food fortified with the vitamin, and those who did had higher amounts in their blood. **The serum levels of three subjects who had been vegan for 6–13 years (long enough theoretically to exhaust liver stores of B_{12}) with no obvious dietary source of B_{12} were also adequate,** at 120–230pg/ml. All the vegans were healthy, none showed symptoms of B_{12} deficiency and all had normal haemoglobin values. The same report lists other surveys of vegans which have failed to show symptoms of dietary deficiency of B_{12}.

Occasional B_{12} Deficiency

Cases of B_{12} deficiency in infant and adult vegans, sometimes resulting in neurological symptoms, have been documented. Results are incomplete in four reports[30-33] and the diagnoses of subacute combined degeneration of the spinal cord in these cases are not convincing, according to Sanders[34]. Fewer than 30 reports of B_{12} deficiency attributable to vegan and vegetarian diets have been described in the medical literature[35], and in several cases underlying disease of the stomach or small intestine, or other contributory factors which could precipitate deficiency, were not ruled out. **It is significant that B_{12} deficiency is so rare among vegans that single cases are thought worthy of publication in the medical journals;** however, it should be pointed out that the relevance of case studies to the vegan population as a whole is not clear. One case reported in 1987 concerned a 14-year-old girl in Israel, who had adopted a vegan diet after witnessing the slaughter of a cow on her farm. Neither she nor her parents had been aware of the need for vitamin B_{12}, and after eight years she had developed severe neurological disturbances — including difficulty in walking, running and climbing stairs. She was "well-developed and well-nourished", but her serum level of B_{12} had fallen to only 50pg/ml. Following injections and supplements of B_{12} and the inclusion of fish and dairy products in her diet the girl returned quickly to health[36]. The use of vegan foods containing natural vitamin, or of fortified foods, would have enabled the girl to continue with a vegan diet in good health.

Ten Rastafarian males aged 18–40 years, who had been vegans for between two and 20 years, were examined at the University of the West Indies and reported to be suffering from B_{12} deficiency[37]. All except two patients had very low serum levels of B_{12}. Neurological and gastro-intestinal symptoms were observed; eight patients had macrocytic anaemia and all had megaloblastic changes in the bone marrow. One patient died, and two still suffered physical effects after several months of treatment. Failure to absorb the vitamin from the gut was excluded as a cause of the condition, which was attributed by the investigators solely to dietary deficiency.

A vegan diet can provide adequate quantities of B_{12} for infants and children, but in cases where the mother, for whatever reasons, has very low body stores of the vitamin or a low current intake, deficiency can develop in exclusively breast-fed infants. This is because they rely for supplies of B_{12} entirely on their own liver stores (derived from their mothers while in the womb) and on B_{12} in their mothers' milk. Two studies conducted in the 1950s (See [39]) suggested that a woman's liver stores of vitamin B_{12} are not transferred to the foetus; if this were so, the foetus would be entirely reliant on the mother's current intake of the vitamin. Since 1978 there have been four case studies — from America, Australia and the West Indies[38–41] — of maternal dietary B_{12} deficiency causing serious problems in exclusively breast-fed infants of vegan mothers. Symptoms were recognized at between three and twelve months of age, when the infants became irritable, lethargic and fed poorly; the mothers were healthy. There was some developmental retardation which was completely reversible in only two out of the four cases. **It is important that women ensure an adequate supply of B_{12} during pregnancy and lactation, and the easiest way to do this is to use foods naturally rich in, or fortified with, the vitamin. Vitamin preparations are another source of B_{12}.**

A 1987 study measured the levels of a metabolite — methylmalonic acid (MMA) — in the urine of breast-fed infants of near-vegan (macrobiotic) mothers, and in the urine of the mothers themselves[22]. High concentrations of MMA in the urine are suggestive of low body levels of vitamin B_{12}. The babies had higher amounts of MMA in their urine than similar babies of omnivore mothers, although no B_{12} deficiency signs were noted. Two mothers opted to give their babies B_{12} supplements, but the third successfully reduced her baby's levels of MMA by including more seaweeds and fermented foods in *her* diet — the extra B_{12} she thus absorbed was passed through her breast milk to the baby.

There have also been cases of vitamin B_{12} deficiency in infants weaned onto *inadequate* vegan diets. In 1982 some 15 cases of deficiency were reported[42] over a 15-month period among babies born to black vegan Americans living in a religious community in Israel. The infants had been weaned onto a diet of over-diluted home-made soya and almond milks, oats, yeast, fruit and vegetables, and were suffering from multiple nutritional deficiencies, including protein and energy malnutrition. In this community weaning began at three months of age, while in the UK it is quite common for vegan mothers to continue breast-feeding for 12 months, and often longer[12]. The authors of the report acknowledged that early weaning contributed to the nutritional deficiencies suffered by these infants.

The body requires only a tiny amount of vitamin B_{12} and is able to conserve the vitamin when supplies are scarce. There is persuasive evidence that, at least in some individuals, there are bacteria present in the small intestine which manufacture B_{12} that is available to the body.

There are numerous fortified foods, and several that naturally contain B_{12}, which are acceptable to vegans, as well as dietary supplements. The accuracy of present tests for the presence of B_{12} in food could usefully be improved, and further studies of the vitamin B_{12} status of vegans would be welcome.

A dietary deficiency of this vitamin in vegans is, despite its notoriety, extremely rare. In general, more cases of deficiency arise through lack of intrinsic factor (required for absorption) than from dietary lack. Nevertheless, the consequences of a deficiency are serious; all vegans should be aware of the varied dietary sources of B_{12} available to them, and should ensure that they use these regularly. Pregnant and breast-feeding women in particular should have an adequate source of vitamin B_{12} and on weaning infants care should be taken to ensure that a dietary supply of the vitamin is provided.

Vitamin C (Ascorbic Acid)

Humans are one of the few species (along with guinea pigs and monkeys) unable to make vitamin C in the body, and therefore we need a dietary source. Small amounts are found in milk and liver, but almost all the vitamin C in the human diet comes from vegetables and fruit, especially potatoes, green leafy vegetables, green peppers, blackcurrants, mangoes, citrus fruits and tomatoes. Although potatoes have a comparatively low content, because they are eaten often they constitute the major source of vitamin C in the British diet. Since the vitamin is easily destroyed during storage, food preparation and cooking, deficiency (eventually leading to scurvy) can occur in the Western diet. Vitamin C

Table 10. Vitamin B_{12} content of some vegan foods

Food	μg of B12/ 100g	μg of B12/ average portion
Dried seaweeds (various)	1.6–100	0.6–29 (1oz)
Spirulina, dried	25.5–74	1.8–5.3 (0.25oz)
Soya bean tempeh	0.02–6.3	0.02–7.2 (4oz)
Soya sauce, miso	<0.5	<0.14 (1oz)
Tofu, seitan	<0.5	<0.57 (4oz)
Wines, ales, bitters, ciders	<0.5	<0.57–1.4 (4–10oz)
Dried yeast	<0.5	<0.04 (0.25oz)
Sprouted pulses, sauerkraut, umeboshi plums	<0.5	<0.29 (2oz)
Fortified yeast extracts/ savoury spreads, e.g.		
Barmene	500	25.7 (0.18oz)
Tastex, Community, Meridian	50	2.57 (0.18oz)
Vecon	13.3	0.67 (0.18oz)
Natex	8.8	0.45 (0.18oz)
Marmite	8.25	0.42 (0.18oz)
Margarine (fortified with B_{12}) e.g.		
Pure, Hawthorn Vale, Suma	5.0	1.4 (1oz)
Soya milks (fortified), e.g.		
Plamil concentrated soya milk	3.2	1.8 (2oz)
Plamil liquid soya milk	1.6	1.8 (4oz)
Soyagen	unspec.	n.a.
Dried TVP & similar mixes (fortified)	1.4–8.0	0.8–4.6 (2oz)

100g = 3.5oz. Values are from various sources including ref. 22 and manufacturers' analyses, and are approximate because of vitamin losses on storage and in cooking and variations due to methods of analysis. Unknown proportions of the vitamin in each food may be in the form of B_{12} analogues which are unavailable to the body. Trade names are in italics.

WHO recommended daily intake: 2μg a day for adults.

is required by the body for the development and maintenance of connective tissues, is needed for the formation of haemoglobin, bones and teeth, and plays a vital role in wound-healing and in resistance to infection. Vitamin C enhances iron absorption. Whether or not high doses are protective against cancer or reduce symptoms of the common cold is still under debate.

The British DHSS recommends a daily intake of 20mg vitamin C for children and 30mg for adolescents and adults, with extra during pregnancy and lactation[2], while the US RDAs[3] are higher at 35–45mg for infants and children, and 50–60mg for adolescents and adults. However, US experts suggested in 1987 that these amounts could be reduced to 30–40mg a day for adults[43].

Given the food sources of vitamin C, it is no surprise to find that a vegan diet contains plentiful amounts of this vitamin. Recent surveys[7–9] indicate that the vitamin C intake of vegans varies between 137 and 210mg a day, with a mean of 162mg; comparable figures for omnivore controls were 78–153mg, with a mean intake of 112mg. **There have been no reports of vitamin C deficiency in vegans.**

Vitamin D (Ergocalciferol D$_2$, Cholecalciferol D$_3$)

Few foods naturally contain vitamin D, and those which do are animal products which contain vitamin D$_3$ (cholecalciferol). The richest of these sources are oily fish, fish liver oils, eggs and butter; margarine is fortified with vitamin D by law, and supplements are available to pregnant and lactating women in the UK. Common plant foods do not contain vitamin D, although **margarines and some soya milks and other foods acceptable to vegans are fortified.** Food sources of vitamin D are relatively unimportant, however, since by far the most significant source is the action of ultra-violet light (daylight) on sterols in the skin to produce vitamin D$_2$ (ergocalciferol). Most people[10], including infants[44], need little or no extra from food. Bright sunlight is not necessary: even the 'skyshine' on a cloudy day will stimulate formation of some vitamin D$_2$ in the skin, while a short summer holiday in the open air will increase serum levels of vitamin D two- or three-fold.

Vitamin D, which is a fat-soluble vitamin, is required for maintaining calcium (and phosphorus) levels in the blood, and it does this by enhancing the absorption of calcium from the intestine and by helping to regulate the movement of calcium between bone and blood. In infancy and childhood, a deficiency of vitamin D causes the deformed bones characteristic of rickets, while in adults a lack of the vitamin causes a softening

Table 11. Vitamin C content of some vegan foods per 100g portion

Food	mg vitamin C/100g	mg/100g after boiling
Blackcurrants	200	150
Green peppers	100	n.a.
Brussel sprouts	90	40
Mango	80	n.a.
Cauliflower	60	20
Cabbage	55	20
Oranges	50	n.a.
Lemon juice	50	n.a.
Grapefruit	40	n.a.
Tomatoes	20	n.a.
Potatoes		
new	16	9
Oct–Dec	19	9
Jan–Feb	9	6
Mar–May	8	5

100g = 3.5oz. Values taken from Ministry of Agriculture, Fisheries & Foods[10].
British DHSS recommended daily intake: 30mg for adults.

of the bones known as osteomalacia. Deficiency is seen more often in high-latitude countries, or where tradition dictates that the body is well covered by clothes, such as in (parts of) the Islamic world. Dark-skinned people may be more susceptible to a deficiency of vitamin D. An excess of the vitamin causes calcium to be deposited in the kidneys.

The exact requirement for vitamin D is not known. As a dietary source is not usually required, UK RDAs[2] exist only for infants, small children and pregnant and lactating women — for whom a daily intake of 7.5–10µg is suggested in winter (10µg vitamin D are equivalent to 400 international units). The US RDAs[3] are for 5–15µg, depending on age. An unpublished report[28] indicated that 91% of vegans (who were keen amateur athletes) obtained vitamin D from fortified margarines and 54% used a proprietary soya milk fortified with the vitamin. Two studies[7,9] measured the intake by vegans of vitamin D in food as 2.5 and 3.2µg (just less than one-third the recommended total amount), compared with 3.7 and 3.5µg for omnivore controls respectively; and British vegan pre-school children were found to have a mean dietary intake of 23% of the estimated total requirement[12]. None of the subjects in these three studies showed signs of vitamin D deficiency; it is likely that vegans, like most people, meet their requirement for vitamin D primarily from regular exposure to sunlight.

An American study compared levels in the blood of a vitamin D metabolite — 1,25-dihydroxyvitamin D — in near-vegan (macrobiotic) lactating and non-lactating women and in omnivore women of similar age[45]. Higher levels of this metabolite were found in lactating versus non-lactating women, and in the near-vegan versus the omnivore women, indicating an adaptation to conserve body supplies of calcium by increasing absorption from the intestine. It was suggested that calcium needed to be conserved for breast-feeding infants on the one hand, and because of a presumed lower calcium intake in the near-vegan women on the other. Levels of calcium in the blood of the near-vegans and omnivores were the same, showing successful adaptation to a lower dietary intake of calcium, while amounts of magnesium were *higher* in the serum of the near-vegan women. Serum levels of vitamin D itself were the same in both dietary groups in the summer, but lower in the near-vegans in the winter months.

Vitamin D Deficiency

Rickets and osteomalacia can be a problem in the Asian vegetarian population in Britain (possibly because of restricted exposure to daylight), but seem to be very rare in Caucasian vegans[46]. A few isolated cases of rickets due to vitamin D deficiency have been reported in infants raised on a vegan diet, and a few also involving vegetarian children. **The prevalence of rickets in infants on vegetarian and vegan diets is unlikely to be any greater than in omnivore children.**

Two reports of rickets in infants raised on vegan diets have been published in recent years. In a black vegan religious community of Americans living in Israel rickets was one of several conditions brought about by nutrient deficiencies[42]. The infants were weaned early onto a diet which was also deficient in protein and Calories, and a 1986 study has suggested that certain forms of rickets may be associated with protein-energy malnutrition[47]. Black-skinned people seem more susceptible to vitamin D deficiency than fair-skinned races and a report[48] of rickets in a black American infant weaned onto an inadequate vegan diet further supports this. The 20-month-old child had been weaned at nine months, after which he had been fed home-prepared soya milk, fruits and vegetables. His exposure to daylight was not mentioned in the report. The authors concluded that breast milk may, in general, contain insufficient vitamin D for infants, especially if other risk factors — such as malnutrition in the mother, dark skin or inadequate exposure to sunlight — are present.

As far as we know, there have been no cases of osteomalacia related to a vegan diet, and no surveys of vegans have suggested any symptoms of this condition. A 1974 report of X-ray examination of the strength and density of the bones of vegans concluded that there was no difference from those of age- and sex-matched omnivores[49]. Of two later studies comparing bone density in vegetarian and omnivore women one found no difference between the two groups at ages 20–49 years[50], while the other[51], which compared older women (aged 50–89 years), found that vegetarians lost only half the bone mass lost by omnivores.

Vegans, young and old, will obtain adequate vitamin D if they spend some time outdoors on bright days; and an intake of the vitamin can be further ensured by consumption of fortified vegan margarines, soya milks and other foodstuffs. The American Dietetic Association has suggested that parents of infants who are solely breast-fed after the age of 4–6 months may, especially if the infants are dark-skinned or seldom in the fresh air, wish to give them a vitamin D supplement.

Vitamin E (Tocopherols)

Vitamin E comprises a number of substances called tocopherols, the most active being alpha-tocopherol. The vitamin is found widely in foods, the richest **sources being vegetable oils, whole grains and flours, wheatgerm, nuts** and eggs; meat, animal fats, fruit and vegetables contain comparatively little. Being a fat-soluble vitamin, it is stored in the body and so a daily intake is not essential, and this, combined with its fairly wide availability, means that deficiency is rare. The precise role of vitamin E in the human body is not known, although it is likely that its anti-oxidant effects are important. An RDA has not been set, but **vegans on a wholefood diet will obtain plenty of this vitamin (and probably more than most omnivores).**

Vitamin K

This vitamin is also fat-soluble, and is **widespread in plant foods such as spinach, cabbage, cauliflower, peas and grains.** It is provided in roughly equal proportions by diet and from **bacterial activity in the gut.** Vitamin K is needed for normal clotting of the blood, but a dietary deficiency is unlikely, partly because of its easy availability in food and partly because our intestinal bacteria can make it. There is no British RDA. The American Recommended Daily Amount Committee has recently proposed a reduction in daily intake to 45μg for adult males and 35μg for females, with more during pregnancy and lactation[52]. This Committee also suggested that infants' diets be supplemented with vitamin K, as breast milk may not contain adequate amounts and infants' intestines will not yet have been colonized with vitamin K-producing bacteria. **As vitamin K is common in plant foods it seems unlikely that vegans will suffer a deficiency.**

Summary

A varied and balanced vegan diet contains all the vitamins necessary for good health with the possible exceptions of vitamins B_{12} and D, but — as has been shown — neither of these need pose difficulties. Only minute amounts of B_{12} are required by the body and it is likely that some is available through the activity of intestinal bacteria. Some plant foods contain B_{12} and numerous proprietary foods are fortified; vitamin supplements acceptable to vegans are also available.

Although a few cases of B_{12} deficiency have been described in vegans, they are very much the exception and vegans of 40 or more years standing — including life vegans — have remained fit and healthy. In the case of vitamin D the Department of Health, which sets nutritional guidelines in Britain, states that both adults and children can obtain sufficient supplies from the action of sunlight on the skin. Furthermore, many vegans use margarines and soya milks which are fortified with an acceptable form of the vitamin (D_2 — ergocalciferol). Other factors — such as poor nutritional status in the mother, dark skin or inadequate exposure to daylight — were also involved in the two reports of rickets in vegan infants. There is no evidence of vitamin D deficiency in adult Caucasian vegans, although it may be a problem among vegetarians of Asian origin.

As applies to adherents of any dietary philosophy, care should be taken by vegans not to limit too narrowly the selection of foods used. A largely wholefood diet, as recommended by the Vegan Society (See *Guidelines on Vegan Diets*) and followed by the majority of British vegans, is the most likely to contain adequate levels of vitamins.

References

1. BOARD OF SCIENCE & EDUCATION, BRITISH MEDICAL ASSOCIATION (1986). *Diet, Nutrition and Health*. London, BMA.

2. DEPARTMENT OF HEALTH AND SOCIAL SECURITY (1979). *Recommended Daily Amounts of Food Energy and Nutrients for Groups of People in the United Kingdom*. London, HMSO.

3. FOOD AND NUTRITION BOARD, NATIONAL ACADEMY OF SCIENCES [USA] (1980). *Recommended Dietary Allowances (9th edition)*.

4. HARDINGE, M.G. and STARE, F.J. (1954). 'Nutritional studies of vegetarians: nutritional, physical and laboratory studies', *J. Clin. Nutr.*, 2, 73–82.

5. HARDINGE, M.G. AND STARE, F.J. (1954). 'Nutritional studies of vegetarians: dietary and serum levels of cholesterol', *J. Clin. Nutr.*, 2, 83–88.

6. GUGGENHEIM, K, WEISS, Y. and FOSTICK, M. (1962). 'Composition and nutritive value of diets consumed by strict vegetarians', *Br. J. Nutr.*, 16, 467–474.

7. RANA, S.K. and SANDERS, T.A.B. (1986). 'Taurine concentrations in the diet, plasma, urine and breast milk of vegans compared with omnivores', *Br. J. Nutr.*, 56, 17–27.

8. SANDERS, T.A.B. and KEY, T.J.A. (1987). 'Blood pressure, plasma renin activity and aldosterone concentrations in vegans and omnivore controls', *Hum. Nutr.: Appl. Nutr.*, 41A, 204–211.

9. CARLSON, E., KIPPS, M., LOCKIE, A. and THOMSON, J. (1985). 'A comparative evaluation of vegan, vegetarian and omnivore diets', *J. Plant Foods*, 6, 89–100.

10. MINISTRY OF AGRICULTURE, FISHERIES AND FOODS (1985). *Manual of Nutrition (9th edition)*. London, HMSO.

11. HUGHES, J. and SANDERS, T.A.B. (1979). 'Riboflavin levels in the diet and breast milk of vegans and omnivores', *Proc. Nutr. Soc.*, 38, 95A.

12. SANDERS, T.A.B. and PURVES, R. (1981). 'An anthropometric and dietary assessment of the nutritional status of vegan preschool children', *J. Hum. Nutr.*, 35, 349–357.

13. PAUL, A.A. and SOUTHGATE, D.A.T. (1978). *McCance & Widdowson's The Composition of Foods (4th edition)*. London, HMSO.

14. ABDULLA, M., ANDERSSON, I., ASP, N-G., BERTHELSEN, K., BIRKHED, D., DENCKER, I., JOHANSSON, C-G., JÄGERSTAD, M., KOLAR, K., NAIR, B.M., NILSSON-EHLE, P., NORDÉN, Å., RASSNER, S., ÅKESSON, B. and ÖCKERMAN, P-A. (1981). 'Nutrient intake and health status of vegans. Chemical analyses of diets using the duplicate portion sampling technique', *Am. J. Clin. Nutr.*, 34, 2464–2477.

15. McLAREN, D.S. (1981). *Nutrition and its Disorders (3rd edition)*, p94. Edinburgh, Churchill Livingstone.

16. FAO/WHO EXPERT GROUP (1970). 'Requirements of ascorbic acid, vitamin D, vitamin B_{12}, folate and iron', *WHO Technical Report Series 452*. Geneva, WHO.

17. HERBERT, V. (1987). 'Recommended dietary intakes (RDI) of vitamin B_{12} in humans', *Am. J. Clin. Nutr.*, 45, 671–678.

18. HERBERT, V., COLMAN N. and JACOB, E. (1980). 'Folic acid and vitamin B_{12}'. In: GOODHART, R.S. and SHILS, M.S., (Eds.) *Modern Nutrition in Health and Disease (6th edition)*, pp229–259. Philadelphia, PA, Lea & Febiger.

19. BAKER, S. J. and MATHAN, V.I. (1981). 'Evidence regarding the minimal daily requirement of dietary vitamin B_{12}', *Am. J. Clin. Nutr.*, 34, 2423–2433.

20. HEYSSEL, R. M., BOZIAN, R.C., and DARBY, W.J. (1966). 'Vitamin B_{12} turnover in man. The assimilation of vitamin B_{12} from natural foodstuff by man and estimates of minimal daily requirements', *Am. J. Clin. Nutr.*, 18, 176–184.

21. VAN DEN BERG, H., DAGNELIE, P.C. and VAN STAVEREN, W.A. (1988). 'Vitamin B_{12} and seaweed', *Lancet* i, 242–243.

22. SPECKER, B.L., MILLER, D., NORMAN, E.J., GREENE, H. and HAYES, K.C. (1987). 'Increased urinary methylmalonic acid excretion in breast-fed infants of vegetarian mothers and identification of an acceptable dietary

source of vitamin B-12', *Am. J. Clin. Nutr.*, 47, 89–92.

23. HERBERT, V., DRIVAS, G., CHU, M., LEVITT, D. and COOPER, B. (1983). 'Differential radioassays better measure cobalamin content of vitamins and 'health foods' than do microbiologic assays', *Blood*, 62(5) *Suppl.*1, 37a.

24. ALBERT, M.J., MATHAN, V.I. and BAKER, S.J. (1980). 'Vitamin B_{12} synthesis by human small intestinal bacteria', *Nature*, 283, 781–782.

25. ELLIS, F.R. and MUMFORD, P. (1967). 'The nutritional status of vegans and vegetarians', *Proc. Nutr. Soc.*, 26, 205–212.

26. ELLIS, F.R. and MONTEGRIFFO, V.M.E. (1970). 'Veganism, clinical findings and investigations', *Am. J. Clin. Nutr.*, 23, 249–255.

27. SANDERS, T.A.B., ELLIS, F.R. and DICKERSON, J.W.T. (1978). 'Haematological studies on vegans', *Br. J. Nutr.*, 40, 9–15.

28. LANGLEY, G.R. and WILCOX, J. (1987). *Nutrient Sources and Health Profile of Vegan and Vegetarian runners*. Unpublished.

29. FULTON, J.R., HUTTON, C.W. and STITT, K.R. (1980). 'Preschool vegetarian children', *J. Am. Diet. Ass.*, 76, 360–365.

30. BADENOCH, A.G. (1952). 'Diet and stamina' (letter). *Br. Med. J.*, 2, 668.

31. BADENOCH, T. (1954). 'The use of labelled vitamin B12 and gastric biopsy in the investigation of anaemia', *Proc. Roy. Soc. Med.*, 47, 426–427.

32. WOKES, F., BADENOCH, J. and SINCLAIR, H.M. (1955). 'Human dietary deficiency of vitamin B_{12}', *Am. J. Clin. Nutr.*, 3, 375–382.

33. SMITH, A.D.M. (1962). 'Veganism: a clinical survey with observations on vitamin B_{12} metabolism', *Br. Med. J.*, 1, 1655–1658.

34. SANDERS, T.A.B. (1978). 'The health and nutritional status of vegans', *Plant. Fds. Man*, 2, 181–193.

35. McDOUGALL, J.A. and McDOUGALL, M.A. (1983). *The McDougall Plan*, p40. New Jersey, New Century Publishers.

36. ASHKENAZI, S., WEITZ, R., VARSANO, I. and MIMOUNI, M. (1987). 'Vitamin B_{12} deficiency due to a strictly vegetarian diet in adolescence', *Clin. Pediatr.*, 26, 662–663.

37. CAMPBELL, M., LOFTERS, W.S. and GIBBS, W.N. (1982). 'Rastafarianism and the vegans syndrome', *Br. Med. J.*, 285, 1617–1618.

38. WIGHTON, M.C., MANSON, J.I., SPEED, I. ROBERTSON, E. and CHAPMAN, E. (1979). 'Brain damage in infancy and dietary vitamin B_{12} deficiency',

Med. J. Australia, 2, 1–3.

39. SKLAR, R. (1986). 'Nutritional vitamin B_{12} deficiency in a breast-fed infant of a vegan-diet mother', *Clin. Pediatr.*, 25, 219–221.

40. HIGGINBOTTOM, M.C., SWEETMAN, L. and NYHAN, W.L. (1978). 'A syndrome of methylmalonic aciduria, homocystinuria, megaloblastic anemia and neurologic abnormalities in a vitamin B_{12}-deficient breast-fed infant of a strict vegetarian', *New Eng. J. Med.*, 299, 317–323.

41. CLOSE, G.C. (1983). 'Rastafarianism and the vegans syndrome' (letter). *Br. Med. J.*, 286, 473.

42. SHINWELL, E.D. and GORODISCHER, R. (1982). 'Totally vegetarian diets and infant nutrition', *Pediatr.*, 70, 582–586.

43. OLSON, J.A. and HODGES, R.E. (1987). 'Recommended dietary intakes (RDI) of vitamin C in humans', *Am. J. Clin. Nutr.*, 45, 693–703.

44. LAWSON, D.E.M. (1978). *Vitamin D*, p304. London, Academic Press.

45. SPECKER, B.L., TSANG, R.C. and MILLER, D. (1987). 'Effect of vegetarian diet on serum 1,25-dihydroxyvitamin D concentrations during lactation', *Obstet. Gynec.*, 70, 870–874.

46. SANDERS, T.A.B. (1983). 'Vegetarianism: Dietetic and Medical Aspects', *J. Plant Foods*, 5, 3–14.

47. BELTON, N.R. (1986). 'Rickets — not only the "English disease"', *Acta. Paediatr. Scand., Suppl.*, 323, 68–75.

48. ANON. (1984). 'Rickets in a breast-fed infant', *Nutr. Rev.*, 42, 380–382.

49. ELLIS, F.R., HOLESH, S. and SANDERS, T.A.B. (1974). 'Osteoporosis in British vegetarians and omnivores', *Am. J. Clin. Nutr.*, 27, 769.

50. MARSH, A.G., SANCHEZ, T.V., MICKELSEN, O., KEISER, J. and MAYOR, G. (1980). 'Cortical bone density of adult lacto-ovo-vegetarian and omnivorous women', *J. Am. Diet. Ass.*, 76, 148–151.

51. SANCHEZ, T.V., MICKELSEN, O., MARSH, A.G., GARN, S.M. and MAYOR, G.H. (1980). 'Bone mineral mass in elderly vegetarian and omnivorous females', in: MAZESS, R.B. (Ed.), *Proceedings of the 4th International Conference on Bone Mineral Measurement*, pp94–98. Bethesda, MD, NIAMMD.

52. OLSEN, J.A. (1987). 'Recommended dietary intakes (RDI) of vitamin K in humans', *Am. J. Clin. Nutr.*, 45, 687–692.

There are 16 minerals known to be essential to the human body and which must be obtained from food. The eight major minerals — calcium, phosphorus, iron, magnesium, sodium, chlorine, potassium and sulphur — are needed in the greatest quantities or are present in large amounts in the body, while the remaining eight trace elements — cobalt, copper, chromium, fluorine, iodine, manganese, selenium and zinc — are equally necessary but in smaller amounts. The three main functions of minerals are as constituents of the skeleton, as soluble salts which help control the composition of the body fluids, and as essential adjuncts to the action of many enzymes and other proteins.

The Major Minerals

Calcium

Calcium is found in dairy milk, cheese and yoghurt, but in only tiny amounts in meat and fish (unless the bones are eaten, as with sardines); white bread is fortified with calcium in Britain. **Good plant sources of calcium include tofu (soya bean curd, which contains more than *four times* the calcium of whole cow's milk), spinach, watercress, parsley, dried figs, seeds, nuts, black molasses and edible seaweeds.** Some proprietary products for vegans are fortified with calcium (e.g. *Plamil* soya milks). For some people drinking **hard water** provides a considerable intake of calcium — the British average being 75mg per person a day.

Calcium is the most abundant mineral in the body (on average 1000g) — about 99% of it being in the bones and teeth in the form of calcium phosphates. As well as providing the structural substance of bones, the bone minerals are also a reservoir for other needs, and there is a continual movement of calcium between the bones and the blood (and hence to other parts of the body), which is under careful control. The 5–10g of calcium not in the bones and teeth are required for muscle contraction, for the functioning of the nerves, for the activity of several enzymes and for blood clotting.

Too little calcium in the tissues of young children causes stunted growth and rickets, and women who lose large amounts of calcium from their bodies during repeated pregnancies and lactation may develop a deficiency which can show as osteomalacia (softened bones). Old people, especially women, often suffer from osteoporosis (thinning of the bones), which is becoming endemic in the British and American populations. However, actual deficiency of calcium in the diet is not common in Britain, especially as the body adapts to low intakes. The main deficiency in rickets and osteomalacia is of vitamin D (*See Section 4 — **Vitamins***), leading to poor absorption of calcium from food.

The British RDAs for calcium are 600–700mg a day for children and teenagers, and 500mg for adults — rising to 1,200mg in pregnancy and during lactation[1]. The comparable US figures are higher, at 360–1,200mg for young people, 800mg for adults and 1,200mg for pregnant and lactating women[2].

Meat, Protein and Calcium Balance

Evidence from laboratory and population studies indicates that a high protein intake, especially from animal foods, can lead to negative calcium balance, a two-fold increase in protein causing 50% more calcium to be lost in the urine. Several human volunteer studies lasting up to 95 days have shown that, on experimental diets with a constant calcium intake, the loss of calcium in the urine increases markedly as protein intake goes up[3–5]. On a low-protein diet adults were in calcium balance regardless of whether calcium intake was 500, 800 or 1,400mg a day[6]. Interestingly, a 1988 study showed that when soya foods (soya milk and tofu) were the primary sources of protein in the diet calcium equilibrium was maintained, even when calcium intake was low and protein intake relatively high[7].

That calcium intake from food is not the whole story is shown by the fact that there are populations whose diets are chronically poor in calcium and yet who have a very low incidence of osteoporosis. For example, among the Bantu of South Africa, whose diet is low in protein and high in phytate (which decreases calcium absorption), very few individuals eat as much as 500mg of calcium a day, and the women have an average of six children, with prolonged lactation. Six pregnancies with long-term breast-feeding are calculated to cause a total calcium loss of 400–500mg, which would be about half the body's stores. Yet osteoporosis was estimated in 1965 to be rare, occurring in about 1 in 200 of the Bantu population[8].

Studies of traditional Eskimos have further implicated high protein intakes, especially from animal foods, in calcium loss and the development of osteoporosis. Elderly Eskimos, whose diet was very rich in meat and animal protein, had less bone mineral mass than omnivore Caucasians of a similar age consuming a less meat-dominated diet, although at younger ages the two groups had bones of similar density[9]. Similarly, a study comparing bone mineral mass in elderly Caucasian omnivore and vegetarian women showed that the vegetarians had significantly higher bone mass than omnivores of the same age, height and weight[10], although the difference may not become apparent until after the age of 50 years[11].

A high-meat diet may have several deleterious effects on calcium in the bones. The higher sulphur (and phosphorus) to calcium ratio of meat increases calcium excretion, and meat may also alter the acid-base balance of the body, causing bone demineralization. A report published in 1988 compared the amounts of calcium excreted in the urine of 15 subjects who followed experimental diets for 12-day periods[12]. The diets contained constant amounts of calcium (400mg/day) and protein (75g/day), but differed with respect to protein sources, which were: animal protein; vegetable and egg protein; and all-vegetable protein. The animal-protein diet caused greater loss of bone calcium in the urine (150mg/day) than either the mixed diet (121mg/day) or the all-vegetable protein diet (103mg/day). These findings suggest that diets higher in vegetable, rather than animal, protein may actually protect against bone loss, and hence osteoporosis.

Vegans, with a slightly lower protein intake (*See Section 1 — Protein and Energy*) and a meat-free diet, probably have a lower requirement for dietary calcium and are better able to conserve the calcium in their bodies.

Calcium Balance and Other Factors

Only 20–30% of calcium in the average diet is absorbed, and the availability to the body of calcium in food is affected by the presence of fibre, phytate and oxalate, which inhibit the absorption of calcium from the intestine. As fibre and phytate are found in unprocessed plant foods, especially in nuts, whole grains, and seeds; and oxalate in green leafy vegetables and nuts, concern has been expressed that vegans may not obtain enough calcium from their diets. The American Dietetic Association is of the opinion that these dietary factors may not have a significant effect — a view shared by the UK Ministry of Agriculture, Fisheries and Foods, which states that because the body is able to adapt to the effects of phytate in the diet this substance is unlikely to cause calcium deficiency[13]. Adaptation to low calcium intakes has also been shown to occur[14,15].

An experiment with twelve post-menopausal Caucasian women suggested that a diet containing high levels of boron may help prevent calcium loss and bone demineralization[16]. The women, aged between 48 and 82 years, lived in a metabolic unit for 167 days and for the first 23 days ate a basal diet, supplemented with some minerals (including calcium) and vitamins, but low in fruits and vegetables. This diet provided 600mg calcium a day, but very little boron. A 3mg supplement of boron strongly reduced excretion of calcium and magnesium in the urine, and raised the levels of oestrogen and testosterone in the blood, thus favouring the conservation of calcium in the bones. The authors concluded that a diet high in fruits and vegetables (and thus containing more boron than the average diet) helps prevent calcium loss and bone demineralization. A vegan diet typically contains large amounts of fruit and vegetables.

Calcium and Vegan Diets

Several surveys have recorded daily calcium intake among British vegans. Studies in the 1950s and 1960s (*See* [17]) found levels of between 500 and 1,000mg, and in a 1985 report[18] the mean intake of ten male and female vegans was lower than that of matched omnivores, but just met the British RDA of 500mg. Two studies[19,20] of 18 and 22 vegans respectively (men and women) also showed mean calcium intakes lower than those of matched omnivores, but adequate at 554mg and 585mg, although there was wide individual variation — with one intake as low as 157mg. None of these studies took into account the contribution made by drinking and cooking water, which supply an average of 15% (75mg) of the recommended daily intake of calcium[18]. An analysis[21] of the diet of six middle-aged Swedish vegans showed a mean calcium intake of 626mg. A 1987 report found that, despite a lower dietary intake of calcium, the blood levels of this mineral were the same in near-vegan women as in omnivore women, because of an adaptation to increase calcium absorption from the intestine[15]. **There have been no reports of calcium deficiency in adult vegans.**

Twenty three British vegan children (aged 12–55 months) were found, on average, to be consuming only 52% of the 600mg calcium a day recommended for their age group, although the amount contained in drinking water was not measured[22]. However, as discussed above, the body adapts to low dietary calcium, and a meat-free and relatively low-protein diet enhances calcium retention in the body. None of the children showed signs of clinical deficiency, and all were in good health, although they tended to be slightly shorter and lighter than standard tables predict. The British standards, using 1965 data, were based on predominantly bottle-fed children whose early rate of growth is greater than that of breast-fed infants, while the vegan children were breast-fed well into the second year of life; this may account for much of the difference in stature. The same is true for children brought up in a vegan community called The Farm, in Tennessee, USA, whose mean intake at

351mg was less than half (41–48%) the US recommendation of 800mg, but who were well and thriving[23]. **A vegan diet can easily provide adequate amounts of calcium for the requirements of children, as shown by diet guidelines (See Table 5) published by nutritionists in America in 1985**[24].

Osteoporosis

Osteoporosis is the major cause of bone fractures in the elderly, and with its associated complications is a serious drain on health resources. It is better prevented than treated, and prevention includes an adequate intake of calcium throughout life; minimization of risk factors, such as smoking and heavy alcohol use; and sufficient physical activity, since this helps strengthen the bones. Osteoporosis in menopausal women is often treated with oestrogen supplementation as this helps preserve calcium balance, but a high (supplemented) intake of calcium as a treatment for osteoporosis seems unlikely to be effective.

Despite an apparently marginal intake of calcium by some vegans, there have been no reports of osteoporosis, and this may be due to the factors in the vegan diet, discussed above, which encourage calcium conservation. **Such studies as have looked at the density and strength of bone in vegans and vegetarians suggest that these groups are not particularly prone to, and in some cases may be protected from, the onset of osteoporosis.** An X-ray examination of the density of the bones of vegetarians and vegans suggested that they were indistinguishable from those of age- and sex-matched omnivores[25]. A later study[11] comparing bone density in vegetarian and omnivore women aged 20–49 years also found no difference between the two groups, while another[10] which compared older women (aged 50–89 years) found that vegetarians lost less than half the bone mass lost by omnivores.

The dietary calcium intake of adult vegans is adequate according to British RDAs, although the intake of some vegan children may be well below the recommended amounts. Vegan parents should take care to ensure that the diets of their children include calcium-rich foods such as tofu, mashed beans, nut and seed 'butters' or spreads using almonds or sesame seeds (tahini), home-made dried fruit 'spreads' and molasses instead of sugar.

There have been no reports of calcium deficiency in vegans, and it is known that the body can adapt to lower intakes of calcium. The high boron content of the vegan diet may help prevent osteoporosis, and the exclusion of meat also assists the body to conserve calcium. Studies of the bones of vegans and vegetarians show that the likelihood of osteoporosis is no greater, and may be less, than for omnivores.

Table 12. Portions of some vegan foods that provide 100mg calcium

Food group	Food	Weight (g)	Weight (oz)
Nuts (shelled)	Almonds	40	1.4
	Brazils	56	2.0
Pulses	Tofu (soya bean curd)	20	0.7
	Soya flour	44	1.6
	Haricot beans, boiled	154	5.4
Grains	Oatmeal	182	6.4
	Wholemeal flour	296	10.1
Seeds (husked)	Sesame	76	2.7
	Sunflower	86	3.0
	Pumpkin	232	8.2
Other	Spinach	17	0.6
	Molasses	20	0.7
	Parsley	30	1.1
	Figs, dried	36	1.3
	Watercress	45	1.6
	Chinese leaves	66	2.3
	Wakame seaweed, raw	66	2.3
	Spring onions, bulbs	71	2.5
	Plamil (concentrated) soya milk	83	2.9
	Currants, dried	105	3.7
	Rhubarb, stewed	108	3.8
	Apricots, dried	109	3.8

100g = 3.5oz. Values taken from Paul and Southgate, 1978[26], Tan *et al*,1985[27] and US Department of Agriculture, 1979[47]. British RDA for adults: 500mg.

Iron

About one-fifth of the iron in the average diet comes from meat. Although eggs contain iron, because they are generally eaten in smaller amounts than bread, flour, other grain products, potatoes and vegetables, the latter are more important sources. Of the plant foods, **dried fruits, whole grains, soya flour, nuts, green leafy vegetables, parsley, watercress, seeds, pulses, black molasses and edible seaweeds** are rich sources. The use of **iron pots and pans** contributes to dietary intake.

The human body normally contains 3–4g of iron, more than half of which is in the form of haemoglobin, the red pigment in the blood. Haemoglobin transports oxygen from the lungs to the tissues, and carbon dioxide in the opposite direction. Iron is a constituent of a number of enzymes. The muscle protein myoglobin also contains iron, which is stored in the liver too — an important source during the first six months of life, because the amount of iron in both breast and cow's milk is low. Many infant feeding formulas and cereals contain added iron, and these contribute a large proportion of the iron intake of many infants. The body's iron balance varies mainly according to dietary intake, as losses from the body are generally small — although women are more susceptible because of blood loss in menstruation. A lack of iron in the diet is partly compensated for by increased absorption rates, but in chronic dietary deficiency the body stores run down, resulting in iron-deficiency anaemia.

The British RDAs for iron are 6–12mg for children and adolescents, 10mg for men and 10–12mg for women[1]. The equivalent US figures were recently reduced from the 1980 recommendations[2] by the 1980–1985 RDA Committee, which now suggests a daily intake of 6.6mg increasing to 10mg up to the age of 18 years, then 10mg for adult men and 15mg for women[28]. Higher levels are recommended for pregnant and lactating women.

Iron Balance and Other Factors

Up to 25% of the iron in meat is absorbed, while less than 5% is absorbed from eggs and plant foods. If body stores fall, the body is able to increase its absorption from foods[27,28]. About 40% of the iron in animal foods is in a form called haem iron, while the remainder, and all the iron in plant foods, is in the less well-absorbed non-haem form. Non-haem iron absorption is elevated by the presence in a meal of animal foods, vitamin C (ascorbic acid) and other organic acids such as malic and citric acids (e.g. in pumpkin, plums and apples; and in citrus fruits respectively), but decreased by tannins (e.g. in tea) and phytates (found in nuts, grains and seeds). These factors can alter iron absorption ten-fold.

Of these substances, all are important to the vegan — with the obvious exception of meat. Laboratory research giving experimental meals to 299 volunteers has shown that the inclusion of foods (such as fresh salad, orange juice or cauliflower) providing 70–105mg of **vitamin C** in each meal increased the absorption of iron. A particularly pronounced effect was seen when 4.5oz cauliflower (containing 60mg vitamin C) was added to vegetarian meals, causing a more than three-fold increase in iron absorption[30]. Earlier studies have shown that, when iron intake from plant foods is relatively high (14–26mg a day), even large amounts of **phytate** do not adversely affect iron balance[31–33]. This level of iron intake is common among vegans (*See* **Iron and Vegan Diets** *below*).

There has been some concern that **fibre** in food, separate from the effect of phytate, inhibits the absorption of iron. However a study with 12 volunteers showed that on diets containing about the same amount of iron (21.8 and 26.4mg), their iron balance was *more* favourable when fibre intake was 59g a day, than on a low-fibre regime of only 9g[34]. These experimental intakes of iron are similar to those found for vegans, while the high-fibre regime exceeded the average 45g of fibre a day consumed by vegans. This suggests that the iron status of vegans is unlikely to suffer from a high fibre intake.

Iron and Vegan Diets

Studies of British vegans have reported daily iron intakes of 22.4mg[18], 31mg[19] and 20.5mg[20], compared with a group of middle-aged Swedish vegans on a deliberately restricted diet whose mean intake was 16.5mg a day[21]. The mean of the British values is 24.6mg — more than double the RDA. At this level of iron intake, fibre and phytate are unlikely to have inhibitory effects on absorption (*See* **Iron Balance and Other Factors** *above*). As vegan diets are high in vitamin C (three times the UK and five times the US recommendations), absorption of iron is enhanced.

A survey of British vegan children aged 1–4 years found a mean iron intake of 10mg a day, mainly from wheat and pulses, which exceeds by nearly a half again the British RDA[22]. A study of American children aged 2–5 years at The Farm, a vegan community in Tennessee, USA, indicated that all children achieved the US RDAs for iron except the 2- to 3-year-old girls, whose intake was 93% of the allowance before contributions from iron cookware were added[23]. The authors of this report acknowledged that studies have shown marginal iron intakes in *omnivore* children of these age groups.

Iron deficiency is believed to be fairly common in the general population, and one survey of young British omnivore women showed that they were consuming, on average, only three-quarters of the recommended intake of iron[35]. A person's iron balance can be measured by several criteria. An early decrease in iron stores is reflected in a drop in plasma ferritin to less than $12\mu g/l$; the next stage is recognised by changes in the content of red blood cells and possibly a reduction in exercise performance, even though haemoglobin levels remain normal; finally, iron-deficiency anaemia is signalled by the presence of microcytic blood cells and abnormally low haemoglobin levels in the blood.

It is generally assumed that haemoglobin concentrations of less than 130g/l in men and 120g/l in women[28] are likely to indicate anaemia, but in 1986 the British Medical Association (BMA)[29] stated that haemoglobin levels as low as 110g/l are not significant to health, and that the importance of maintaining haemoglobin at the previously recommended levels has been exaggerated. The BMA also pointed out that high levels of haemoglobin in the blood carry health hazards.

The Swedish vegans already mentioned[21] had haemoglobin levels in the normal range, with a mean of 143g/l (men) and 124g/l (women), and 23 out of 26 British vegans studied in 1970 also had average haemoglobin levels[36]. A report of haematological studies on vegans showed mean haemoglobin levels of 143.5g/l in men and 135g/l in women, which compared with mean values of 149g/l and 130g/l in omnivore men and women respectively[37]. All the vegans in these studies were healthy. An investigation[38] of 56 Seventh Day Adventist Canadian women who had followed a *vegetarian* diet for a mean of 19 years, showed that their iron intake was considerably *lower*, at an average 12.5mg a day, than that of the vegans described. Despite this, and the fact that 92% of their dietary intake of iron was from less well-absorbed plant sources (as is the case with vegans), the women were well and in good iron balance, with a mean haemoglobin concentration of 131g/l.

Vegans have a high dietary iron intake — more than twice the recommended amount. Although iron from plant sources is less well absorbed than that from meat, vitamin C enhances iron absorption and vegan diets contain high levels of this vitamin. The large amounts of fibre and the presence of phytate in plant foods have been shown not to interfere with iron absorption when dietary intake is at the levels measured in vegan diets studied to date. Studies of the iron status of vegans indicate that they are healthy in this respect and rarely suffer from iron deficiency.

Table 13. Portions of some vegan foods that provide 2mg iron

Food group	Food	Weight (g)	Weight (oz)
Nuts (shelled)	Pistachios	14	0.5
	Almonds	48	1.7
	Cashews	53	1.9
Pulses	Soya flour	22	0.8
	Haricot beans, boiled	80	2.8
	Butter beans, boiled	118	4.2
	Broad beans, boiled	200	7.0
Grains	Barley, whole, raw	33	1.2
	Oatmeal, raw	48	1.7
	Wholemeal flour	50	1.8
	Rye flour, 100%	74	2.6
	Wholemeal bread	80	2.8
Seeds (husked)	Pumpkin	13	0.5
	Sesame	26	0.9
	Sunflower	29	1.0
Other	Molasses, black	22	0.8
	Parsley	25	0.9
	Ladies fingers (okra), canned	37	1.3
	Figs, dried	48	1.7
	Apricots, dried	49	1.7
	Spinach, boiled	50	1.8
	Kelp seaweed, raw	67	2.4
	Chinese leaves	69	2.4
	Endive, raw	71	2.5
	Wakame seaweed, raw	100	3.5
	Currants, dried	111	3.9
	Watercress	125	4.4
	Dates, dried	125	4.4
	Raisins, dried	125	4.4
	Peas, fresh, boiled	167	5.9
	Mushrooms, raw	200	7.0

100g = 3.5oz. Values taken from Paul and Southgate, 1978[26], Tan *et al*, 1985[27], US Department of Agriculture, 1979[47]. British RDA: 10–12mg for adults.

Magnesium

Magnesium is widespread in foods, particularly in **green vegetables** because it is a constituent of chlorophyll, but also in **nuts, whole grains (including wholemeal bread) and yeast extracts**. Most of the magnesium in the body is in the bones; it is an essential component of all cells and is required for the functioning of some enzymes. Deficiency is rare, the most likely cause being not dietary insufficiency but excessive loss through diarrhoea. There is no British RDA for magnesium, while the US guidelines suggest 50 and 400mg a day for children and teenagers, and 300mg for women and 350mg for men. An extra 150mg is suggested for pregnant and breast-feeding women[2].

Less than half the magnesium eaten is absorbed from the intestine, and a high-fibre diet can cause some of the mineral to be unavailable to the body, although a degree of adaptation occurs[34]. The magnesium content of vegan diets has not often been measured. In 1981 the mean intake of middle-aged Swedish male and female vegans was found to be 542mg a day[21] and in 1987 the daily intake of British male and female vegans was reported to be significantly higher than matched omnivore controls, at 516mg compared with 398mg[20]. A 1987 study of near-vegan and omnivore women showed higher blood levels of magnesium in the near-vegans[15]. **The average intake of magnesium by vegans is considerably higher than suggested by the US standards; any binding effect of fibre is therefore unlikely to be significant.**

Phosphorus

Phosphorus is present in nearly all foods, particularly good sources for vegans being **nuts, whole grains (including wholemeal bread) and yeast extracts.** It is the second most abundant mineral in the body after calcium, and is essential in all cells for the utilization of energy from food. In the form of phosphates it plays a vital role in the bones and teeth. Dietary deficiency of phosphorus is unknown, but an excess of phosphorus over calcium in the first few days of life, as is found in cow's milk compared to breast milk, can cause muscular spasms in infants[13]. There is no British RDA for phosphorus; the US RDAs are 240mg for infants, rising to 1,200mg at age 18 years, and 800mg for adults, with more for pregnant and lactating women[2]. There are few reports of measurements of phosphorus intake of vegans. One, of children aged 2–5 years at The Farm, a vegan community in Tennessee, USA, showed that all age groups met or exceeded the recommended intake, except in the case of the 2- and 3-year-old girls, whose intake was 94% of the recommended level[23]. **It seems likely that a vegan diet generally contains adequate phosphorus.**

Sodium and Chlorine

Sodium and chlorine levels are relatively low in unprocessed foods, but salt (sodium chloride) is added to very many prepared foods. For example, salt is low in fresh meat but high in bacon, sausages and other processed meat products. Salt is added to canned vegetables and most butter, margarine, cheese, bread and some breakfast cereals during manufacture, and many people add further salt in cooking and at the table. Sodium bicarbonate and monosodium glutamate are also dietary sources of sodium. Sodium chloride is found in all fluids, inside and outside the cells, and is involved in maintaining the fluid balance of the body. Sodium is also essential for muscle and nerve activity. It is important that concentrations of sodium and chlorine in the blood are kept within close limits, and control of sodium is achieved by excretion through the kidneys.

In a temperate climate an adult needs less than 3g of salt a day[13], although more is needed during exertion, especially in hot weather, because of loss of sodium in the sweat. The required intake can be achieved from the salt naturally present in food, but most people consume 5–20g a day. A habitually high salt intake has been associated with high blood pressure, itself a major risk factor in heart disease and strokes. The long-term decrease in salt intake suggested by the National Advisory Committee on Nutrition Education[39], to 3g a day, might substantially reduce the prevalence of high blood pressure and deaths from it. A high potassium intake minimizes the effects of sodium on blood pressure, so the sodium/potassium ratio may be important in preventing hypertension.

The intake of sodium and chloride by a group of 22 British vegans was found to be 4.4g and 2.6g respectively, compared to significantly higher levels for matched omnivores, of 5.4g and 3.5g[20]. A similar sodium intake of 4.2g was found for a group of Swedish vegans[21]. **Evidence suggests that a vegan diet is lower in sodium chloride than the typical omnivorous diet, which may help protect vegans against high blood pressure and associated diseases.**

Potassium

The main sources of potassium in the average diet are **vegetables,** meat and milk, but **fruits and fruit juices** have a high potassium to sodium ratio. Potassium has a complementary action with sodium in cell function, and its level in the body is also closely controlled, excess being excreted by the kidneys. Potassium deficiency can result from the use of diuretics and purgatives, or from protracted diarrhoea, and in severe potassium depletion heart failure may result. There is no recommended daily intake of this mineral. Plant foods in general have a higher potassium to sodium ratio, which may be important in protecting against high blood pressure[39]. The potassium intake of a group of British vegans was 2.9g — significantly higher than that of matched omnivores at 2.4g[20]. The intake of Swedish vegans was measured at 2.6g[21].

Sulphur

Sulphur is incorporated in two amino acids, methionine and cystine, and two B vitamins, thiamin and biotin. Its role in the body is not clearly understood, although it is considered essential. The best sources are **protein-rich foods** (*See Section 1 — Protein and Energy and Table 2*). No recommended daily intake has been set and no deficiency state is known.

The Trace Elements

Knowledge of the exact requirements for and the functions of some of the trace elements is incomplete, either because they have only relatively recently been found to be essential, or because dietary deficiencies of many are unknown, or because the utilization of one trace element may be affected by the amounts of other elements present. The trace elements include zinc, selenium, iodine, copper, cobalt, chromium, fluorine and manganese.

Zinc

Zinc is present in a wide variety of foods, and meat and dairy products are very rich sources. Vegan sources of zinc include: **wheatgerm, *whole* grains (such as wholemeal bread, rice, oats and cornmeal), brewer's yeast, yeast extracts, nuts, pulses, tofu (soya bean curd), soya protein, miso (fermented soya bean paste) and some vegetables (e.g. peas, parsley, bean sprouts)**. Zinc is required for wound healing and is associated with a number of enzymes in the body, but most of this mineral is found in the bones. Less than half the zinc in the diet is absorbed, and this proportion is lower in the case of plant foods containing fibre and phytates (*But see below*). A deficiency of zinc can cause stunted growth and delayed wound healing, and possible causes include dietary lack, alcoholism, malabsorption, chronic renal disease and the use of certain drugs.

A Ministry of Agriculture, Fisheries and Foods survey published in 1981 showed that the average British diet contains 10.5mg of zinc a day[40]. This compares with the US recommended daily intakes of 3–10mg up to the age of 10 years; 18mg for male and female teenagers and for most women; and 10mg for men[2]. The recommendations made by the Canadian Dietary Standards are lower, at 9mg of zinc for women[41]. The World Health Organization (WHO) suggests that a normal adult needs 5.5–11mg a day[42]; there is no British RDA.

There is controversy over whether the fibre and phytate found in plant foods affect the body's ability to absorb zinc; some studies indicate that phytate does not have an inhibitory effect. An abundance or lack of zinc in the soil influences the zinc content of plants. Four studies have found slightly lower levels of zinc in the bloodstream of Caucasian vegetarians than in omnivores and one unpublished study suggests the same may be true for vegans (*Reviewed in* [43]), even though zinc intakes from food were similar to or greater than those of non-vegetarians. Whether or not this is significant remains to be seen.

At the time of writing the author knows of only one published study measuring the zinc intake of adult vegans[21], in which the average daily intake of middle-aged Swedish vegans was found to be 13mg for men and 10mg for women — slightly higher than the intake from a typical British omnivorous diet[40], and satisfying Canadian and WHO recommendations. The amount of zinc in the diets of 23 British pre-school vegan children varied from 1–8mg, with an average of 4mg a day — slightly below Canadian and US standards but similar to the intake of omnivore children[22]. A diet plan for vegan infants which provides adequate zinc has been published[24].

The intakes of zinc by vegans (and vegetarians) appear to be equal to or greater than those of omnivores. Zinc levels in the bloodstream of vegetarians and vegans, while generally within the normal range, *may* be slightly lower than those of omnivores. There have been no reports of zinc deficiency in vegans, but more studies of the zinc intake and status of vegans would be useful.

Selenium

The main dietary sources of selenium are meat, fish and **grains**, but the amount of selenium in the soil, which varies widely within and between countries, affects the level of this mineral in plants. Selenium is required for an enzyme found in the red blood cells, but deficiency is not common, especially in countries whose foods come from a wide variety of sources. A minimum daily intake of selenium has not been recommended by either the UK or USA.

There have been two studies of selenium in vegan diets — both from Sweden, whose soil has a low selenium content. A 1982 report[21] on middle-aged male and female vegans measured very variable intakes, whose mean was 9.6μg — compared with a mean intake of 25μg a day by average Swedish omnivores, and 65μg by Swedish vegetarians[44]. A later study[45] accurately measured dietary intakes of selenium by all three groups as well as levels of selenium in the bloodstream. The results showed, interestingly, that although selenium *intake* was lowest in the vegans and highest in vegetarians, the mean *serum level* of selenium in vegans was not significantly different from that of the omnivores, while the vegetarians did have significantly lower levels. The serum levels of selenium in vegans was close to the mean of healthy omnivores from eight different countries.

Although population studies have suggested that selenium intake has a major influence on serum levels of the mineral, other factors also affect this, including the rate of turnover of plasma proteins and urinary excretion of selenium. In the second Swedish study[44], both vegetarians and vegans lost less than half the amount of selenium in their urine compared with omnivores, suggesting that the body can conserve supplies. Further research into selenium and its distribution in the body in general is needed before firm conclusions can be drawn. **Studies so far suggest that selenium *may* be present in smaller amounts in a vegan diet, although serum levels in vegans are the same as in omnivores.**

Iodine

The most reliable source of iodine is sea food, and this includes **edible seaweeds such as *nori, wakame* and *hijiki*** — which are used by an estimated 11–16% of vegans[46]. There is iodine in **vegetables and grains**, and hence in animal foods, although amounts depend on the level in the soil. Because of the widespread use of iodides in animal feed, milk is the main source of iodine in the average British diet; milk products, meat and eggs are also important sources. Iodine is an essential component of hormones produced by the thyroid gland, and a deficiency leads to goitre, which is characterized by a swelling of the thyroid gland.

There is no British recommended daily intake of iodine, while the US minimum level is 150μg for adults[2]. One study[21] of Swedish vegans indicated a mean intake of 70μg, with a nutrient density per 1000 Calories only one-quarter of that found in the Swedish omnivore diet. There have been no reports of iodine deficiency in vegans, but further studies would be interesting.

Copper

Shellfish and liver are particularly rich sources of copper, but the main sources in the average diet are meat (28%), **bread and other grain products** (24%), and **vegetables** (21%). Whole grains are a better source than refined grains (such as white flour and bread), and **wheatgerm** especially so. Households with copper piping may obtain some copper from their drinking and cooking water. Copper is associated with a number of enzymes in the body. Deficiency has only occasionally been observed in malnourished infants, especially those who have been fed solely on cow's milk for a prolonged period, as it contains less copper than most foods. This particular problem would not arise with vegan infants.

There is no British standard for dietary copper intake; the WHO has proposed that a normal adult needs about 2mg a day[42], and the results of a large survey published in 1981 indicated that the average British diet contains 1.8mg[40].

One study of Swedish vegans found their dietary copper intake to be 3.6mg[21]. To the author's knowledge, there have been no other reports on copper intake by vegans.

Cobalt, Chromium, Manganese, Fluorine

Cobalt is utilized by the human body only in the form of vitamin B_{12} (*See Section 4 — Vitamins — for a detailed discussion of this vitamin*). **Chromium** is required for the utilization of glucose, and is fairly widely distributed in foods. **Manganese** is associated with a number of enzymes, and plant foods such as **nuts, whole grains and spices** are much better sources than animal products. **Tea** is very rich in this mineral. It is not known if flouride is an essential nutrient or not. It helps prevent tooth decay, but has toxic side effects at relatively low levels. **Drinking water** contains variable amounts. Other sources of fluoride are **tea and sea foods** (and some toothpastes, if swallowed). To the author's knowledge, there have been no studies of the levels of these minerals in vegan diets.

Summary

A vegan diet can provide all the minerals that the human body is known to need. In a few cases — such as calcium, selenium and iodine — levels in the vegan diet *may* be slightly lower than in the typical British diet. Some vegan children are consuming less calcium than the RDA (as do many omnivore children), and although they are healthy it makes sense for parents to ensure that calcium-rich foods are included in their children's diets. There have been no reports of calcium deficiency in vegans; the exclusion of meat and the slightly lower amounts of protein in their diets may help protect against this.

Vegans have a high dietary intake of iron, which — combined with high amounts of vitamin C — seems generally able to counteract any effects of fibre or phytate in inhibiting iron absorption. Vegan volunteers have been found to have adequate stores of iron in their bodies and rarely suffer from iron deficiency. The lower levels of sodium chloride found in the diets of vegans are advantageous and may help protect against high blood pressure and associated diseases. Selenium intakes may be low, but research suggests that the level of this mineral in the bloodstream of vegans is normal. For zinc, amounts in the vegan diet are adequate but its absorption may be inhibited by the fibre in plant foods, although no deficiency has been reported in vegans. The content of iodine and cobalt in a vegan diet may be lower than average, but again there have been no reports of deficiency. Further research on the importance of certain trace minerals in general, and in particular in the vegan diet, would be useful.

References

1. DEPARTMENT OF HEALTH AND SOCIAL SECURITY (1979). *Recommended Daily Amounts of Food Energy and Nutrients for Groups of People in the United Kingdom*. London, HMSO.

2. FOOD AND NUTRITION BOARD, US NATIONAL ACADEMY OF SCIENCES (1980). *Recommended Dietary Allowances (9th edition)*. USA.

3. WALKER, R. M. and LINKSWILER, H.M. (1972). 'Calcium retention in the adult human male as affected by protein intake', *J. Nutr.*, 102, 1297–1302.

4. ANAND, C.R. and LINKSWILER, H.M. (1974). 'Effect of protein intake on calcium balance of young men given 500g calcium daily', *J. Nutr.*, 104, 695–700.

5. ALLEN, L.H., ODDOYE, E.A. AND MARGEN, S. (1979). 'Protein-induced hypercalcuria: a long-term study', *Am. J. Clin. Nutr.*, 32, 741–749.

6. LINKSWILER, H.M., ZEMEL, M.B., HEGSTED, M. and SCHUETTE, S. (1981). 'Protein-induced hypercalcuria', *Fed. Proc.*, 40, 2429–2433.

7. ZEMEL, M.B. (1988). 'Calcium utilization: effect of varying level and source of dietary protein', *Am. J. Clin. Nutr*. In Press.

8. WALKER, A.R.P. (1965). 'Osteoporosis and calcium deficiency', *Am. J. Clin. Nutr.*, 16, 327–336.

9. MAZESS, R.B. and MATHER, W. (1974). 'Bone mineral content of North Alaskan Eskimos', *Am. J. Clin. Nutr.*, 27, 916–925.

10. SANCHEZ, T.V., MICKELSEN, O., MARSH, A.G., GARN, S.M. and MAYOR, G.H. (1980). 'Bone mineral mass in elderly vegetarian and omnivorous females', in: MAZESS, R.B. (Ed.), *Proceedings of the 4th International Conference on Bone Mineral Measurement*, pp94–98. Bethesda, MD, NIAMMD.

11. MARSH, A.G., SANCHEZ, T.V., MICKELSEN, O., KEISER, J. and MAYOR, G. (1980). 'Cortical bone density of adult lacto-ovo-vegetarian and omnivorous women', *J. Am. Diet. Ass.*, 76, 148–151.

12. BRESLAU, N.A., BRINKLEY, L., HILL, K.D. and PAK, C.Y.C. (1988). 'Relationship of animal-protein rich diet to kidney stone formation and calcium metabolism', *J. Clin. End.*, 66, 140–146.

13. MINISTRY OF AGRICULTURE, FISHERIES AND FOODS (1985). *Manual of Nutrition (9th edition)*. London, HMSO.

14. FAO/WHO (1961). 'Calcium requirements', *Nutr. Meetings Rep. Series no. 30*. Rome, Food and Agriculture Organization; Geneva, WHO.

15. SPECKER, B.L., TSANG, R.C. and MILLER, D. (1987). 'Effect of vegetarian diet on serum 1,25-dihydroxyvitamin D concentrations during lactation', *Obstet. Gynec.*, 70, 870–874.

16. NIELSEN, F.H., HUNT, C.D., MULLEN, L.M. and HUNT, J.R. (1987). 'Effect of dietary boron on mineral, estrogen, and testosterone metabolism in postmenopausal women', *FASEB J.*, 1, 394–397.

17. ELLIS, F.R. and MUMFORD, P. (1967). 'The nutritional status of vegans and vegetarians', *Proc. Nutr. Soc.*, 26, 205–212.

18. CARLSON, E., KIPPS, M., LOCKIE, A. and THOMSON, J. (1985). 'A comparative evaluation of vegan, vegetarian and omnivore diets', *J. Plant Foods*, 6, 89–100.

19. RANA, S.K. and SANDERS, T.A.B. (1986). 'Taurine concentrations in the diet, plasma, urine and breast milk of vegans compared with omnivores', *Br. J. Nutr.*, 56, 17–27.

20. SANDERS, T.A.B. and KEY, T J.A. (1987). 'Blood pressure, plasma renin activity and aldosterone concentrations in vegans and omnivore controls', *Hum. Nutr.: Appl. Nutr.*, 41A, 204–211.

21. ABDULLA, M., ANDERSSON, I., ASP, N-G., BERTHELSEN, K., BIRKHED, D., DENCKER, I., JOHANSSON, C-G., JÄGERSTAD, M., KOLAR, K., NAIR, B.M., NILSSON-EHLE, P., NORDÉN, Å., RASSNER, S., ÅKESSON, B. and ÖCKERMAN,

P-A. (1981). 'Nutrient intake and health status of vegans. Chemical analyses of diets using the duplicate portion sampling technique', *Am. J. Clin. Nutr.*, 34, 2464–2477.

22. SANDERS, T.A.B. and PURVES, R. (1981). 'An anthropometric and dietary assessment of the nutritional status of vegan preschool children', *J. Hum. Nutr.*, 35, 349–357.

23. FULTON, J.R., HUTTON, C.W. and STITT, K.R. (1980). 'Preschool vegetarian children', *J. Am. Diet. Assn.*, 76, 360–365.

24. TRUESDELL, D.D. and ACOSTA, P.B. (1985). 'Feeding the vegan infant and child', *J. Am. Diet. Assn.*, 85, 837–840.

25. ELLIS, F.R., HOLESH, S. and SANDERS, T.A.B. (1974). 'Osteoporosis in British vegetarians and omnivores', *Am. J. Clin. Nutr.*, 27, 769.

26. PAUL, A.A. and SOUTHGATE, D.A.T. (1978). *McCance & Widdowson's The Composition of Foods (4th edition)*. London, HMSO.

27. TAN, S.P., WENLOCK, R.W. and BUSS, D.H. (1985). *Immigrant Foods. 2nd Supplement to McCance & Widdowson's The Composition of Foods*. London, HMSO.

28. HERBERT, V. (1987). 'Recommended dietary intakes (RDI) of iron in humans', *Am. J. Clin. Nutr.*, 45, 679–686.

29. BOARD OF SCIENCE AND EDUCATION, BRITISH MEDICAL ASSOCIATION (1986). *Diet, Nutrition and Health*. London, BMA.

30. HALLBERG, L., BRUNE, M. and ROSSANDER, L. (1986). 'Effect of ascorbic acid on iron absorption from different types of meals', *Hum. Nutr.: Appl. Nutr.*, 40A, 97–113.

31. WALKER, A.R.P., FOX, F.W. and IRVING, J.T. (1948). 'Studies in human mineral metabolism. 1. The effect of bread rich in phytate phosphorus on the metabolism of certain mineral salts with special reference to calcium', *Biochem. J.*, 42, 452–462.

32. CULLUMBINE, H., BASNAYAKE, V., LEMOTTEE, J. and WICKRAMANAYAKE, T.W. (1950). 'Mineral metabolism on rice diets', *Br. J. Nutr.*, 4, 101–111.

33. HUSSAIN, R. and PATWARDHAN, V.N. (1959). 'The influence of phytate on the absorption of iron', *Ind. J. Med. Res.*, 47, 676–682.

34. KELSAY, J.L., BEHALL, K.M. and PRATHER, E.S. (1979). 'Effect of fiber from fruits and vegetables on metabolic responses of human subjects. II. Calcium, magnesium, iron and silicon balances', *Am. J. Clin. Nutr.*, 32, 1876–1880.

35. BARBER, S.A., BULL, N.L. and BUSS, D.H. (1985). 'Low iron intakes among young women in Britain', *Br. Med. J.*, 290, 743–744.

36. ELLIS, F.R. and MONTEGRIFFO, V.M.E. (1970). 'Veganism, clinical findings and investigations', *Am. J. Clin. Nutr.*, 23, 249–255.

37. SANDERS, T.A.B., ELLIS, F.R. and DICKERSON, J.W.T. (1978). 'Haematological studies on vegans', *Br. J. Nutr.*, 40, 9–15.

38. ANDERSON, B.M., GIBSON, R.S. and SABRY, J.H. (1981). 'The iron and zinc status of long-term vegetarian women', *Am. J. Clin. Nutr.*, 34, 1042–1048.

39. NATIONAL ADVISORY COMMITTEE FOR NUTRITION EDUCATION (1983). *Proposals for Nutritional Guidelines for Health Education in Britain*. London, Health Education Council.

40. MINISTRY OF AGRICULTURE, FISHERIES AND FOODS (1981). 'Survey of copper and zinc in food' (*Food Surveillance Paper no. 5*). London, HMSO.

41. DEPARTMENT OF NATIONAL HEALTH AND WELFARE (1975). *Dietary Standards of Canada (revised)*. Ottawa, Department of National Health and Welfare.

42. WHO EXPERT COMMITTEE ON TRACE ELEMENTS IN HUMAN NUTRITION (1973). 'Trace elements in human nutrition', *WHO Technical Report Series 532*. Geneva, WHO.

43. SANDERS, T.A.B. (1983). 'Vegetarianism: Dietetic and Medical Aspects', *J. Plant Foods*, 5, 3–14.

44. ABDULLA, M., ALY, K-O., ANDERSSON, I., ASP, N-G., BIRKHED, D., DENKER, I., JOHANSSON, C-G., JÄGERSTAD, M., KOLAR, K., NAIR, B.M., NILSSON-EHLE, P., NORDÉN, Å., RASSNER, S., SVENSSON, S., ÅKESSON, B. and ÖCKERMAN, P-A. (1984). 'Nutrient intake and health status of lactovegetarians: chemical analyses of diets using the duplicate portion sampling technique', *Am. J. Clin. Nutr.*, 40, 325–338.

45. ÅKESSON, B. AND ÖCKERMAN, P.A. (1985). 'Selenium status in vegans and lactovegetarians', *Br. J. Nutr.*, 53, 199–205.

46. LANGLEY, G.R. and WILCOX, J. (1987). *Health Profile and Nutrient Sources of Vegan and Vegetarian Runners*. Unpublished.

Cow's Milk Allergy

Iron-deficiency Anaemia in Children

Milk-induced Bleeding in Infants

Lactose Intolerance

Milk and Heart Disease

Milk and Other Health Problems

Summary

References

Although cow's milk contains useful amounts of protein and minerals, there are two major health problems associated with it: direct effects on the health of infants fed dairy milk, and longer-term problems of degenerative artery disease and immune function to which milk can contribute.

Cow's Milk Allergy

Allergy to cow's milk may affect as many as 75 in every 1,000 babies, causing frequent diarrhoea, vomiting, persistent colic, eczema and urticaria, catarrh, bronchitis and asthma. Babies fed with cow's milk develop antibodies to it in their blood, which can cause problems later in life.

A group of eight infants (7–46 weeks old) was referred to a University Department of Pediatrics in Belgium because of **chronic sleeplessness**[1]. During an average night they slept about 4.5 hours and woke their parents about five times. They were described as "fussy" and cried a lot during the day, and two had been given medication without effect. Standard medical and psychological tests found no cause for insomnia. Studies showed that the infants were allergic to cow's milk protein. When this was excluded from their diets the infants slept normally; when it was reintroduced, sleeplessness recurred. Rarer complications of milk protein allergy in children include **thrombocytopenia**, a disorder of the blood[2] and **lung disease** (pulmonary hemosiderosis)[3].

A meeting of the American Society of Microbiologists suggested that some of the many thousands of cot deaths occurring in the USA each year may be attributable to cow's milk allergy, as babies who are breast-fed are less likely to succumb to **cot death**[4].

Infants with documented cow's milk allergy need to be taken to the doctor more than twice as often during the first year of life as infants without milk allergy, and they are also hospitalized more often[5].

Iron-deficiency Anaemia in Children

The consumption of whole cow's milk in the first year of life — which was common fifteen years ago — is linked with iron-deficiency anaemia. Cow's milk contains about 0.5mg of iron per litre, of which only 5–10% is actually available for use by the body (breast milk contains slightly more iron and it is better absorbed). If cow's milk is fed as the sole or major source of nutrition during the first year **it cannot provide enough iron** for the growing infant. In addition, **cow's milk appears to decrease the absorption of iron from other foods,** compounding the iron-deficiency problem[6,7].

A study of infants in a clinic reported that 60% (two out of three) of those fed whole cow's milk at an early age developed iron-deficiency anaemia, and 33% (one in three) developed iron-deficiency without anaemia. This occurred despite the infants being fed iron-fortified cereal and while receiving personal pediatric care[8]. Another study found that the longer feeding with whole cow's milk was postponed, the less chance there was of infants aged 9–12 months developing iron deficiency. Of infants fed cow's milk before six months of age, two-thirds had insufficient iron, and one-third had insufficient iron when cow's milk was introduced between six and nine months of age[9].

Milk-induced Bleeding in Infants

In the 1970s a series of studies of infants led to the conclusion that feeding with whole cow's milk is associated with iron deficiency — not only because it is a poor source of iron, but also because it increases a baby's need for iron by causing hidden bleeding from the stomach and intestine. In a 1971 study, 44 out of 100 infants receiving whole cow's milk had **blood in their faeces**, and the authors concluded that cow's milk may be unsuitable for babies[10]. In a 1974 report, 17 out of 34 infants (aged 6–25 months) with iron-deficiency anaemia had **gastro-intestinal bleeding** caused by whole cow's milk. Bleeding stopped when a soya milk formula was substituted[11]. Other **doctors recommended that unmodified cow's milk should not be given to infants** before the age of four months because of the risk of gastro-intestinal bleeding[12], and the practice is no longer widespread in the UK and USA.

Lactose Intolerance

In the majority of the world's population the ability to digest milk sugar (lactose) decreases after the age of five years and drinking milk can lead to bloating, cramps, wind and diarrhoea. Four reports suggest that 20%-40% of patients aged 5–17 years with **repeated abdominal pains in childhood** suffered from lactose intolerance, which can often be relieved by excluding dairy milk and derivative products from the diet (See [7]).

Milk and Heart Disease

A five-year survey in Bogalusa, USA, of children aged 2.5–14 years included a study of the relationship between diet and health in 185 ten-year-olds[13]. Fat accounted for 38% of their energy intake, compared with the NACNE long-term recommendations of 30%[14]. The ratio of their intake of polyunsaturated to saturated fats (P/S ratio) was 0.3, compared with the COMA recommendations of a P/S ratio of 0.45[15]. 18% of the children's total fat intake was contributed by dairy milk, as was 26% of their intake of saturated fats — more than twice the amount provided by any other food group. Levels of blood cholesterol were linked with milk intake: children with the highest levels of blood cholesterol had significantly higher intakes of total fat and saturated fats than children with low cholesterol levels.

The process of heating milk in order to pasteurize it may cause proteins in cow's milk to denature. These denatured proteins are known to be **linked with atherosclerosis**, and hence with heart disease[16]. **Milk and other dairy products account for about half the saturated fats eaten in this country** (meat contributes most of the rest). The UK has the highest level of heart disease in the world, and with only 20% of the population of the EEC it consumes about 40% of EEC milk. **A high intake of saturated fat is linked with heart disease.** In Switzerland, a falling death rate from heart disease is partly due to a drop of nearly a half in milk consumption between 1951 and 1976, and the story is similar in other countries[17]. Four studies have implicated **cow's milk in heart disease** (See [18]). **Milk and dairy products were the major source of saturated fat and cholesterol for 75 adult vegetarians living in the USA, whose blood levels of cholesterol were higher than those of vegans who ate no dairy products**[19].

Milk and Other Health Problems

Antigen/antibody complexes in the blood, formed as a result of feeding babies with whole or modified cow's milk, may be involved in the later development of **allergy and recurrent infections** and with atherosclerosis[20]. Immune complexes of this sort are also known to be capable of **damaging the joints and kidneys**[20]. A report from London's Hammersmith Hospital described a patient with **rheumatoid arthritis and multiple drug allergies** who improved markedly when milk and cheese were excluded from the diet and relapsed when they were reintroduced[21].

Summary

Cow's milk is a common, but sometimes still unrecognized, cause of allergy in infants and children, with symptoms ranging from diarrhoea and vomiting to eczema, asthma and chronic sleeplessness.

Infants under one year who are given cow's milk as the sole or major food often develop iron deficiency, not only because it is a relatively poor source of iron but also because it can cause iron loss through gastro-intestinal bleeding. Lactose intolerance is a significant cause of repeated abdominal pain in children.

Milk and other dairy products account for about half the saturated fat intake of omnivores in the UK, and a high intake of saturated fat is a risk factor for heart disease. Some studies have directly implicated cow's milk consumption in heart disease. Other health problems have also been associated with the consumption of dairy milk.

References

1. KAHN, A., MOZIN, M.J., CASIMIR, G., MONTAUK, L. and BLUM, D.(1985). 'Insomnia and cow's milk allergy in infants', *Pediatr.*, 76, 880–884.

2. JONES, R.H.T. (1977). 'Congenital thrombocytopenia and milk allergy', *Arch. Dis. Child.*, 52, 744–745.

3. LEE, S.K., KNIKER, W.T., COOK, C.D. and HEINER, D.C. (1978). 'Cow's milk-induced pulmonary disease in children', *Adv. Pediatr.*, 25, 39–57.

4. DUNEA, G. (1982). 'Beyond the Etheric', *Br. Med. J.*, 285, 428–429.

5. GERRARD, J.W., MACKENZIE, J.W.A., GOLUBOFF, N., GARSON, J.Z. and MANINGAS, C.S. (1973). 'Cow's milk allergy: prevalence and manifestations in an unselected series of newborns', *Acta Paediatr. Scand. Suppl.*, 234, 1–21.

6. WHO (1985). 'Control of nutritional anemia with special reference to iron deficiency', *World Health Organization Technical Report Series, no. 580*. Geneva, WHO.

7. OSKI, F.A. (1985). 'Is bovine milk a health hazard?', *Pediatr.*, 75, 182–186.

8. HUNTER, R. (1970). 'Iron nutrition in infancy', in (p22): *Report of the 62nd Ross Conference on Pediatric Research*. Columbus, Ohio.

9. SADOWITZ, P.D. and OSKI, F.A. (1983). 'Iron status and infant feeding practices in an urban ambulatory center', *Pediatr.*, 72, 33–36.

10. ANYON, C.P. and CLARKSON, K.G. (1971). 'A cause of iron-deficiency anaemia in infants', *N. Z. Med. J.*, 74, 24–25.

11. WILSON, J.F., LAHEY, M.E. and HEINER, D.C. (1974). 'Studies on iron metabolism. V. Further observations on cow's milk-induced gastrointestinal bleeding in infants with iron-deficiency anemia', *J. Pediatr.*, 84, 335–344.

12. FÖMON, S.J., ZIEGLER, E.E., NELSON, S.E. and EDWARDS, B.B. (1981). 'Cow milk feeding in infancy: Gastro-intestinal blood loss and iron nutri-

tional status', *J. Pediatr.*, 98, 540–545.

13. BERENSON, G.S. (1980). 'Dietary studies and the relationship of diet to cardiovascular disease risk-factor variables in children', in (pp289-307): *Cardiovascular Risk Factors in Children: the Early Natural History of Atherosclerosis and Essential Hypertension.* Oxford, Oxford University Press.

14. NATIONAL ADVISORY COMMITTEE ON NUTRITION EDUCATION (1983). *Proposals for Nutritional Guidelines for Health Education in Britain.* London, Health Education Council.

15. COMMITTEE ON MEDICAL ASPECTS OF FOOD POLICY (1984). 'Diet and cardiovascular disease', *DHSS Report on Health and Social Subjects 28.* London, HMSO.

16. ANNAND, J.C. (1986). 'Denatured bovine immunoglobulin pathogenic in atherosclerosis', *Atherosclerosis*, 59, 34–351.

17. SEGALL, J. (1982). 'Communicable disease associated with milk and dairy products' (letter), *Br. Med. J.*, 285, 575.

18. DAVIES, D.F., REES, B.W.G. and DAVIES, P.T.G. (1980). 'Cow's milk antibodies and coronary heart disease' (letter). *Lancet* i, 1190.

19. SACKS, F.M., ORNISH, D., ROSNER, B., McLANAHAN, S., CASTELLI, W.P. and KASS, E.H. (1985). 'Plasma lipoprotein levels in vegetarians: the effect of ingestion of fats from dairy products', *J. Am. Med. Ass.*, 254, 1337–1341.

20. DELIRE, M., CAMBIASO, C.L. and MASSON, P.L. (1978). 'Circulating immune complexes in infants fed on cow's milk', *Nature*, 272, 632.

21. WOO, P. (1982). 'Anti-inflammatory drugs are the key', *Gen. Pract.*, 17th September, 55.

A number of studies have investigated the general health of vegans, as distinct from specific health indicators which have already been mentioned in other sections of this book. In 1970 Ellis and Montegriffo[1] examined 26 vegans of between one and 18.5 years standing and compared various parameters of health with matched controls, finding no abnormal symptoms or signs of definite significance which could have been related to nutritional status. In the same year they also published a review of surveys of the health of British vegans compared to omnivores, and concluded that physical fitness and the incidence of disease were similar. Apart from the vegans being slightly lighter in weight, and having lower blood cholesterol and urea levels, there was little difference between the two groups[2].

The health status of 72 British vegans compared with 72 matched omnivores was assessed by the Cornell Medical Index questionnaire and the results were published in 1976[3]. These suggested that there was no difference between the men in the two groups, but that the **vegan women tended to be healthier than the omnivore women**, particularly with respect to cardiovascular disease, frequency of illness and number of days away from work due to illness. A review published in 1978 confirmed that vegans tended to be **lighter in weight and less obese than omnivores**[4], and were more likely to be closer to their ideal weight. They had lower serum cholesterol and triglyceride concentrations, normal blood formation, but showed differences in electroencephalograms which did not, however, appear to affect health. There were obvious differences in plasma lipid levels (*See Section 3 — **Fats** — for a fuller discussion of this*), and **a vegan diet may have protected against ischaemic heart disease**.

A similar review published in 1983[5] supported these views, pointing out that **children brought up as vegans are healthy**, although they tend to be smaller and lighter than average — while still within the normal range. This may reflect the effect of prolonged breast-feeding rather than bottle-feeding and is not necessarily a bad thing, given the prevalence of obesity-related disease. A survey of the health of ten British vegans compared with vegetarians and omnivores published in 1985 found that there was no statistical difference between the groups in pulse rate, blood pressure, or incidence of allergies or other clinical parameters[6]. Haemoglobin levels, mean corpuscular haemoglobin, mean blood corpuscle volume, haematocrit and corpuscular haemoglobin concentration were similar in all groups. Four vegans and two omnivores had slightly low haemoglobin levels, but all participants were in good health.

The health and well-being of vegan women during pregnancy has been a topic of some concern among nutritionists. **Several studies have indicated that babies born to vegan women and reared on vegan diets thrive.** A 1987 report[7] of a survey of pregnant women at The Farm, a community in Tennessee, USA, has stated that the **incidence of pre-eclampsia was extremely low** (one in 775). Pre-eclampsia is characterized by increased vasoconstriction, reduced blood flow to the placenta and premature delivery. The authors concluded that, **far from being harmful during pregnancy, a well-planned and varied vegan diet could be beneficial in reducing the incidence of pre-eclampsia.**

In a report published in 1980, of 28 American pre-school vegetarian children (2–8.4 years old), six were macrobiotic vegans and 22 were vegetarians, including Seventh Day Adventists and macrobiotics[8]. The above-average mean IQ for all subjects was 116, while the mean for the vegan children was 119. The average mental age of the vegan children was 16.5 months ahead of their chronological age, compared to 12.5 months for all the children together. The authors concluded that **the above-average IQs and mental development of the children were as likely to reflect the educational level of the parents as any nutritional factors, but showed that the vegan and vegetarian diets had obviously had been able to support this advanced development.** Anthropometric and clinical measurements were normal in all the children.

The opinion has been expressed that there may be some link between veganism/vegetarianism and *anorexia nervosa*. This has *not* been supported by a recent study of 116 consecutive patients with this condition who were seen by doctors at a hospital in New South Wales, Australia[9]. While 54% of the patients were found to be avoiding red meat, in only four cases did this precede the onset of *anorexia nervosa*. There were no vegans in this series of anorexic patients.

Vegetarians, including vegans, are **less at risk from non-insulin-dependent diabetes,** partly because they are leaner than omnivores and partly because their high intake of complex carbohydrates lowers basal glucose levels. Vegetarians and vegans also **suffer less from osteoporosis, kidney stones, gallstones and diverticular disease**[10].

References

1. ELLIS, F.R. and MONTEGRIFFO, V.M.E. (1970). 'Veganism, clinical findings and investigations', *Am. J. Clin. Nutr.*, 23, 249–255.

2. ELLIS, F.R. and MONTEGRIFFO, V.M.E. (1971). 'The health of vegans', *Plant Fds. Hum. Nutr.*, 2, 93–103.

3. ELLIS, F.R., WEST, E.D. and SANDERS, T.A.B. (1976). 'The health of

vegans compared with omnivores: assessment by health questionnaire', *Plant Fds. Man.*, 2, 43–52.

4. SANDERS, T.A.B. (1978). 'The health and nutritional status of vegans', *Plant Fds. Man.*, 2, 181–193.

5. SANDERS, T.A.B. (1983). 'Vegetarianism: Dietetic and Medical Aspects', *J. Plant Foods.*, 5, 3–14.

6. LOCKIE, A.H., CARLSON, E., KIPPS, M. and THOMSON, J. (1985). 'Comparison of four types of diet using clinical, laboratory and psychological studies', *J. Roy. Coll. Gen. Pract.*, 35, 333–336.

7. CARTER, J.P., FURMAN, T. and HUTCHESON, H.R. (1987). 'Preeclampsia and reproductive performance in a community of vegans', *Southern Med. J.*, 80, 692–697.

8. DWYER, J.T., MILLER, L.G., ARDUINO, N.L., ANDREW, E.M., DIETZ, W.H., REED, J.C. and REED, H.B.C. (1980). 'Mental age and IQ of predominantly vegetarian children', *J. Am. Diet. Assn.*, 76, 142–147.

9. O'CONNOR, M.A., TOUYZ, S.W., DUNN, S.M. AND BEUMONT, P.J.V. (1987). 'Vegetarianism in anorexia nervosa? A review of 116 consecutive cases', *Med. J. Australia*, 147, 540–54.

10. HAVALA, S. and DWYER, J. (1988). 'Position of the American Dietetic Association: vegetarian diets — technical support paper', *J. Am. Diet. Assn.*, 88, 352–355.

As research into possible health benefits of veganism increases, more studies of the role a vegan diet may play in the treatment of various diseases are likely to be conducted. At present only a handful of such studies have been published, although there is much anecdotal evidence that the adoption of a vegan diet may be helpful in a number of conditions. Since several population studies have indicated that a vegetarian or vegan diet can lower **blood pressure**, three reports are of particular interest in this connection. In 1983 the results of a controlled trial of the blood pressure-lowering effect of a vegetarian diet were published[1]. In Australia 59 healthy omnivore volunteers with normal blood pressure followed a vegetarian diet for six weeks. After adjusting results for variations in age, obesity, heart rate, weight change and blood pressure, it was found that systolic blood pressure fell by 5–6mm of mercury, and diastolic pressure by 2–3mm, while subjects were on a vegetarian diet, but not while on an omnivorous diet.

Following this, a randomized controlled trial was conducted in Australia on the effect of a vegetarian diet on patients with raised blood pressure[2]. 58 subjects with mild untreated hypertension were put on such a diet for six weeks, during which time their systolic (but not diastolic) pressure fell by about 5mm of mercury. While on an omnivorous diet, the subjects experienced a fall of only 1–2mm. Greater changes would be expected with patients suffering higher blood pressure, and effects on diastolic pressure were also possible. A reduction of 5mm of mercury in systolic blood pressure might result in a 7% reduction in the number of major coronary illnesses in a middle-aged population.

A 1984 report from Sweden documented the effect of a vegan diet on 26 patients with long-established hypertension[3]. All the patients had been taking medication and while this had brought the pressure of most into the normal range, eight still had high blood pressure. The patients followed a strict vegan diet for one year, with the further exclusion of coffee, tea, chocolate, and added sugar and salt. Vegetables were eaten mainly fresh and raw, and the volunteers were also given herbal preparations and encouraged to take physical exercise.

After one year 22 subjects reported freedom from all adverse symptoms and the other four claimed that they had fewer symptoms; 20 of the patients had been able to give up their medication completely. There was a general reduction in systolic (7–9mm of mercury) and diastolic (5–10mm) blood pressure and in pulse rate, and blood levels of triglycerides and cholesterol decreased. Although there were many factors involved in this study and no single one can be identified, the authors believe that a vegan diet can be beneficial for hypertensive patients. In contrast, it must be mentioned here, a 1987 report[4] found when a group of 22 British vegans was compared with omnivores of similar age, sex and body build, the vegans had slightly *higher*, although still normal, blood pressure. In general, recent research has suggested that the factors in a vegetarian or vegan diet which contribute to the blood pressure-lowering effect include a high ratio of polyunsaturated to saturated fats, high fibre and low protein intakes.

A report in 1977 reviewed the health of four patients with severe *angina pectoris* who had followed a vegan diet as treatment for their condition[5]. Although this condition is known to remit spontaneously, the authors thought it unlikely that this would occur in all four patients. One patient aged 65 years experienced complete remission of angina symptoms while on a vegan diet, which he followed for five years until death from pulmonary embolism. A second patient aged 48 years adhered to a vegan diet for several years during which time his condition improved markedly, but after giving up the diet his symptoms gradually recurred. The remaining two patients aged 44 and 46 years, who experienced severe angina on exertion, followed a vegan regimen for several years and were able during that time to take fairly vigorous exercise without pain or shortage of breath. To the author's knowledge, there have been no controlled trials of the effect of a vegan diet on angina.

Two Swedish studies have looked at the effects of fasting and a strict vegan diet on **rheumatoid arthritis**. Under medical supervision 13 women with rheumatoid arthritis followed one week on a juice fast and then three weeks on a vegan diet, with the further exclusion of coffee, tea, chocolate, cereals, soya and wheat products, and added sugar and salt; 13 matched women received conventional food[6]. The **clinical results after a month's dietary therapy showed significant and pronounced improvement in the vegan (but not in the control) group, in spite of the withdrawal of almost all pain-relieving medication.**

Biochemical measurements also indicated improvement in the condition of the subjects on the vegan diet. A later report[7] concerned 20 patients with rheumatoid arthritis who followed a similar dietary regimen for three to four months. Twelve patients reported an improvement, five no change and three felt worse while on a vegan diet, and these subjective reports corresponded fairly well with the views of the investigator. Patients felt less pain and experienced improved function in the affected joints, although objective measurements of grip strength and joint tenderness showed no change. The authors concluded that many patients with mild or moderate rheumatism might benefit from adopting a vegan diet of this sort.

A vegan diet has also been prescribed by Swedish doctors in an effort to treat **bronchial asthma**[8]. 24 volunteers with long-established asthma were instructed how to follow a vegan diet which excluded tea, coffee, chocolate, added sugar and salt, and restricted certain fruits and vegetables, as well as cereals. With only a few lapses, the subjects followed the diet for a year and their health was assessed twice in that period. After one year, 92% of patients reported an improvement in or freedom from symptoms of asthma, with the number and severity of attacks having decreased. Clinical measurements confirmed the improvement. Some of the volunteers who had also suffered from rheumatism found a lessening of these symptoms.

These studies have not clarified precisely which features of a vegan diet may be effective in improving certain medical conditions. It is to be hoped, however, that the generally encouraging results of these pilot investigations will stimulate further research.

References

1. ROUSE, I.L., BEILIN, L.J., ARMSTRONG, B.K. and VANDONGEN, R. (1983). 'Blood pressure-lowering effect of a vegetarian diet: controlled trial in normotensive subjects', *Lancet* i, 5–10.

2. MARGETTS, B.M., BEILIN, L.J., VANDONGEN, R. and ARMSTRONG, B.K. (1986). 'Vegetarian diet in mild hypertension: a randomised controlled trial', *Br. Med. J.*, 293, 1468–1471.

3. LINDAHL, O., LINDWALL, L., SPÅNGBERG, A., STENRAM, Å. and ÖCKERMAN, P.A. (1984). 'A vegan regimen with reduced medication in the treatment of hypertension', *Br. J. Nutr.*, 52, 11–20.

4. SANDERS, T.A.B and KEY, T.J.A. (1987). 'Blood pressure, plasma renin activity and aldosterone concentrations in vegans and omnivore controls', *Hum. Nutr.: Appl. Nutr.*, 41A, 204–211.

5. ELLIS, F.R. and SANDERS, T.A.B. (1977). 'Angina and vegan diet', *Am. Ht. J.*, 93, 803–804.

6. HAMBERG, V.J., LINDAHL, O., LINDWALL, L. and ÖCKERMAN, P.A. (1982). 'Fasting and vegetarian diet in the treatment of rheumatoid arthritis — a controlled study', *Rheuma*, 4, 9–14.

7. SKÖLDSTAM, L. (1986). 'Fasting and vegan diet in rheumatoid arthritis', *Scand. J. Rheum.*, 15, 219–233.

8. LINDAHL, O., LINDWALL, L., SPÅNGBERG, A., STENRAM, Å. and ÖCKERMAN, P.A. (1985). 'Vegan regimen with reduced medication in the treatment of bronchial asthma', *J. Asthma*, 22, 45–55.

The evidence presented in this book clearly demonstrates that there is no known essential dietary nutrient which cannot be supplied by a varied and balanced vegan diet — a conclusion also supported by the fact that there are now third-generation vegans enjoying good health.

Pulses, nuts, seeds and grains provide protein at recommended levels, as shown by numerous surveys of proteins and amino acid intake by vegans over the last 20 years. The perceived need to combine protein at each meal has been shown to be a myth; eating a range of protein-rich foods on a daily basis will ensure adequate intake as long as energy needs are met. Only two occurrences of protein and energy deficiency in vegan infants of vegan parents have been published, which the observance of simple guidelines for feeding infants — not to over-dilute, and to ensure that suitably-prepared energy-dense foods are given — would have prevented. Successive generations of healthy, slim and bright vegan children are clear proof of the ability of a vegan diet to support growth and development.

Numerous expert committees have advised an increased intake of complex carbohydrate foods, high in fibre, to help protect against heart disease, diverticulitis and bowel cancer, among other common illnesses. According to studies published to date, vegans are the only dietary group to achieve the intake of complex carbohydrates *and* fibre recommended by the National Advisory Committee on Nutrition Education (NACNE).

Consumption of fats, especially saturated fats, is higher in Britain than expert committees recommend. Meat, milk, cream, cheese, butter and margarine contribute 78% of the saturated fats consumed by the average omnivore. The total fat intake of vegans is within the limits proposed by the Committee on Medical Aspects of Food Policy (COMA Report, 1984) at 34% of energy consumed, while both vegetarians and omnivores exceed this level. Polyunsaturated fatty acids, which have a beneficial effect on levels of blood cholesterol, are more abundant in a vegan diet. Of vegans, vegetarians and omnivores, vegans have the lowest levels of total cholesterol and low-density lipoprotein-cholesterol in their bloodstream, and their risk of coronary heart disease is substantially lower.

When it comes to a discussion of vitamins and veganism, B_{12} is still a controversial area. Yet there is no difficulty in ensuring an adequate dietary intake of this vitamin, since it is naturally present in useful amounts in some plant-derived foods and in fortified form in many others. Cases of B_{12} deficiency in long-term vegans remain very rare indeed.

Vitamin D, which is not known to occur naturally in plant foods (although added by law to margarines), is manufactured in the skin in response to daylight, so regular exposure to fresh air is the prescription for omnivores and vegans alike. Vitamin A (as carotene), the B group, and vitamins C, E and K, are plentiful in a wholefood vegan diet.

Iron and calcium are often cited as minerals which are scarce in vegan diets. In fact, they generally contain *above*-average amounts of iron, whose absorption is enhanced by the substantial levels of vitamin C also consumed by vegans. Although fibre and phytate theoretically may interfere with iron absorption, some evidence suggests that at the levels of iron and vitamin C eaten by vegans a significant deleterious effect is unlikely. Studies of vegans have shown them usually to be in good iron balance.

Regarding calcium, reports indicate that adult British vegans achieve the recommended daily intake set by the Department of Health, although some children's intake may fall below these levels — without, however, documented signs of deficiency. Parents should ensure that their children's diet contains calcium-rich foods — such as tofu, beans, nut and seed spreads (e.g. tahini), green leafy vegetables (e.g. spinach, parsley and watercress), and molasses instead of sugar. By avoiding animal protein, which increases calcium excretion, vegans are better able to conserve calcium in their bodies. There have been no reports of osteoporosis in vegans and studies suggest that vegetarians, and possibly vegans too, may be less likely than omnivores to suffer from osteoporosis in old age.

The higher potassium-to-sodium ratio found in plant foods may help protect against high blood pressure. Amounts of selenium and iodine may be lower than in omnivore diets, but no deficiencies have been recorded. The general health of vegans is good, and certain vegan diets have been used with some success in the treatment of high blood pressure, angina, rheumatoid arthritis and bronchial asthma.

Although veganism is now a well-recognized, and increasingly widely-practised way of life, with ethical, economic, ecological and health benefits, scientifically it is still rather poorly understood. For 30 years it has been a source of surprise to many scientists that so many long-term vegans remain healthy with no apparent dietary source of vitamin B_{12}. Do bacteria in the small intestine provide usable amounts of the vitamin? How much of the B_{12} measured in assays is biologically active in humans? Does boron (abundant in vegan diets) help conserve the body's calcium? What is the incidence of osteoporosis in elderly vegans? What is the nutritional status of vegans with regard to zinc and selenium? Does a vegan diet protect against disease? If so, which diseases and which nutrients are protective? There is a wide scope for further research, which would be welcomed by the Vegan Society and is of enormous potential benefit to the community as a whole.

I hope this book has presented a persuasive argument for the ability of a vegan diet both to support and foster good health, and useful information for those seeking to know more than the minimum. Health professionals need no longer recommend the inclusion of *"just a little* milk" to ensure the survival of those who have chosen a vegan way of life! For readers who would like to learn about aspects of veganism beyond the nutritional, or who would like to read more popular authors on the subject, as well as discover the delights of vegan cookery, a further reading list is supplied. Many of the titles are available direct from the Vegan Society. (*Please send an SAE for a current list.*)

FURTHER READING

General

THE VEGAN. Magazine and offical organ of the Vegan Society. Published quarterly since 1946.

AKERS, K. *A Vegetarian Sourcebook: The Nutrition, Ecology and Ethics of a Natural Foods Diet*. Vegetarian Press, Virginia. With tables, figures, 19 pages of references both popular and academic.

BRAUNSTEIN, M.M. *Radical Vegetarianism*. Panjandrum/Aris Books, Berkeley, California. Diet and ethics, vegan-oriented. With various religious perspectives, short bibliography.

GIEHL, D. *Vegetarianism — A Way of Life*. Harper and Row, New York. Areas covered include: nutrition, health, ethics, economy, ecology; vegetarianism in history and literature. 21 pages of references both popular and academic.

GOLD, M. *Living Without Cruelty*. Green Print, London. A cohesive philosophy with practical advice and information on avoiding animal products and animal testing in the kitchen and other spheres of life.

HOWLETT, C. (Ed.). *The Vegan Holiday & Restaurant Guide*. Vegan Society, St Leonards. Lists UK eating places and holiday accomodation catering for vegans. With special-interest and foreign holidays sections.

HOWLETT, L. (Ed.). *The Cruelty-Free Shopper*. Bloomsbury, London. Comprehensive and regularly updated guide to 100% animal-free foods, toiletries, cosmetics, etc.

KAPLEAU, P. *A Buddhist Case for Vegetarianism*. Anchor Press, Tiptree. Religious, humanitarian and scientific reasons for vegetarianism. With further reading list, references.

KLAPER, M. *Pregnancy, Children and the Vegan Diet*. Gentle World Inc., Florida, USA. Written by an MD, contains nutritional advice with recipes and nutrient analyses, plus photos of vegan parents and children.

McDOUGALL, J.A. and McDOUGALL, M.A. *The McDougall Plan*. New Century, New Jersey. Detailed exposition of health benefits of a low-fat vegan diet. With tables, diagrams, original references, food values, recipes and index.

MORAN, V. *Compassion: The Ultimate Ethic*. Thorsons, Wellingborough. History and philosophy of the vegan movement.

WYNNE-TYSON, J. *Food for a Future*. Thorsons, Wellingborough. A classic work which powerfully argues all aspects of the vegan case — moral, economic, ecological, nutritional. With bibliography and index.

Cookbooks

BATT, E. *Vegan Cookery*. Thorsons/Vegan Society. With general information and practical advice.

BRADFORD, P. and BRADFORD M. *Cooking With Sea Vegetables*. Thorsons, Wellingborough. Recipes are both vegan and macrobiotic.

BRUSSEAU, P. *Healthy Eating for Diabetics*. Century, London. Mainly vegan (some vegetarian) recipes. With total carbohydrate and Calorie values.

D'SILVA, J. *Healthy Eating for the New Age*. Wildwood House, London. Simple and tasty vegan recipes.

HAGLER, L. *Tofu Cookery*. The Book Publishing Co., Tennessee. Highly imaginative ideas for tofu in both savoury and sweet dishes. Colour illustrations, large format. Calories, protein, fat and carbohydrate values given for each recipe.

HILL, D. *Vegan Vitality*. Thorsons, Wellingborough. Emphasis on unusual vegan recipes.

HUNT, J. *The Compassionate Gourmet*. Thorsons, Wellingborough. Exotic vegan dishes from around the world.

HUNT, J. *The Caring Cook*. Vegan Society, St Leonards-on-Sea. Low-cost vegan cookbook for beginners. Many practical hints included.

HURD, F.J. and HURD, R. *Ten Talents*. F. & R. Hurd, Minnesota. Natural foods cookbook with mainly American-style recipes, nutritional information, colour illustrations.

LAMONT, H. *The Gourmet Vegan*. Gollancz, London.

LENEMAN, L. *Soya Foods Cookery*. RKP, London. Adventurous introduction to the subject, with recipes for soya yoghurts, soft vegan 'cheese', mayonnaise; tofu and tempeh dishes; miso.

LENEMAN, L. *The International Tofu Cookery Book*. RKP, London. Tofu recipes from America, Britain, the Caribbean, the Far East, India, the Mediterranean and Mexico.

RHOADS, S.A. *Cooking with Sea Vegetables*. Autumn Press, Massachusetts. International recipes with seaweeds, plus history of their use.

SCOTT, D. and GOULDING, C. *The Vegan Diet: True Vegetarian Cookery*. Rider & Co., London. Gourmet-oriented, with over 250 recipes.

SWEET, A. *The Vegan Health Plan*. Arlington Books, London. With nutritional information, advice on buying and storing food, reading list, useful addresses.

WAKEMAN, A. and BASKERVILLE, G. *The Vegan Cookbook*. Faber and Faber, London. Recipes graded by cost and ease of preparation. Calories, protein, fat, carbohydrate and fibre given for each dish. Nutritional information, useful addresses.

WHOLEFOOD COOKERY SCHOOL. *Weaning Your Baby with Wholefoods*. Wholefood Cookery School, Leicester. A 12-page booklet with vegan recipes.

INDEX

LIVERPOOL POLYTECHNIC
I. M. MARSH CAMPUS LIBR
BARKHILL ROAD, LIVERPOO
L17 6BD 051 724 2321 ext

NOTES